"Generosity is a critical issue in the life of the church and in the lives of believers. In *Giving Away the Collection Plate*, John Richardson gives a great apologetic for believers and the church to be generous agents engaged in God's mission."

—Ed Stetzer
President of LifeWay Research

"I do not recommend anyone reading *Giving Away the Collection Plate*, unless you are prepared for God to bring deep conviction regarding the shallow commitments and passivity that characterize too many churches today. This book will confront you with the clear biblical mandates of what the church, as the body of Christ, is to be in the world. You will be forced to reevaluate traditional church programs and rethink what the call to discipleship and sacrifice really means."

—Jerry Rankin
President Emeritus
International Mission Board, SBC

"Obedience to Jesus's teachings on generosity has been a struggle for the American Church for some time now. John Richardson and Traceway Church have embraced a level of generosity that few others would even be willing to consider. What might happen in our communities if we would actually trust God for daily bread and live completely open-handed lives? Read this book only if you want your norm to be wrecked by the generosity of Jesus."

—Jason C. Dukes
Author of *Live Sent: You Are a Letter* and *Beyond My Church*

GIVING
AWAY
THE COLLECTION PLATE

GIVING AWAY

THE COLLECTION PLATE

REGIFTING GOD'S LOVE AND MONEY

JOHN D. RICHARDSON

TATE PUBLISHING
AND ENTERPRISES, LLC

This book is designed to provide accurate and authoritative information with regard to the subject matter covered. This information is given with the understanding that neither the author nor Tate Publishing, LLC is engaged in rendering legal, professional advice. Since the details of your situation are fact dependent, you should additionally seek the services of a competent professional.

The opinions expressed by the author are not necessarily those of Tate Publishing, LLC.

Published by Tate Publishing & Enterprises, LLC
127 E. Trade Center Terrace | Mustang, Oklahoma 73064 USA
1.888.361.9473 | www.tatepublishing.com

Tate Publishing is committed to excellence in the publishing industry. The company reflects the philosophy established by the founders, based on Psalm 68:11,
"The Lord gave the word and great was the company of those who published it."

Book design copyright © 2012 by Tate Publishing, LLC. All rights reserved.
Cover design by Kate Stearman
Interior design by Christina Hicks

Published in the United States of America

ISBN: 978-1-62024-105-9
1. Religion / Christian Church / Administration
2. Religon
12.03.22

DEDICATION

To my grandfathers, James Richardson and Alvin Word Jr., whose passion for God and extravagant generosity have shaped generations of the Church

ACKNOWLEDGMENTS

JD, you will never cease to amaze me with your faith and encouragement. Thank you for sharing this life-long journey with me.

Mom and Dad, in my better moments, I am a shadow of you. Thank you for the family you have developed and for the missional faith you have always displayed (even before it was called missional).

The Traceway community, this is your story. It is such an honor to serve as a co-laborer with you and to proclaim your faithfulness to the world.

All who invested in ReGifting, there is not enough space to acknowledge you all. You believed in God's plan long before you saw the evidence of his movement. You also loved many neighbors that you had never even met. I am so proud to be associated with each of you.

All who have come before us in this journey, the vast majority of your stories will never be in print, but you are the heroes of the faith. You labor daily to invest in the lives of those who are missing out on life with God. Behind closed doors, you have discipled and prayed for more Jesus followers than I will ever meet. I pray that these words represent you well. I look forward to hearing even more of your stories.

The incredible staff at Tate Publishing, you provide a voice for the everyday followers. Thank you for your trust, your insight, and your vision.

TABLE OF CONTENTS

PART THREE: IN THE WAKE

INTRODUCTION

THE CHANGING CHURCH

> God is building a home. He's using us all—irrespective of how we got here—in what he is building. He used the apostles and prophets for the foundation. Now he's using you, fitting you in brick by brick, stone by stone, with Christ Jesus as the cornerstone that holds all the parts together. We see it taking shape day after day—a holy temple built by God, all of us built into it, a temple in which God is quite at home.
>
> Ephesians 2:19-22 (MSG)

What would happen in your church if you gave away all of the tithes and offerings for a week? There are huge implications in that question—from both giving and receiving perspectives. And considering the awkward conversations that may surface from this question, there are plenty of reasons to avoid the subject altogether.

But while we are playing the "what if" game, let me ask you another question. What if God pushed you beyond a one week offering? What if God pushed you to become radically generous? What if God asked you to give everything away for an entire year? What would happen in your church? What would happen in your community? How would you invest God's money? How would you use it to make disciples?

At the end of 2009, God asked our church to walk down that road. He moved us to give everything away for one entire year. And while this is not a biography, the pages that follow will introduce you to many of the principles that we learned along the way.

Giving Away the Collection Plate will push you to dream with God. It will ask you to step away from the American Dream and look at your financial motivations through a new lens. It will ask you to rethink church and discipleship apart from the bondage of money.

TURNING THE PAGE

Money is not a new struggle for the church. As long as we have been called Christians, we have staggered between the love of God and the love of money. But at our current place in church history, we have a window of opportunity unlike many generations before us. As the church is being deconstructed and ultimately reconstructed, we have a chance to focus on the things that are of utmost importance to God.

In case you did not get the memo, we have just closed a major chapter in church history. The church that defined our childhoods is no longer found on every street corner. In some cases, it is no longer found in entire cities in North America. Things have changed.

Some historians compare the current developments of the church to the insurrectionist days of Martin Luther or the defining days of Constantine. Some say the church is moving back to the ways of the first century and others say that the twenty-first century holds more promise for the church than any previous time in its history.[1] Regardless of our positions on this current revolution, it is clear that the church has started writing on a new page. We have entered a new chapter.

My grandfather was a pastor throughout the previous chapter. He was a hero to many, and even after his passing, he remains a hero of mine. In the 1950s, he moved to a small town in northeast Mississippi and started working as the pastor of a new mission church. Every Saturday, he would walk the streets of West Point. He knocked on doors and sat on front porches. In his down-to-earth manner, he told people about God and invited them to the new church. After five years of my grandfather laboring in this manner, there were over five hundred people in that church.

That was at the climax of the previous chapter of church history. It was period of gathering. A period defined by fellowship and characterized by the statement, "Let's go to the church."

That chapter of church history has ended. People no longer look to the church as a primary social gathering place. Knocking on doors, even by pastors, is viewed as intrusive and bothersome. Front porches have been traded for privacy fences. Communities are more active in the virtual world than they are in the physical world. As a result, local churches have been forced to adapt.

And the major chapter of gathering and fellowship has concluded. The page has been turned. Some are still fighting its demise, but for all practical purposes, the church has opened a new chapter.

HERE IS THE CHURCH

The current chapter in church history began with something of an identity crisis. The church started examining her roots to figure out her identity. We were asking questions like "What is the church," or more appropriately, "Who is the church?" "How does she become all that God intended her to be?" "How can a group of people begin to look like the incarnation of Christ?" With thousands of people dissecting scripture and digging into church history to look for answers, we came up with numerous, and sometimes confusing, results. But, overall, the process has been a beneficial one. We have refined our thinking. We have gone back to the fundamentals. And after wading through some interesting mud holes, the church is starting to resurface with a new identity.

While the descriptive phrases of the previous chapter in church history were *gathering* and *fellowship*, the important phrase of the current chapter is *missional*. The church is rediscovering and committing to the mission of God. We have realized that we can no longer talk about *going* to church, but rather we must think in terms of *being* the church. We have recognized that the church is not a building or an entity as much as it is a people group. The church is not contained in a location; it is contained in the lives of believers.

When I was a child, I was taught a cute saying that identifies the church of the previous chapter. We were taught to put our hands together, interlocking our fingers, and say, "Here is the church, here is the steeple"— as we formed a steeple with our pointer fingers—"open the door and here are the people." That was the symbol of gathering and fellowship. But today, we are more conscious that the church starts (and ends) with the people and not the building. The church is not a place to gather, but it is the everyday lives of the believers. It is not an event that happens on Sunday mornings, but it is a way of life that occurs 168 hours a week.

You may find the church on the front lawn speaking to a neighbor. You may experience the church over a meal or in the office. But whatever she is, the physical representation of Christ (the body of Christ) is not found in entities and structures. She is found in Jesus followers.

DAY AFTER DAY AFTER DAY

When Jesus gave us the Great Commission, He was giving us a description of the church. He said,

> God authorized and commanded me to commission you: Go out and train everyone you meet, far and near, in this way of life, marking them by baptism in the threefold name: Father, Son, and Holy Spirit. Then instruct them in the practice of all I have commanded you. I'll be with you as you do this, day after day after day, right up to the end of the age.
>
> Matthew 28:18-20 (MSG)

His commission was to invest in people—day after day after day—wherever you may find them, near or far. In other words, whether you are at home, in the office, in a meeting across town, or on a plane to the other side of the earth, love people enough to make disciples. And through the power and authority of Jesus, train them in the way of life and mark them with baptism.

If you look at the most effective evangelistic methods throughout the history of the church, you will find that they are marked by this distinct form of discipling. In fact, I am the product of people who live as the church 168 hours a week. My dad was a deacon, my mom played hand bells, and they both sang in the choir. But more importantly, they lived as the church at home.

When I was ready to accept the way of Jesus, I did not run to an edifice. I talked to my dad as he lay beside me to pray before bedtime. I had seen my parents' love for God. I had witnessed a genuine relationship between God and humanity. As I lived with my parents, they discipled me and led me to follow Christ. Their influence eventually played a major role in my relationship with God.

Most people who call themselves Christians have similar stories. They can name a few critical people who cared enough about them to invest in them and show them the ways of Jesus. The church of our time is one that is gravitating back to the fundamental concept of living as the church during everyday life rather than focusing on the few hours each week that we gather.

Before I go any further, let me clarify one thing. Gathering is important. The gathering of believers is something that we all need. It was a major part of the early church (Acts 2:42) and the gathering of believers is noted as important to God (Hebrews 10:25). Please do not hear me saying anything to the contrary. However, gatherings are an *activity* of the bride of Christ, not her definition. Gathering for worship is one thing that the church does, not the encompassing view of her purpose.

The present chapter of Church history is unfolding before our eyes. This is a period of decentralizing— moving out—rather than assembling.* It is characterized by intentionally investing in relationships. In the present chapter of church history, you are more likely to hear the statement, "It's time to live as the church," than the statement, "Let's go to the church." Leaders in this movement are as inclined to say, "Grab someone and take them to lunch" as they are to say, "Grab someone and bring them to church."

GENEROUS CHURCH

The Church is, once again, rebirthing an ancient movement. We are rethinking our terminology and looking at new definitions of success. We are finding ways to measure the boundaries of God's Kingdom apart from budgets, buildings, and statistics. We are feeling our way through what it means to live together, under the mission of God.

---

*In some cases, decentralization is taking place over entire cities rather than just individual congregations. Local church groups are purposefully uniting for the good of the Gospel in their city. They are looking to the prayer of Jesus in John 17 and building on the fact the all of the churches of the New Testament are churches of a city (church of Galatia, church of Jerusalem, church of Philippi, etc). For a great example, see www.thechurchofwestorange.com.

It is in this context that *Giving Away the Collection Plate* materialized. One small, local church decided to live—day after day after day—with the intention of making disciples. The surprising way God asked us to do this was by giving away all of our tithes and offerings for an entire year. He asked us to *regift* his kindness. And unlike the negative "regifting" connotations from *Seinfeld*, this generosity did not involve label makers and unwanted gifts.[2] Instead, this form of regifting meant taking God's remarkable gifts to the church and giving them away for the good of his mission.

There is nothing new about the idea of investing in relationships for the purpose of discipling. There is nothing new about the concept of caring for the disadvantaged (Jesus was frequently found among the poor and outcasts). But the thought of uniting the financial resources of a local church with a heart for intentional disciple-making has proven profound. Generosity provided a foundation for an entire group of people to start living missionally. Radical giving opened the door to relationships that were otherwise infertile.

Throughout *Giving Away the Collection Plate*, you will be introduced to many of these relationships. Fair warning: you may be frustrated by their stories.

With any good story, it is natural to want to know how it ends. Unfortunately, you may not always see the conclusion to the stories. If closure is imperative to you, this book may send you over the edge. You may soon be ministering to your neighbors in the insane asylum.

Many of the regifting stories are open-ended. It is not that I want to hide the results from you. I cannot tell you "the rest of the story" yet, because the conclusion has not been written. We are still walking with these people. We are meeting them at McDonald's, talking with them on Facebook, interacting with them in their homes and worshiping with them on Sundays. We are wading through messy spirituality. So, we do not necessarily expect a bow-wrapped conclusion before this book is published.

Instead of fixating on the end of their stories, I am going to ask a favor of you. Let God speak to you about the story unveiling around you. As you read, ask God to reveal how he wants to use generosity in your story. Ask how he can turn the page in your life as you follow his lead.

What happens when we use Jesus as our model for day to day living? What happens when a church decides that they care more about discipling than they do about salaries? What would occur if a local church decided to invest significant time and financial resources into those who are struggling through abusive relationships, medical difficulties, and unemployment? How will the community respond to the Gospel after they see the love of Christ in a material way?

These questions are only answered by missional giving. When giving becomes missional, the church regains community respect. Maybe more importantly, when giving becomes missional, the church learns to look at their ball and chain budget as a rallying point for ministry.

Regardless of the history of your local church, *Giving Away the Collection Plate* will inspire you to become more missional. It will force you to ask, "How can we become a better physical representation of Christ to our community?" Maybe it will even arouse you to the point that you become radically generous, as he is generous toward us.

PART ONE:
PREGIFTING

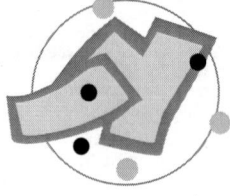

THE HUNGER TO GIVE

If your heart is broken, you'll find God right there;

If you're kicked in the gut, he'll help you catch your breath.

Psalm 34:18 (MSG)

God draws near to the brokenhearted. He leans toward those who are suffering. He knows what it feels like to be wounded and abandoned.

When I was in seminary, I met a college student living just north of San Francisco. My church had been trying to connect with some of the local unchurched students. A mutual friend introduced us, and he soon started coming to our church.

Many people in that part of California are highly affluent. They have either inherited money or created wealth through the years. The average home price, even after a recent, deep recession, is still a little over seven hundred thousand dollars. I cannot comprehend that type of money, and neither can my friend. Maybe that is why we connected well from the start.

Within a few months of visiting the church, he accepted Christ and was baptized—wetsuit and all—in the Pacific Ocean. Those present at his baptism will tell you that I took the brunt of the baptism. Waves seven to eight feet tall engulfed us, and by the end of the baptism, I was the one who washed up fifty feet down shore.

As time passed, our friendship grew, but our lives moved down divergent paths. I graduated from seminary and moved with my new wife away from California. God called us to join a church in rural Mississippi. But my friend stayed. Marin County was his home. He had never really known life outside of Northern California, and he had no plans to leave. He eventually graduated from college and started working toward a graduate degree.

During his first year of graduate studies, his life unraveled. One sad event followed another, and his dreams for a life in the performing arts fell apart. He experienced significant time without work and eventually hit rock bottom. His mother told him he needed to learn to survive on his own and she could not send any help. His brother, who lived nearby and worked as an attorney, told him to stand on his own feet. And my college-educated friend wound up on the streets.

With no place to turn, he eventually found himself in a homeless shelter. One morning soon after he arrived, he got out of the shower to discover that all of his worldly possessions had been stolen. His only connections to "normal" life—a laptop computer, a wallet, and a few other small possessions—were forever lost.

He would e-mail me from the library and update me on his condition. He found a local church that occasionally forgot to lock the foyer doors at night. When there was no room at the shelter, he would sneak in and sleep on the floor. Other nights, he would hide in a corner of the library and hope the staff would not notice him. In the middle of one of the wealthiest communities in the world, he struggled to survive.

Through e-mail conversations, he would periodically ask for help—money to get a prepaid cell phone or to buy a few groceries. His pleas from the other side of the country broke my heart and left me feeling despondent.

THE HUNGER TO HELP

I did not realize it at the time, but God was using the pain of my friend to shape me. He was opening my eyes to an enormous need. Through the life of my friend God was helping me understand that desperate suffering is incredibly common. It is far more common than the bloated bellies of compassionate infomercials can convey. In every community across the globe—from the wealthiest counties of California to the rural towns in Mississippi, from the poverty stricken nations of Africa to the streets of Afghanistan—there are numerous people who are grinding through life. People in each of our communities and behind the closed doors of our neighborhoods are daily facing abuse, neglect, and poverty. Pain is far more prevalent than prosperity. Suffering is a universal language.

Even though most of us have not experienced the desperation of homelessness, we can empathize with the struggle of life. It seems like we all have a deep hunger to help those in need. Sometimes our sympathy is overpowered by our selfishness, but in the pit of our being, it exists. We have a natural, instinctual desire to give.

When our children are hurting, we will go to the ends of the earth to provide what they need. When a friend encounters anguish, we want to help. If a good person is in a desperate situation, we feel a natural pull toward generosity.

In the oldest records of the Bible, Job suffers through a few days of unimaginable loss. His herds are stolen, his servants are slaughtered, and his children— all ten of them—are tragically killed. After his entire body breaks out in sores, his friends come to his side, yearning to help. Even though they eventually prove to be abysmal counselors, they sit with him in silence for seven long days. They mourn with him. Something inside of each of these friends prompted a desire to alleviate suffering. They wanted to end the torment in Job's life.

And while a lot has changed in the world since the days

"PAIN IS FAR MORE PREVALENT THAN PROSPERITY. SUFFERING IS A UNIVERSAL LANGUAGE."

of Job, humanity still has a basic urge to relieve suffering. Thousands of years later, we still have a natural longing to help. After the fall of Adam, we somehow retained the genetics of a compassionate Creator.

DRAWING NEAR

As I dealt with my friend in California, this God-shaped compassion coursed through me. I just did not know how to help. He was 2,300 miles away; I was broke. So, I did all that I knew to do. I helped when I could, encouraged him in his faith and consistently reminded him that his regular participation in a church community was critically important.

Thankfully, he listened. After some long, deep struggles, he is back on his feet. He has a consistent income and is surrounded by a faith community. But he will never be the same, and neither will I.

My wife was not as close to that particular friend, but she has compassionate longings very similar to mine. The only difference is that she handles them substantially better than I do. Every month or two, JD finds a way to extend her hand to someone in need. Just this week, a former prostitute found her way to our church as she sought assistance. She was the kind of person you try not to stare at when you see her on the street. Her past has taken a toll on her body. Her hair, which was braided at some point, is now a tangled mess. She no longer has any teeth. Her purple outfit is wearing thin, and her short sleeves expose several homemade tattoos. But the most prominent signs of her past were the sores which littered her arms. According to her story, they are the result of full-blown HIV. Her sad appearance startled a few people in our church, but it came as no surprise that JD was the one to show her kindness. She took this sin-abused woman to the store, bought her some food, and gave her a ride home.

JD sees these as opportunities. These situations present occasions for kindness, for giving. And at the core of her being, JD is a giver. She, like all of us, has an ingrained desire to help people. But unlike so many, she acts on it.

I have another friend who has this same type of magnetic pull toward giving. Phil is in his early sixties and is at the point in life when most Americans are thinking about retirement. He has worked hard as the owner of a painting business and later as a sales representative to make a good living. He has earned the right to slow down and take life easy, but that thought never crosses his mind. Phil is too busy giving things away to consider the comforts of life.

Over the last several years, Phil has become a regular missionary to Honduras. With the support of his Sunday school class and intentional flexibility in his work schedule, he has been able to travel to Central America many times. He goes with one mission— to give.

Phil has forewarned his kids that they will not have anything to inherit when he dies. Since they are all self-sufficient, Phil plans to work as long as he can and give away everything that he earns. He has told me on more than one occasion that he hopes the last check he ever writes bounces, so that he can literally go out the way he came in.

I admire people like JD and Phil. They offer a glimpse into the culture of God. When people are suffering, they lean in. They are not afraid to draw near. And their generosity regularly awakens my hunger for God's culture, God's kingdom. They challenge me to be more thoughtful. They make me want to be a better humanitarian, to be a better me.

To be honest, I do not fully understand why this giving hunger has survived from the days of Job until today. Maybe we long to give because of the gratitude that radiates from those who cannot repay you. Maybe it is tied to our deep longing for community. Maybe it is tangled in our desire to be (re)conformed to the image of God. But it seems to be a universal desire. A quick search of the Internet shows the wide expanses of philanthropy. A glimpse of Christmas morning displays the joys of giving as quickly as it does the joys of receiving. From the poorest among us to the wealthiest, we all have some desire to share.

Anytime there is an earthquake, a hurricane, or a devastating storm, the news is flooded with stories of individuals and organizations that shift into charitable mode. We help with housing and healthcare. We give food and toiletries. We come together to work for the good of others.

In 2005, after hurricanes Katrina, Rita, and Wilma hit US shores, over two billion dollars of assistance was donated to the American Red Cross.[3] Religious groups teamed up to organize shelters and meals. Foreign countries stood up to offer aid. And on top of all of this, thousands of individual groups trekked to these locations to offer help.

Those events demonstrate our desire to intercede. Where there is a worthy cause or an extenuating circumstance, there is also an appetite for giving. There is a hunger to help.

SACRIFICIAL CHARITY

But what happens when the level of giving passes the "feel good" stage and becomes costly? What happens when you feel like you are supposed to give more than you really want to give or can afford to give? What happens when you are not sure if the recipient is being honest?

Do you remember the rich young man in the New Testament? He approaches Jesus and asks what he needs to do in order to inherit eternal life. Jesus addresses the heart of his question by letting him know how to become a disciple. Jesus informs him that abundant life and eternal life are bound up in relationships. "If you want to be perfect, go, sell your possessions and give to the poor, and you will have treasure in heaven. Then come, follow me" (Matthew 19:21). In essence, Jesus says, "First of all, stop loving your stuff and start loving people." *Sell your possessions and give to the poor.* "Second," Jesus says, "fall in love with God. Show your love for God by joining him in his work." *Follow me.*

Considering all that he owned, the young man dropped his head and walked away. That kind of giving was costly. That extent of giving moved past the "feel good" stage. And as far as we know, it was too high a price in the mind of the young man.

Toward the end of this past year, our church leadership faced a predicament similar to that of the rich young man. We were by no means wealthy. Financial excess was never a concern. But when we ran to God and asked what we should do to better follow Him, we encountered a similar response from Jesus.

As we went to God to ask how we could better follow Him, economies across the world were sagging. The United States was in the middle of one of the most devastating recessions in memory. And our small church group was not immune from the recession, either. Five of our families had recently experienced layoffs.

So when we came to God and asked, "Father, what do we need to do to be more like you this year?" we were not feeling as confident as the rich young man. We were worried about cutting back our missions efforts. We were struggling with the idea of reducing our children's ministries. We were confident that our already bi-vocational ministers would endure pay cuts. Nevertheless, we asked honestly and waited for a response.

Maybe we should have anticipated God's answer. After all, we knew the story of the rich young man. But it still took us by surprise.

JOINING GOD'S MISSION

The answer actually came through a blurb in a magazine. It is no more than a quarter of a page—a condensed story from *USA Today*. The title of the story is "Bypassing the Plate." The article begins by saying, "The offering at Waterfront Community Church in Schaumburg, Illinois, doesn't cover salaries, utilities, or the church's mortgage: 100 percent of the weekly collection goes to people in need."[4]

The short commentary goes on to mention a single mother whose daughter is struggling with cerebral palsy. Because of the church's heart for giving, this mother will receive help with her rent, her financial planning, and parental advice for the next two years—free.

I am typically skeptical of circumstantial answers from God. I do not start praying and let my Bible fall open to a random passage for direction. While I know that God can speak through many avenues, I tend to want something a little more substantial, something that cannot be easily contrived. In this case, I did not open the magazine looking for an answer. I was simply looking to pass the time at work.

Contrary to my skepticism, God made it clear that his answer to our prayer was coming in the form of a magazine article and a church plant in the suburbs of Chicago. "Give your possessions to the poor. Then, come follow me."

In other words, God was saying, "Take all of the tithes and offerings that are given each Sunday and use them to minister to the hurting in Clinton."

As awe-struck as I was over the answer, I felt like I must have been misreading the signs. Logic said that I was jumping to conclusions. Our budget said that we could not afford to give. Therefore, I talked to mentors. I sought second and third opinions. And with each passing conversation, this answer came back: "I don't know. How would that work? Maybe you need to keep praying."

I agreed. And the more I prayed, the more I realized what God had been doing in my life over the past few years. God was molding me through the homelessness of my friend in California. He joined me to a wife who is a natural giver. He placed me in the path of Phil. I knew God was leading *me* in this direction, but was the entire church ready for such a radical step of faith? Moving from one man's convictions to an entire congregation's generosity is a massive leap.

Eventually, I felt certain enough of God's direction to approach the rest of our leadership with the idea of giving everything away. Although they shared some of my feelings of initial skepticism, they agreed to pray and pray desperately.

For weeks, we all wrestled with God over this vision. *Give everything away? Apparently, you didn't catch the part about our church needing financial help, God.* We struggled with the logical restraints on our finances. We wondered how we would handle a mountain of requests. We fasted and waited. And in the midst of our praying, God persistently responded with the same answer, "Give your tithes and offerings to the hurting this year. Then, come follow me."

Through circumstances in our lives, through Biblical gleanings and gifted communicators, God humbled us with a simple reminder: As Philip Yancey says, "There is but one true Giver in the universe; all else are debtors."[5]

With only one month left in the year, our church leadership consented to God's way. We would hand over the tithes and offerings; we would start to *regift* the offerings of God for the good of the community.

Within a few weeks of that decision, the rest of the church cautiously came onboard. If we wanted to become more like Christ over the next year, we were to pursue strategic, missional generosity. We should seek out the abused, neglected, and poor of Clinton so that we could walk with them. We should help meet their needs and do life with them day after day after day. God was teaching us to lean into the lives of the brokenhearted. He was inviting us to join his mission.

COEXISTENT
FEAR

Whoever trusts in his riches will fall, But the righteous will thrive like a green leaf.

Proverbs 11:28

God is limitless. We are not. That makes it hard for us to follow his generosity. He owns all that we see. We are not so fortunate. What if we give too much away? What if we are not able to pay the bills? What if something unexpected comes up after we give? Does sharing liberally really qualify us as being wise stewards, or should we be preparing for future opportunities? What if we give to others and they abuse the gift?

All of these questions surfaced as God led us to become givers in the vein of his generosity. As a church, we struggled with money dependence just as any normal family or individual struggles when they are asked to give. We wanted to give, but we also wanted to ensure we would have our needs met. More accurately, we wanted to be known for our generosity, but we also wanted to have access to the latest church resources and gadgets. It was tough to make our convictions and our actions align.

Over the last few years, one man has become the face of intentional generosity for US Christians. Shane Claiborne has been teaching the Jesus followers in Philadelphia how to give. He has demonstrated a life free of financial pursuit. He has pointed a spotlight on our worship of the material life. Maybe more importantly, he has demonstrated that our statements about generosity and our correlating actions are often inconsistent. In his book, *The Irresistible Revolution*, he noted that "the great tragedy of the church is not that rich Christians do not care about the poor but that rich Christians do not know the poor."[6] The beliefs and actions divide is not created by theology. We know the teachings of scripture, and we experience the hunger to help. But fear drives a wedge between what we think and what we do.

TREPIDATION

For every hunger we have toward giving, there is a coexistent and possibly more powerful fear of actually following through. We have an obvious hunger toward helping the poor, but we fear getting too close to them. We worry about unstable minds and irrational violence. With almost every impulse toward generosity, we fear what will become of us if we give too much—if we risk too radically. For all of our good intentions, there is an equal and opposite feeling of trepidation.

As a child I learned about this fear of loss through baseball cards. In the small baseball card society that my friends created, self-esteem was bought and traded with the faces of great players. We were fanatics. Every spare dollar was marked for upgrading our card collections. Every sleepover produced a trading frenzy. And when I mistakenly traded away a valuable card, I suffered. I lost.

Most of us feel the same way about money today. The only difference is that we are not trading paper faces of athletes; we are trading paper faces of former presidents. When we give too much, we lose. We sacrifice a little piece of ourselves and our futures. We forfeit what was good for virtually nothing in return.

In the classic novel *The Great Gatsby*, F. Scott Fitzgerald explores the connections between personal wealth and self-esteem. One character, named Daisy, was born into an affluent family. Throughout her life, her major decisions revolved around the ability to maintain an opulent lifestyle. She marries a man named Tom, not because of his character, but because of his inherited wealth. And although she maintains a relatively unhappy existence (Tom is openly having an affair), the thought of living without his money is a risk she is unwilling to consider. Eventually her pursuit of abundance leads her to commit murder and ultimately leads to the death of the man she really loves. Fitzgerald sums up Daisy's and Tom's lives by saying,

They were careless people, Tom and Daisy—
they smashed up things and creatures and then
retreated back into their money or their vast
carelessness…and let other people clean up the
mess they had made.[7]

Fitzgerald's summarization is true of millions of
Americans who worship at the altar of money. In pursuit
of the American Dream, cash is hunted and hoarded
recklessly, to
the detriment
of the entire
society. With
frightening reg-
ularity, we trade
the real joys and
love of life for the perceived safety of wealth.

> **"WITH FRIGHTENING REGULARITY,
> WE TRADE THE REAL JOYS AND
> LOVE OF LIFE FOR THE PERCEIVED
> SAFETY OF WEALTH."**

RISKY BUSINESS

Throughout the gospels, Jesus tells numerous stories
about the false security of wealth. In fact, he talks more
about this subject than he does about heaven or hell.
Pointedly, Jesus himself is a man who "has no place to
lay his head" (Luke 9:58). He, by choice, has no home.
So while his perspective on wealth may not match the
American Dream, he understands the weight of this
issue. He knows what money means to our families and
to our ministries. He clearly comprehends how heavily
this subject impacts our daily decisions.

In one instance, Jesus tells a story of a very wealthy
man who entrusts three of his servants with some of

his money. To the first servant, he entrusts a sum of five talents, the second receives two, and to the third, he hands over one talent. For all three men, this is probably more money than they have ever held at one time. The wealthy owner instructs the servants to handle his money wisely, and he prepares to go out of town.

The first two servants decide that in order to please the master, they need to take some calculated risks. In one way or another, they invest the money that they have received.

I don't know about you, but there are times in the Bible when I wish we had a little more detail. This is one of those points. I wish Jesus would have told us what type of risks these servants took. I wish I knew how far out on the financial limb they wandered. But Jesus does not give those details. All we know is that risk—and conquering the fear that accompanies risk—was necessary to please the owner.

We know that much with certainty, because the third servant did not take any risks. He promptly went out and buried the money. He took fear out of the equation. The money was hidden. Loss was virtually impossible. Fear was restrained.

Many of us have the mind of the third servant. When it comes to handling money, especially the money of the church, we hold safety as the highest value. The absence of risk is known as financial wisdom.

Apparently, this is not the mindset of the master. When he came back into town, he settled his accounts with the servants. The first two, which had taken risks and doubled their money, were told, "Well done, good and faithful servant! You have been faithful with a few things; I will put you in charge of many things. Come and share your master's happiness!" (Matthew 25:21, 23).

The servant who avoided fear and avoided risk heard a dramatically different response;

> His master replied, "You wicked, lazy servant! So you knew that I harvest where I have not sown and gather where I have not scattered seed? Well then, you should have put my money on deposit with the bankers, so that when I returned I would have received it back with interest.
>
> "Take the talent from him and give it to the one who has the ten talents. For everyone who has will be given more, and he will have an abundance. Whoever does not have, even what he has will be taken from him. And throw that worthless servant outside, into the darkness, where there will be weeping and gnashing of teeth."
>
> Matthew 25:26-30

Wicked and lazy are two words that we do not throw around lightly. Can you remember the last time you called someone wicked and lazy...*to their face*? John Ortberg says these words are indications of "the sin of unrealized potential...the willful refusal to choose risk and obedience and to choose comfort and safety instead."[8] The master calls this man lazy and wicked as a result of his fear.

Further, we can infer from other places in the Bible that God is not simply pleased by the positive financial results of the first two servants. Instead, he is delighted by their willingness to take a risk for him.

There is a widow in the book of First Kings that graphically illustrates this truth. We do not know much about her life, but I am pretty sure that she was not producing money for God's kingdom. She did not have resources even comparable to those of the wicked, lazy servant. In fact, when Elijah encounters the widow, he asks her for a simple snack—a jar of water and a piece of bread. Her response is, "I don't have any bread—only a handful of flour in a jar and a little olive oil in a jug. I am gathering a few sticks to take home and make a meal for myself and my son, that we may eat it—and die" (1 Kings 17:12). In other words, she is not too optimistic about her wealth. She is desperately poor and is not looking to do anything special with her few remaining resources. She intends to eat one last meal with her son and then die.

Elijah responds by saying,

> Don't be afraid. Go home and do as you have said. But first make a small cake of bread for me from what you have and bring it to me, and then make something for yourself and your son. For this is what the LORD, the God of Israel, says: "The jar of flour will not be used up and the jug of oil will not run dry until the day the LORD gives rain on the land."
>
> Kings 17:13-14

At her point of hunger and despair, she has to choose between a guaranteed meal and a curtain of fear. She chooses to take a monumental risk for God and bake some bread for this stranger before eating the final, leftover scraps. She chooses to regift from her pantry; she chooses faith over the security of her last financial covering. God is so pleased with this generosity and her pecuniary risk that he spares her life and her son's life until the famine lifts. In other words, God is more glorified by appropriate monetary risk than he is by financial gain.

VEIL OF FEAR

In the short history of Traceway Baptist Church, we have regularly rested on the comforts of a financial cushion. Risk has been the perceived enemy of our fiscal planning. This was never our overarching intention. We did not sit in committee meetings looking for ways to deny God's power. It was simply a matter of ritual.

Each year, we prayed diligently before the budget was developed and eventually went with the numbers that we felt God wanted us to employ. We honestly wanted to take up a budget based on faith. However, after the adoption of each budget, we would practice financial safety. We were careful to spend only what was coming in regardless of the faith in our initial budget. And if we ran into a shortfall during the year, we were thankful that we had controlled our spending. We accepted the shortfall and assumed that our controlled spending led to the appropriate conclusion—a balanced ledger sheet. As is typical in accounting, we monitored the cash flow and installed safety buffers to make sure that we did not fall into the red. Our budgeting process was based on faith and our financial practices were driven by the coexistent fear.

Maybe that is why God began to tell us to give away our offerings. Maybe this is why God directed us toward the process of regifting. We desperately needed to become dependent on God rather than sitting in the mud of fear. In order to move forward with God, we had to follow his voice in every area, including finances. We had to walk through the frightening veil of security and surrender to the ways of God instead of the ways of Mammon.

There was at least one man in first-century Israel who enjoyed the security of money. Because he was good at his job, he had a large security blanket—a nice-sized nest egg. Zacchaeus may have been small in stature, but he was high on the hog. He was on top of a prosperous tax collecting pyramid. As collectors under him made money, he received a portion.

I imagine it was a little bit surprising to the lower-ranking collectors when they found out that Zacchaeus, their financial leader, wanted to hang out with a homeless man, Jesus. And the religious people were equally shocked that Jesus would stay in the house of a "sinner."

This is another one of those stories that I wish included more detail. We know the part about Zacchaeus climbing the tree and the interaction he and Jesus had on the road. We also know the conclusion of the story. But we do not know what Jesus said to Zacchaeus in the meantime. We do not know what conversations they shared over meals. We do not know if Zacchaeus came to the sycamore-fig tree looking for a new way of life or looking for the latest spectacle. We just do not know.

Somewhere in their conversations, the subject of money comes up. Somewhere between the roadside tree and the parting steps out of the house, Jesus talks to this man about his financial practices. Apparently, he helps Zacchaeus realize that his financial practices are intimately tied to his spiritual experiences. Taking and hoarding is affecting his relationship with God. So Zacchaeus boldly steps through the curtain of fear and proclaims, "Here and now I give half of my possessions to the poor, and if I have cheated anybody out of anything, I will pay back four times the amount" (Luke 19:80).

At that point, Jesus makes one of those statements that are almost hard to believe. He says something so shocking that the disciples probably would not have believed it if they had not heard it firsthand. Jesus replies, "Today salvation has come to this house, because this man, too, is a son of Abraham. For the Son of Man came to seek and to save what was lost" (Luke 19:9-10).

Salvation? Are you kidding me? The man gives back what was not even rightfully his, and Jesus says this is the door to salvation?

Well, not exactly. Jesus said salvation came to the house of Zacchaeus because he was a child of Abraham. In other words, he was a man of faith. He had more faith in Jesus, a previously unknown Savior, than he did in the coins in his pocket. He had enough faith to risk his financial security for the good of others. And to demonstrate this trust, he took the coins out of his pocket and gave them away.

The Master, the Father, was pleased. *Well done, good and faithful servant.*

Philip Yancey captures the heart of our struggle well. Speaking on a personal level, he says,

> I feel pulled in opposite directions over the money issue. Sometimes I want to sell all that I own, join a Christian commune, and live out my days in intentional poverty. At other times, I want to rid myself of guilt and enjoy the fruits of our nation's prosperity.[9]

While all of us may not dream of joining a Christian commune, we recognize God's promptings toward a more generous existence. Apparently, the primary thing keeping our churches from practicing the radical generosity of God is anxiety. And the only wedge that separates our actions from his leadership is a thin veil of fear.

THE WAY OF GOD

I can't stand your religious meetings.
I'm fed up with your conferences and conventions.
I want nothing to do with your religion projects,
your pretentious slogans and goals.
I'm sick of your fund-raising schemes,
your public relations and image making.
I've had all I can take of your noisy ego-music.
When was the last time you sang to me?
Do you know what I want?
I want justice—oceans of it.
I want fairness—rivers of it.
That's what I want. That's all I want.

Amos 5:21-24 (MSG)

Last Christmas, our family decided to start a new holiday tradition. Immediately after opening our presents, we went out and gave one of these brand new gifts away. I have to admit that I would have hated this tradition as a child, but we thought it would be a great way to teach (and learn) an invaluable lesson. True generosity consists of giving from your best, not your leftovers. This was a true family test of regifting.

To be honest, I was not sure how our girls (four, three, and one year) would handle this. So we started preparing them for this potentially traumatic event about a month in advance. We taught them about children that do not receive gifts at Christmas or any other time of year. We tried to help them understand that some people are suffering and would really appreciate a new gift. We told them Bible stories to show how God always gives us his very best gifts, even giving us his own Son. But we knew that asking small children to act like God was a bit of a stretch. They had given away old toys in the past, but to give away an untouched toy was another story.

On Christmas morning, we passed out the presents and ripped off the wrapping paper with gusto. The girls were thrilled with their princess dolls, DVDs, and dress up clothes. Then came the moment of truth. We asked each what they wanted to give away to less fortunate children. One by one, they picked out presents that were still in their original boxes. Surprisingly, they did not complain or fuss. In fact, they were actually excited about giving gifts away.[10] So, on Christmas morning, two children in a local children's hospital received brand new gifts. One gas station clerk was given a DVD to take to his young girl. Local firemen who were working Christmas morning received new presents. And our family received the momentary pleasure of acting like God—giving away some of our best possessions.

WHOLLY DIFFERENT

One thing was abundantly clear to me through this process. My ways are not like God's ways. My thoughts are not like his thoughts. I do not instinctively give away the best of my lot. I do not naturally act with the graciousness of the Father.

Apparently, I am not the only one, either. Newspapers are regularly filled with stories of men and women who are caught up in the pursuit of stuff. I recently saw an article about a woman who faked cancer to get gifts. Because of her lie, she was given a dream wedding and honeymoon. After announcing that she only had mere months to live, people showered her with affection and provisions.[11] Later the husband confessed to the ruse, much to the horror of the donors.

If we are going to follow in the footsteps of Jesus, we need Divine intervention. His footsteps are too deep for us; his stride is too long. There is no natural way for a man, with all the stains of sin, to become like the unblemished, holy God. It can only happen through the work of the Holy Spirit. Although we are made in the image of our Creator, God and humanity are wholly distinct.

At only a few months old, my youngest daughter already exuded the marks of humanity. Even though she could not walk and could not speak more than a couple of words, she was a magician with her possessions. She would sit with a toy in her hands and confound her older sisters. As they ran around her trying to steal the toy, she would pass it between her hands, behind her back, under her leg and make the toy dance like a jumping bean. Eventually, the older girls would lose interest and move on to the next, unoccupied toy.

Meanwhile, the ten-month-old would grin and revel in the prize of her selfishness.

JD and I never demonstrated those amazing moves to our child. We never taught her to be self-centered. Instead, we passed it to her naturally as an inheritance. From the moment she took her first breath, she felt desires for self-preservation. As part of humanity, selfishness came naturally at birth.

The more I pursue God, the more I realize that he is inherently different from us. He does not protect his possessions and hoard his toys. He does not look for ways to make us jealous of him, though he, the God Most High, is jealous for us. While we are limited by time and space, he is boundless. Where we are faithless, he is faithful. While we often live in fear and worry, he always reigns in power.

This separation is so wide, the Bible indicates that apart from the sacrifice of Jesus, we are all actually enemies of God (Colossians 1:21-22). We are self-absorbed and arrogant. But God is, by nature, giving. At the core of his disposition, he is gracious. Generosity is simply the way of God. And while it is a respectable part of our culture, giving is contrary to our selfish nature.

THE AMERICAN DREAM

Standing in New York Harbor, there is a gift from France, which ironically displays America's struggle between selfishness and generosity. The Statue of Liberty stands tall as one of the great symbols of America. She stands for freedom, liberty, and opportunity. She cries to the world,

GIVING AWAY THE COLLECTION PLATE

Give me your tired, your poor,

Your huddled masses yearning to breathe free,

The wretched refuse of your teeming shore.

Send these, the homeless, tempest-tost to me,

I lift my lamp beside the golden door![12]

As a nation, we embrace this thinking, and we display a hunger to give. We desire to see people come out of hardship to a place of security. We are willing to take in the poor and give them a portion of our wealth. We, with the Statue of Liberty, stand with one hand always open to a hurting world.

Conversely, this magnificent statue is also the prevailing symbol for the American Dream. She represents the desire for opportunity, upward mobility, and financial prosperity. She stands tall for developing and gathering wealth. And in that sense, she represents a self-indulgent American culture that generally keeps one hand closed.

The American Dream has cultivated a mindset that we deserve a life of comfort. Being naturally selfish, I struggle with these feelings of entitlement. I feel like my hard work permits me a certain amount of selfishness. When I make the most of my opportunity, I should reap the reward. I should be free to pursue the cars that I want and the houses that I desire. I should be able to provide my children with the same vacations and pleasures that their friends experience. I should be able to occasionally eat well at the restaurants of my choice. I have earned that right.

The American Dream has taught me that making the most of my opportunity leads to the satisfaction of my possessions. And when we are satisfied with our possessions, they become exceedingly hard to relinquish. Generosity is tough for the hand that is closed.

Our congregations naturally languish in the same struggle. We want to be kind. We post plaques on our building walls to show that we live with an open hand toward all peoples. We honestly pursue charity and often buy necessities for the poor who walk through our doors. But we also keep one hand closed behind our backs.

American church communities wrestle with the discrepancies between missions giving and personal spending. We debate how freely to spend on foreign missions at the expense of personal building projects. We walk the tightrope between clothing ministries for the poor and six-figure salaries for decorated ministers.* We are in a constant battle between kindness and selfishness. Ironically, our church entities, much like the Statue of Liberty, stand as beacons toward both giving and hoarding.

---

*Every minister deserves his wages. In a God-cultured church, the congregation will work with each minister to joyfully cover their all their needs. In turn, as a lead servant, the minister will honestly evaluate the disparity between his needs and desires. Ezekiel 34 stands as a profound indictment of the lavish lifestyles of many decorated ministers. It states, "Woe to the shepherds of Israel who only take care of themselves! Should not shepherds take care of the flock? You eat the curds, clothe yourselves with the wool and slaughter the choice animals, but you do not take care of the flock. You have not strengthened the weak or healed the sick or bound up the injured. You have not brought back the strays or searched for the lost. You have ruled them harshly and brutally. So they were scattered because there was no shepherd, and when they were scattered they became food for all the wild animals."

OPENHANDED GENEROSITY

It was in the midst of this struggle that Traceway felt the call to give everything away. Somehow, by the grace of God, we grasped the irony of our situation. We began to understand the incredible riches that had been lavished upon us. At the same time, we started to realize the weight of our selfish nature.

When we asked God how we could become more like him, he responded by showing us his openhanded generosity. He made us conscious of the fact that he is always giving. He does not wrestle with selfishness.

Even while we were still his enemies, even while we persisted in sin, he gave his life for us. Even though he inhabited the riches of heaven, he did not hold on to those personal pleasures. He wrapped himself in flesh. For our benefit, he became an indescribable gift. As Jesus walked on the face of the earth, he deliberately lived to serve, not to be served. He is generous by nature. At the core of his being, he is gracious.

In Luke 6, Jesus speaks about the way of God. Some of the things that Jesus says at the end of this chapter are so familiar to believers that we have stopped paying attention to his words. He says things like,

> Love your enemies, do good to those who hate you, bless those who curse you, pray for those who mistreat you. If someone strikes you on one cheek, turn to him the other also. If someone takes your cloak, do not stop him from taking your tunic.
>
> Luke 6:27-29

Typically, when we hear these things, our minds shift into autopilot. We have become so accustomed to these sayings that we almost dismiss them as nice thoughts—Jesus thoughts. We expect this type of talk from Jesus, but because of its familiarity, we typically distance it from everyday life.

In truth, we would prefer that Jesus altered these statements for us. We would prefer Him to say, "When you encounter those who hate you and those who curse you, take your cloak, walk away, and avoid your enemies." We prefer to practice passive Christianity. We will often get out of the way or ignore our enemies, but to love them means taking a proactive step of faith. Where Jesus says, "Do good," we prefer to keep our distance.

Interestingly, these ideas were not just passive thoughts to Jesus. They were not Twitter-esque statements that he thought his followers would enjoy. In reality, Jesus would soon put these radical phrases into action. He would live them out on the way to the cross. He demonstrated the power of these statements on the road to his death.

"If someone strikes you on the one cheek..."

Soon after he was arrested, they mocked him and struck him in the face. He had every right to lash out or call on legions of angels to take him out of this situation. But he did not walk away from the attackers. He stayed the course and turned the other cheek.

"If someone takes your cloak..."

They took the cloak off his back, and he did not fight to retain his possessions. Instead, he gave them his tunic and his undergarment as well.

"Love your enemies; do good to those who hate you..."

In the ultimate act of love, he gave his life for his enemies.

In the face of extreme adversity, he gave. In the time of pain, he did not pride himself on passive reactions.

"THIS IS THE WAY OF GOD— GIVING HIS BEST, EVEN TO THOSE WHO ARE ENEMIES." He actively engaged his most boisterous opponents with openhanded generosity and grace. He took his own statements of kindness and demonstrated their weight as he went to the cross.

That type of generosity is staggering. It goes against everything that is human. It swallows all pride and shoves aside any form of selfishness. This is the way of God—giving his best, even to those who are enemies.

I gave away a few presents last Christmas morning, but honestly, I did not give my best. I did not give away the house. I never thought of offering my car. I would not even entertain the thought of giving away one of my children for the benefit of someone else. And I did not attempt to give to people who disliked me. But, astonishingly, that was God's plan. He never entertained the thought of giving us anything less. He gives his best, even to those who are his enemies.

In Luke 6, Jesus does much more than offer a thoughtful soliloquy. He shows us the heart of God. He demonstrates that generosity is a conscious decision and a proactive way to live. He goes on to say, "Give to everyone who asks you, and if anyone takes what belongs to you, do not demand it back. Do to others as you would have them do to you" (Luke 6:30-31).

GOD'S KINDNESS

Andy Stanley has aptly noted that most of us have established unwritten levels of generosity.[13] We determine what we are going to give based on the worthiness of the recipient. We give generously when we have confidence that the gift will be used properly.

For example, the bottom tier of my giving pyramid is comprised of homeless people and those who are asking for handouts. In downtown Jackson, there is a homeless man who is probably sixty years old. His exposure to the elements has aged him beyond his years. Every time I see him, he is leaning on his cane and donning a big, silly grin on his face. To every person that passes, he calls out, "Hey, give me a dollar. Give me a dollar." His smile is nice, but he still falls to the bottom giving rung. I do not trust that he will use the money appropriately. So he may get a cup of coffee if I am in a good mood.

The next level of giving is reserved for reciprocating generosity. When an acquaintance gives me a small Christmas gift, I may know them well enough to trust them, but I really do not consider them a gift-giving type friend. So I reciprocate. I stop by the dollar store and find the nicest thing on the shelves. I spend just enough to get by.

Then the levels of giving increase. Legitimate friends get nice gifts. Best friends, brothers, and sisters get better gifts. Parents and children get gifts that approach extravagance (for my budget). And my wife is going to get the best that I have to offer.

I, along with millions of others, approach giving with this tier system in mind. But apparently Jesus does not approach giving in this manner. Instead, he says, "Give to everyone who asks you." *Everyone.* Wow. That puts a big strain on my giving system. Beyond that, he tells us not to demand back our possessions that have been stolen. Do not worry about these things.

Finally, Jesus sums all of these statements up by saying,

> But love your enemies, do good to them, and lend to them without expecting to get anything back. Then your reward will be great, and *you will be sons of the Most High, because he is kind to the ungrateful and wicked.*
>
> Luke 6:35 (Italics mine)

In other words, if you want to be known as children of the Most High, be generous as he is generous. Be giving as he is giving. Even to the ungrateful and wicked. Even to those who will take your gift and use it the wrong way. This is the way of God.

When the leadership of Traceway began to ask, "How can we become more like You?" we genuinely wanted to follow God. We honestly wanted to be known as the incarnation of Christ, the physical representative of God in our city. But we had no idea what we were asking. We were oblivious to the gravity of our question and to the depth of God's love.

Following the way of God was clearly going to be harder than we anticipated. The generosity of God extends well beyond the tithes and offerings from Sunday morning. We were only beginning to scratch the surface of God's kindness. We were only beginning to comprehend how different we are from God.

"How great is the love the Father has lavished on us, that we should be called children of God! And that is what we are!" (1 John 3:1).

PART TWO: REGIFTING

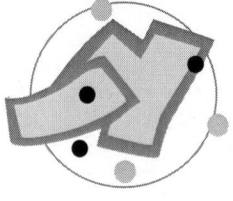

FROM RADICAL TO PRACTICAL

God can do anything, you know—far more than you could ever imagine or guess or request in your wildest dreams! He does it not by pushing us around but by working within us, his Spirit deeply and gently within us.

Ephesians 3:20-21 (MSG)

Generosity is always a choice. Every church can practice radical generosity. Any church can transform their community through strategic giving. Regardless of congrega-

tion or budget size, generosity only happens as a result of a conscious decision.

Toward the beginning of our ReGifting Project, a woman named Jamie called me to ask about our church. Although she called while I was at my "day job," I had some free time and was able to introduce her to the heart of our ministry. She had heard about some of the things that we were doing and was intrigued by the way we approached church.

It did not take long to figure out that Jamie was not just interested in our theology. I do not remember if it was on that first phone call or not, but she eventually divulged that she was fighting a desperate battle and needed assistance to keep going. Only a short time before hearing of our church, Jamie found out that her marriage was in deep trouble. Her husband had been away on business and had been unfaithful to the marriage. He was now talking about leaving his family and was restricting their access to his income.

When I met Jamie, she was living with relatives and was fighting for her marriage as well as some understanding of God's role in this mess. She was penniless and broken. She couldn't even afford gas to get around town.

Over time, Jamie became a regular at our worship gatherings. She started attending small groups and even started a women's Bible study for a few friends.

Her life did not turn around overnight, but with some financial assistance and the support of a community, she was eventually able to get back on her feet. Her husband left his job and his mistress to reunite with his family. Through some friends, we found Jamie a job and assisted them in getting an apartment.

Today, Jamie is pursuing a career in ministry and is starting to talk to a few churches about youth ministry positions. While we cannot accept the credit for Jamie's life-change, we were able to help her walk through some of the deeper valleys. We were able to take the gifts that God had given to us and use them for the good of a family in our community.

God used our obedience to display His glory.

HOW DID YOU DO THAT?

As Traceway started the ReGifting Project, we averaged fifty to sixty people in worship. By virtually any standard, we were a small church. And according to some, it is easier for a small church to practice radical generosity. When budgets are in the thousands rather than the millions, giving everything away seems easier. There are not as many obligations. There are not as many staff members or immovable budget constraints. And to some extent that is true. But, as we have found, there are a number of ways to practice radical generosity.

When God called us to give away all of our tithes and offerings for a year, we did not know how to make this dream become a reality. Although we were overwhelmed by the thought, eventually 100 percent of our receipts would go to the hurting of our community. Every dollar that went into the offering plates would be used to minister to the community. But, somehow, we still had to pay the bills.

In spite of our size and in spite of the fact that our ministers were already bi-vocational, we had to cover certain expenses. There was no option but to maintain our insurance. We still needed to purchase some small group materials. We needed a way to supplement our ministers' ten-dollar-per-hour jobs. So, in order for this process to become a reality, we knew that we had to find ways to accomplish two things: first, reduce our budget, and second, find outside sources of income.

As we began to follow God into these unknown depths, I knew we would have to move beyond our comfort zones to accomplish his mission. We would be forced to release our dependence on money. We would have to let go of pride. As soon as we said yes, we were bobbing in deep, scary waters. (Although that is scary, it is a pretty cool place to be.)

Reducing the budget was not too difficult. In fact, we were already beginning to shift the direction of our children's ministry before we were led to radical giving. In God's remarkable foreknowledge, he was leading us to a less expensive form of inspiring children before we ever realized this particular call to generosity. And by shifting to a children's environment based on parental leadership, we reduced our budget by fifteen thousand dollars.

In addition to the children's ministry makeover, God was also paving the way for increased involvement with another local church. The largest church in our city, Morrison Heights Baptist Church, came to us and made a staggering offer. For the last few years, God had been shaping them for more extensive local missions' efforts, and now they felt led to include our church plant in those plans. In a remarkable act of generosity, they renovated one of their older buildings and let us move in—for free. No strings attached. We did not have to worship like Morrison Heights. We did not have to answer for the type of people that came to our gatherings. They expected nothing of us except that we would glorify God. And once again, through God's astounding foreknowledge and through the generosity of Morrison Heights, we were able to reduce our budget even further.

In the end, we were able to reduce our previous year's budget by a little over twenty thousand dollars. Without much effort on our part, and with the obvious interventions of God, our expenses for the year went down to fifty thousand dollars—a 30 percent reduction. Now, in order to give everything away we would have to form partnerships and find creative ways to cover our fifty thousand dollars of obligations.

If you've seen the movie *Jaws*, you will never forget the opening scene. An attractive, blonde-haired woman is swimming alone in the ocean. The music is deep and haunting. The water is dark. As she treads upright, you can only see her head and shoulders. The rest of her body is submerged in the deep. You get a sense of her legs waving through the water, when suddenly, something grabs her from below. Her shoulders dip into the water. She comes back upright and starts to panic. She is grabbed again and her head is pulled below the surface. When she pops up this time she is screaming. You can feel her terror. Her face tells the story of a woman being eaten alive by a great white shark.

When I watch that scene, I get a rush of adrenaline. My heart rate increases, and my stomach starts feeling uneasy. Before the movie is five minutes old, I am privately recounting how I will never swim in the open ocean again. *Jaws* is famous for the incredible sense of dread that it instills from the opening moments.

As our church leaders discussed covering the remaining budget, I knew we were venturing into frightening territory. Reducing the budget was one thing, but raising funds moved us to a whole new level of discomfort. As we talked about asking untold numbers of friends for money, I felt the same type of dread that I felt watching *Jaws*—sweaty palms, nervous stomach, and a racing heart. Stepping into the shoes of a beggar is rarely easy.

For some professional fundraisers, fifty thousand is pocket change. There are people that raise that much in a single week and do it all over again before the end of the month. But for me, anytime fundraising is mentioned, I feel a little bit sick at my stomach. When I have to ask for money, my heart starts to race. I start to feel like the guy at the mall who tracks down unassuming shoppers and sprays them with cologne, hoping to drum up a sale. And I do not like that guy.

I am generally better at talking people out of giving money than I am at talking them into giving. I do not have any problem teaching financial concepts. I do not hesitate to teach about stewardship and tithing, but this is different. I hate to pressure people, especially knowing that they are already giving in other places and understanding that most of them are not wealthy (or more accurately, do not *feel* wealthy). I am the type of person who would rather give the money myself, if possible, than to ask for it from friends and relatives. For me, this was another giant step in a journey of faith.

At first, we talked about finding five or six large donors to cover the budget obligations. We talked about local "celebrities" that we could approach and also considered a few wealthy believers in our city.

Eventually, after seeking God's wisdom, we determined that collecting large donations would be the quickest method but maybe not the most effective. So we opted to go in the complete opposite direction. We realized that we should include as many people as possible in this process. We decided to present this as a unique opportunity for ministry. It would become a ministry that could be experienced by the wealthy, the financially struggling, and everyone in between.

As we did the math, we realized that if 2,500 families or individuals could offer a onetime gift of twenty dollars, our obligations would be covered. Within a few days of this decision, we created an invitation letter and started messaging all of our friends on Facebook. Additionally, we videoed a simple invitation with a personal camcorder and sought a select few individuals who would be willing to share this video with their small groups or Sunday school classes. We clearly emphasized that we did not want these people to reduce their tithes to their local church for our benefit.

These gifts were to be a small sacrifice above what they were already putting into God's kingdom.

In all honesty, we never heard back from the majority of the people we contacted. They did not "de-friend" us, but the subject simply never came up again. And we did not push it any further with those individuals.

On the other hand, we did hear from people that we never thought would donate. And those who decided to participate jumped in with both feet. Not only did they provide financial support, but they provided incredible encouragement for us as we began this journey.

One friend, who also serves as a church leader, responded by saying,

> Not only do I applaud and admire you for what Traceway is doing, but I am inspired and affirmed. We are walking through—maybe better said struggling through—the same process. We don't want Amos 4 and 5 to be read about us. We want to love the poor and the broken as Jesus did, not just band aid social issues—one family at a time. Love how you guys are doing this.

Another friend who was enduring unbelievable hardships of her own sent twenty dollars and a personal note saying, "I am so happy and thankful to be able to help with the church's ministry in this way. I only wish I could do more…I hope that His love spreads like wildfire and touches a multitude of people!"

In the end, we did not have 2,500 families participate, but approximately two hundred families or individuals donated the required fifty thousand dollars. Many donated twenty dollars. Others gave more excessively. And every donation received above the fifty thousand dollar goal was designated toward our missional giving efforts.

As a small staff, we tapped into our circle of friends and trusted God with the rest. For large churches, there are larger circles of friends and larger numbers of people who may be willing to participate in the fund raising process. The task may look daunting, but taking up a cross was never presented as simple. Sweaty palms and a nervous stomach should never be the determining factors in your decision to "go with God."

THE JOY OF THE UNKNOWN

I'll never forget the joy of following God into this uncharted environment. He did not hand us the funds in one lump sum (as I hoped he would). He did not even provide the entire year's funds before we started the ReGifting Project. In fact, we even had a few moments of serious doubt. We briefly considered delaying the project until we could raise all of the funds. But God convinced us to move ahead as planned. Remarkably, he always gave us money and resources in proportion to the needs around us.

At one point during the year, a friend asked if he could talk to me. That part did not strike me as strange, but it was a little odd that he did not want to talk in public. Over a period of a few days, we played phone tag, and I eventually ended up driving to his house.

I really did not know what to expect as I drove over. Although we are friends, we do not hang out regularly.

So, I walked into their home and we made small talk for a few minutes. Finally, with some hesitation, he brought up the real reason for our meeting.

A few months earlier, as the economy sagged, his sales job had been cut. Their previously healthy income had taken a nose dive. He had been looking for new work and had already been through several rounds of interviews, but the job did not come quickly enough.

As the kids played in their rooms, this man and his wife sat with me in the living room of their two-story home and showed me a bank-endorsed foreclosure notice. They were several months behind, and even with the prospects of a new job they were not going to be able to catch up in time to save the house.

"John," he said, "we have wrestled with this for months. We have looked at all of the options, and we really have nowhere else to turn. We are making payments each month but it is not enough to satisfy the bank. Is there anything Traceway can do?"

During the previous month, the requests for assistance had been remarkably quiet. We were not getting any new nominations, and our ReGifting account was steadily growing. We had wondered why God was building this surplus; as I sat on the couch of their home, I finally understood.

Within a couple of days, the family had been nominated for assistance and was approved by the funding team. Within a week, the mortgage company had received a cashier's check and the family was no longer behind on their house payments. What an incredible joy it was to look those people in their teary eyes and tell them, "*God was planning your deliverance before you ever knew you had a problem.*"

Doesn't that just sound like God? Isn't it amazing that he always has the answer before we ever see the problem? And as we walk by faith, he affords us these unique moments where we experience faith incarnate. He allows us to be his body—his vehicle—as he interrupts our neighborhoods with his glory. He invites us to walk in his footprints, to encounter his movement, to bask in his sovereignty.

That is joy; God-shaped joy.

As we came to learn through all of the regifting scenarios, the "how" of regifting was not tremendously important. We could have developed a thousand different methods to give away God's love and money. The thing that really mattered was that this was God's plan. And in the end, he would carry it out in his (better than we could have ever designed) fashion.

> "GOD ALLOWS US TO BE HIS BODY—HIS VEHICLE—AS HE INTERRUPTS OUR NEIGHBORHOODS WITH HIS GLORY."

MISSIONAL REGIFTING

> We loved you so much that we were delighted
> to share with you not only the gospel of God
> but our lives as well, because you had become
> so dear to us.
>
> 1 Thessalonians 2:8

During the week, I work in a downtown office
building. Outside of our thirteen-story building, there
are people that walk the streets all day and sleep in the
alleys at night. You can identify them by their unkempt
hair and tattered clothing. Some of them smell of urine
and seem lost in a sea of confusion.

Stories circulate of a man walking around the local
streets completely nude. Others tell of a homeless man
that sat in the bushes, almost hidden to the eye, who
would laugh and giggle as people passed by. One man
played his own football games—standing on the street

corners, he would frighten unsuspecting bystanders with the deafening cadence of a quarterback. "Down… Set…Hike! Hike! Hike!" Then he would take off running across streets and through courtyards, periodically looking over his shoulder for the imaginary pass coming his way. Meanwhile, the people with leather briefcases and Kiton suits stared in amazement.

The typical homeless population struggles with issues much deeper than budgeting and unemployment. Schizophrenia and dementia dominate the landscape of their lives. Their worlds are riddled with the wounds of war, mental disease, and overwhelming trauma. Their minds are revolting against the harshest realities of life. And they have proven to be a vast mission field, even since the days of Jesus.

In the suburbs, where I live, finding a homeless person is as rare as finding a twenty-dollar bill in my pocket. There are no tattered people walking the streets, but behind the privacy fences and closed doors, there is a wealth of pain. The working poor, the divorced, the abused and neglected are strewn throughout our neighborhoods. In the four or five houses surrounding my own, there is a recently divorced woman, a divorced father with a small child, and an often lonely widow. So, whether I step into my driveway or out in front of my office, I am surrounded by suffering.

The opportunity to regift God's generosity—in the cities, in the suburbs, and in the country—is always available. Jesus himself noted that the poor will always be with us. As long as there is life on this earth, there will be suffering. And while there is no one simple answer to the problem of human suffering, there is a question that points toward God's heart in this matter. *How do we provide assistance that really changes lives? How do we lighten suffering, regardless of the situation, with the result of transformation?*

A monetary gift alone rarely changes the recipient. Government handouts simply do not provide life change; they perpetuate existence. Even though the United States government hands out millions of dollars to the distressed, they cannot seem to change the lives of these people. The government provides rations, not revolutions. They are good at bridging the temporary gap, but they will never succeed at filling the void.

Our King, on the other hand, is in the business of transformation. He is not nearly as interested in our temporary comforts as he is in our permanent life change. So he does something that a systematic government cannot do—he takes our pain personally. He joins us in our struggle. He takes on flesh to walk with us. He tears open the curtain to the holy of holies so that, like the Father of the prodigal, he may run toward and embrace us. It is an act of passion. It flows from a heart of love. And one day, he vows to transform us eternally by making "the dwelling of God with men" (Revelation 21:3). It is the presence of God that changes the lives of men.

DIVINE IMAGE

God is obsessed with the mission of molding people. His ongoing mission is to share His love with us and invite us into his joy. And the method that he has chosen to accomplish this is a practice of regular gift giving. God uses strategic, missional gifts to shape our lives.

"For God so loved the world that he gave…"

Life renovation is found in God-infused charity. It cannot come through the law, and it does not happen through increasing forms of discipline. According to the ways of God, it happens through strategic giving.

Paul says it was God's gift that persuaded him to change the entire course of his life. "I became a servant of this gospel by the *gift* of God's grace" (Ephesians 3:7). In the same way, the indwelling of God that overrides our old, sin nature is the "*gift* of the Holy Spirit" (Acts 2:38). And when God wants to initiate the evolution of a society, he does it not by sheer force but rather by dispensing love in the form of spiritual *gifts*. He changes individuals and entire societies through calculated and sometimes astonishing generosity.

"LIFE RENOVATION IS FOUND IN GOD-INFUSED CHARITY."

So it only makes sense that God would tell our church to become generous as he is generous. It is by reflecting God's missional generosity that our church could gain influence in the lives of the unchurched. Further, it is through missional generosity that church members found brokenness and were remolded into the image of Christ.

I recently had a church member come into my office and tell me a story of financial generosity. He did not intend to tell me a story of transformation, but his body language conveyed much more than a simple story of giving.

Joshua was away from his house around noon and decided to grab a quick lunch. As he was driving, he came to a local burger joint. Against his better judgment, he stopped and went inside to eat. As he was sitting alone, enjoying his meal, he noticed a disheveled man enter the side door. The man glanced around quickly and moved toward the garbage bins. Reaching inside, he fumbled through the trash and eventually found a partially consumed drink. Without ever looking up, he took the cup and walked back outside to drink the remainder.

Since the restaurant has a primarily glass exterior, Joshua could watch the man's movements. After finishing the drink, he started walking around the exterior of the building. When he came to the other side, he once again entered and cautiously searched the remaining garbage bins for leftovers. By this time, people were staring and starting to show their disdain. Finding nothing salvageable and knowing he was unwanted, the man walked outside and found a quiet place to sit, alone.

Having watched the entire scene unfold, Joshua was moved with compassion. He walked through the door, caught the man's attention, and called him back to the restaurant. He asked if he was hungry. The man indicated his craving with a simple nod of his head. So Joshua led him to the cashier and invited him to order whatever he desired. After receiving the food, Joshua escorted him to sit in the restaurant with dignity and enjoy his meal.

As Joshua sat in my office relating that story to me, he was overcome with emotion. His voice was broken.

He periodically removed his glasses and wiped away the tears. Because of his gift, he was a changing man. I do not know if that stranger's life is any different after his meal, but I know that Joshua experienced a life-shift. He is starting to understand, in a new way, what it means to love a neighbor in the same way that he loves himself. Grasping the love of the Almighty (and occasionally letting go of the almighty dollar) is the real reason a change is happening in his life.

On the receiving end of the relationship, the same principle is true. God's love is what changes the recipient. Money is simply the conduit for building a friendship. Money is not love, but it can act as the handle on the door to love.

Properly relating to God's love is the only thing that really transforms people.

DIVINE THEATER

When God wants to make profound contentions in the Bible, he often does it on the stage of human life. It is almost as if God invites men and women to serve as the lead characters for his divinely written scripts. He takes certain lives and develops a drama to act out his most important truths.

When he wanted to emphasize the impending arrival of the Messiah, he instituted the feasts of Leviticus. He developed the feast of Passover and commanded the Jews to literally act it out year after year. He scripted the time line for watching over a lamb to make sure it was unblemished, the time for taking it to the slaughter, and the importance of leaving its bones unbroken. Year after year, the Jews took the stage of God to demonstrate (to the precise hour) how the perfect lamb would be treated while he was on earth. Further, God commanded his people to celebrate the feasts of Trumpets, Booths, and the Day of Atonement as they physically acted out the prophecies of the coming Christ.[14]

When God wanted to warn of the coming shame for Egypt and Ethiopia, He initiated an R-rated exhibition unlike any other. Isaiah was directed by God to climb the stairs of the divine theater and preach naked—for three years (Isaiah 20:1-6). God brought Ezekiel on the same stage and asked him to bake his bread over human excrement in order to show the defilement of his people (Ezekiel 4). At another point, God led Jeremiah to place a wooden yoke around his neck and speak to the leaders of Judah about their impending slavery to Babylon (Jeremiah 27:1-2).[15]

God loves to see his truths acted out. In one of the most memorable theatrical pictures of scripture, God tells the prophet Hosea to take a prostitute for a wife. She would leave him and return to prostitution, forcing Hosea to buy her back for a handful of silver and a few bushels of barley. Her continual infidelity portrayed the affairs of Israel and Judah with common idols. After depicting this wickedness on the stage of Hosea's life, God goes on a tirade over the sinfulness of his people. He warns, "You walk away from your God at the drop of a hat and like a whore sell yourself promiscuously at every sex-and-religion party on the street" (Hosea 9:1, MSG).

For eleven chapters, God rants against the wickedness of his people. He is grief-stricken over their sinfulness and shame. He is mortified at the sight of their self-inflicted wounds. Their suffering has caused him pain. And in the end, he reminds them that there is really only one hope for sustained change: "I am like a luxuriant fruit tree. Everything you need is to be found in me" (Hosea 14:8, MSG).

Life transformation only really happens in the presence of God. It is the demonstrative love of God that changes sin-wounded people. In a way that nothing else can, God's radical love renovates the heart.

REDEEMING DIGNITY

As our church began to actively distribute financial gifts, we knew that they would only be beneficial when they were packaged in the "luxuriant fruit" of God's presence. We knew that handing out money was only the beginning of regifting the presence of God. We wanted to approach local heartache with an outpouring of genuine empathy so that our gifts would not equate to a "resounding gong or clanging cymbal." We wanted the recipients to know the identity of the true Giver. We wanted them to see the Imago Dei (image of God) rather than a charitable handout. We desired that they would feel cherished rather than ashamed.

Speaking of feeling cherished, there is a fine line between a good gift and an offense. Generosity, delivered poorly, can feel like an insult. That is why needy people make statements like "I don't need your pity" or "Please don't make me your charity case." Fifty million

Americans currently depend on government assistance in the form of health care or food stamps, but very few of them feel pride over their support. Instead, neediness comes with a level of shame, and shame is easily inflamed to bitterness. So how do we provide support without insult? How do we use these gifts to redeem the dignity they have already lost?

Our church is privileged to have a strong relationship with a local rehab center. This relationship has afforded us many great men over the course of our existence. They have served in our praise band, freely offered help with construction and maintenance projects, and have been leaders in befriending timeworn soldiers at the local VA Medical Center. However, for a few of them, the battle with addiction never seems to diminish.

At one point, a couple of these men yielded to their cravings and were resultantly discharged from the rehab center. Through conversations the following Sunday, I found out that they had traded in the hope of rehab for a dingy, rundown motel room. Often, after guys are expelled from their rehab "home," they become transient and may change locations daily. Thankfully, these men were in the same motel room when I went to find them that afternoon. They had consumed more alcohol in one weekend than many adults consume in a lifetime. There were forty-ounce liquor bottles littering the tables and floor. There were even a few half-consumed bottles spilling out onto the bed. It was the grace of God that allowed them to survive that weekend. And it was the kindness of my wife that brought them back to our home.

In their drunkenness, they told us that they loved us and expressed the shame of their condition. After sleeping off the alcohol, one of the men headed out, adamant that he could not stay. The other lingered, at our insistence, for a couple weeks.

In their hole of sin, we worked to restore their dignity and remind them of their innate value. We wanted to do what God always does—lean into their suffering. But beyond that, we wanted to present opportunities for them to recognize the character of God. We wanted them to know that God had already offered redemption. After all, his presence was their only hope of transformation.

As God has demonstrated throughout history, this kind of redemption requires presence. The redeemer has to be on site to pay for his treasure. The act of redemption forces the redeemer to walk into the valley of the suffering. Buying back dignity and reminding people of their God-given value requires physical attendance and time. It means that we cannot simply hand out a check or offer a cliché statement of hope. We must walk into the pit of suffering with them and encourage them until they emerge on the other side.

Becoming a generous church requires much more than a financial program. When we hurt, God does not typically hand us cash to make the problem go away. He does not offer a simple gift to bridge the gap, but instead offers a missional gift to renovate our lives. His greatest gifts come packaged in his companionship. His presence is what really makes the difference.

In order for our financial gifts to be truly beneficial, we have to echo the missional work of God. We have to take the divine stage and reenact the empathetic love that God has demonstrated for so long.

A truly generous church cannot be bound to handouts. We cannot be constrained to the transfer of property. Paul profoundly noted that physical property and personal comforts amount to rubbish or garbage in light of knowing Christ (Philippians 3:8). There is no earthly substitute for intimacy with the Almighty. So, as we practiced church-wide generosity, our biggest hurdle was not diverting the budgeted funds. Our greatest challenge was diverting our time for missional living. Giving gifts is easy enough, but it is not our mission. It is the means to a more important end. Presenting the Imago Dei is what makes a financial gift truly transformational.

THE WEALTH OF THE CHURCH

> …But we ourselves are like fragile clay jars containing this great treasure…
>
> 2 Corinthians 4:7 (NLT)

In the year 258, the Church was thriving despite the severe persecution of ancient Rome. There was a growing society of Jesus followers. At the same time, Rome was developing an equally intense lust for paganism. As a result, Valerian, the emperor of Rome, decided to confiscate the property of the church and kill all known bishops, priests, and deacons. After sending the majority of these leaders to horrific deaths,

Valerian encountered a deacon named Lawrence, who controlled the wealth of the church.

In a bold move, Lawrence asked the emperor to spare his life for three days. In exchange, he would collect the church's greatest treasures and present them as a gift to Valerian himself. Valerian's eyes glazed over with greed. He agreed to grant Lawrence three days to collect the wealth before he would meet his impending death.

Leaving the presence of the highest Roman official, Lawrence fled to the streets of Rome and began to gather the destitute, the abused, and the sick that depended on the church for survival. Over three days he assembled a ghastly multitude, and when he finally revisited Valerian, Lawrence stood among the pitiful crowd, which still groaned for alms.

Valerian was furious at the sight and would eventually punish this demonstration by slowly cooking Lawrence to death on a public griddle. But before his execution, Lawrence explained his dramatic parable to the emperor.

> These poor of ours are sick and lame,
> But beautiful and whole within.
> They bear with them a spirit fair
> And free from taint and misery.
> These humble paupers you despise
> And look upon as vile outcasts,
> Their ulcerous limbs will lay aside
> And put on bodies incorrupt.
> When freed at last from tainted flesh
> Their souls, from chains of earth released,
> Will shine resplendent with new life
> In their celestial fatherland.
> Not foul and shabby, or infirm,

As now they seem to scornful eyes,
But fair, in radiant vesture clad,
With crowns of gold upon their heads.[16]

The bold statement of Lawrence to the emperor was that the wealth of the church could not be measured in gold, but only on the scales of human sanctity. Investing in the poor, and the work of God among the broken, was the greatest treasure of the early church.

In much the same way, contemporary church generosity cannot be adequately measured in paper currency, but only in terms of God's radiance among his earthen vessels.

It did not take us long to recognize the ribbon of God's glory flowing among the people affected by ReGifting. God

> **"GENEROSITY CANNOT BE ADEQUATELY MEASURED IN PAPER CURRENCY, BUT ONLY IN TERMS OF GOD'S RADIANCE AMONG HIS EARTHEN VESSELS."**

made one thing abundantly clear—when we would get out of the way and pursue simple obedience, he would baptize us with his presence. He would go to work. We did not always understand his timing or agree with the human responses, but we never had to question who was in control. It was abundantly clear that God never really needed us in this process. He brought us into these scenarios so that we could experience his glory. He wanted us to know that he is still the God Most High, the Sovereign Lord.

The following stories are a sample of the wealth produced by God in Clinton, Mississippi.

LEGAL INTERVENTION

On a Tuesday evening, JD went to support the work of a friend. She arrived at the Mary Kay party with empty pockets and a joyful freedom only understood by mothers of small children. As the party progressed, she initiated a conversation with Cathy. Cathy was a new face to JD. She was a face that was also clearly enjoying the freedom of the ladies' night out. They discussed the nuances of makeup, laughed, and forged a quick friendship.

The next day, Cathy called JD to reveal that her world was not as happy as it appeared the night before. In order to attend the party, she concealed the bruises on her face. She had been careful to cover the results of a beating from her husband. She was afraid. She was confused. She did not know anything about the work of our church, but she knew that she needed a confidant.

Around the same time, word began to spread at my day job that I was a pastor and our church was trying to help the hurting of our city. One particular paralegal from the law firm e-mailed me and said she needed to talk. She included her cell phone number and told me when I could reach her. I was expecting the worst— another form of abuse, another hurting woman. It took a couple of days for us to connect, but when we did, I was shocked by the conversation.

This paralegal formerly worked as an attorney in a neighboring state. She had been a victim of abuse.

In an act of desperation, she packed up her belongings and fled to Mississippi. Since she was not licensed to practice law here, she jumped on the opportunity to serve as a paralegal in this law firm. Over the years, she obtained her law license in Mississippi and was once again able to serve as an attorney. But at this point, she did not want the full time responsibilities of a lawyer. Instead, she wanted to offer her services to battered women. She contacted me because she wanted to offer free legal counsel, including filing for protective orders, to any abused women that we might encounter.

As this paralegal told me her story and offered her services, I sat with chills dancing across my spine. Cathy had revealed her predicament to JD earlier that same day. God was showing us how he was involved and was showing off his radiance.

CANCER SURVIVOR

In the middle of this project to help the hurting, a leader in our church nominated a friend for help. Donna and her husband were struggling to stay financially afloat. He was battling liver cancer and had endured debilitating side effects as the cancer was treated. Operations and ongoing medical treatments for the liver cancer forced him to leave his job, and although Donna was working full time, they could not cover their expenses. It would be several weeks before his disability income would be available to them.

During this time of crisis, Donna approached her friend from our church with tears in her eyes. It was a humbling moment, but she desperately needed help.

Within a few days, our church was able to bridge the financial gap for them as they waited on his disability income. But God was orchestrating more than a transfer of funds. He was preparing this family for a valuable, loving friendship.

The weekend after we began assisting Donna's family, a couple joined our church from another local congregation. Phillip and Ginger agonized over leaving their church home but knew that God wanted them to join his work at Traceway. They did not know anything about our work with Donna's family and had no intentions of intervening in this situation. But God had other plans. He brought them to Traceway with a missional assignment already in place.

Ginger came into our church as a survivor. Over twenty years prior, she had endured a liver transplant and now was able to boast that she was the longest surviving single transplant patient. So, when Donna visited Traceway for the first time, she was able to connect with one of the only liver transplant survivors in our city. She found encouragement, and Ginger found a new outlet for sharing the love of God.

God was displaying the wealth of his kingdom.

AN OPEN HOME

A family in our church owned a rental house in addition to their personal home. After enduring a few substandard tenants, they were no longer enthusiastic about being landlords. Unfortunately, the economy was so bad at this time that selling the home was unlikely. So they began to pray and seek God's direction.

In spite of the economy, they felt as if God was directing them to stay away from new tenants. The couple trusted God in this and assumed that he would further lead them to sell the house. But, in order to get to that point, they knew they would have to go in and make some significant repairs. They had to patch holes in walls, repaint several sections of the rooms, replace some broken tile, and clean the place thoroughly. Because of their already demanding schedules, this repair work was going to take a few weeks to complete. As they tried to follow God's leadership, they dove in and started the work.

As the house was nearing completion, I received a phone call from a leader in our church named Cindy. She stated that a coworker's daughter was in desperate need of help. Over the last five years, this woman had been the victim of ongoing domestic violence. The husband was so controlling that she had only seen her parents a handful of times during those long years. Her children hardly even knew their grandparents.

Eventually, Cindy told me that the situation had climaxed and this abused spouse fled with nothing more than her children and the clothes on their backs. Since she was no longer a practicing Jehovah's Witness, her father would not take her into his home. So they needed a place to live and a way to survive.

As this situation was presented to our church, the owners of the rental home realized what God had planned for their property. They now understood that God wanted the house available and properly repaired for this mistreated family. Within a few days' time, the abused family moved into their new home.

After walking into the house, the three-year-old daughter squealed and leapt across the house like it was Christmas morning. She could not believe they were living in a house with new carpet. We could not believe how God was humbling us and displaying the fortunes of his church.

Over a period of several months, Traceway paid all of the rent and utilities for this family. They not only received some of life's most basic necessities, but they also received a ready-made group of loving friends. Most important, they amassed an invaluable picture of the love of God.

DENTAL FELLOWSHIP

On a hot August weekend, I met a man who was eking out a sad existence. Previously, I knew him by name but had never seen his face. He was a felon and had spent considerable time at Parchman—Mississippi's only maximum-security prison for men. After serving his time, Ty started trying to pull his life back together.

I met Ty as he sought financial help. He had a hard time convincing employers to take a risk on a convicted felon. So he often resorted to asking friends and churches for help. He found a ride to Traceway and sat with me for over an hour before the Sunday gathering started. As we talked, Ty told me of his need to pay an overdue electric bill. But his main request was for his girlfriend. "If you don't ever help me with anything else, do this one thing for me," he said. Not knowing what the request was, I could not make any promises, but I told him to continue.

"Stephanie works hard. She has a job as a receptionist but doesn't earn much. If you would go to her house and look at pictures, you would see that Stephanie used to be a healthy, nice-sized woman."

I smiled, and he continued. "Some men would not like that, but she is beautiful in my eyes. But Stephanie has diabetes. And because her diabetes is so bad, she lost all of her teeth. Some government assistance got her a pair of dentures a while back, but they don't fit. And they're tearing her mouth up. She can't even eat solid food without terrible pain. Most days now she hardly eats anything at all."

Now I understood what Ty was asking, and I knew we did not currently have the thousands of dollars necessary for new dentures.

"Please, Pastor," he said. "If you can't do anything else for me, just help me get her some new dentures."

Honestly, I was a little annoyed by the request. I knew Stephanie was in need, but Ty was so accustomed to begging that in the short hour we talked, he had already sought our help in several other ways—books, bills, clothes, and even a television set. I informed him that we did not have the money but I would see what I could do.

Every day, Ty called to get an update on the dentures. I had not talked to anyone about this request yet and wanted God to consent to my inaction. By Wednesday's phone call, I knew I had to do something.

After hanging up the phone, I turned to God. "What do I do, Father? How do I tell him that we do not have the money or any useful contacts?"

Almost instantly, I had a clear impression of what God wanted. *You told him you would look for help, so look for help, and I'll take care of the rest.* As I said "Okay," I wondered where to turn first.

Not having any good ideas, I went to Twitter. In less than 140 characters, I made a quick plea for assistance: "Anyone aware of a dentist or group of dentists in the US who performs missionary dental services?" I knew we could not pay for the dentures, but I thought we might be able to fly Stephanie to a missionary dentist.

Within an hour, I had a response from someone that I had never met before. He pointed me to The Baptist Medical Dental Fellowship in Oklahoma City. I went to their website hoping that they would have a list of affiliate dentists. But the only names I could find were those of the Board of Directors. So, in order to fulfill my promise, I scrolled through the list of names and looked for any name followed by "DDS."

The first one listed was Dr. William. I e-mailed him explaining our situation. A short time later, I had a response from Dr. William. He simply stated, "Call my office and see if they can schedule her with me. Is her income less than $30,000/year?"

As simple as those two sentences were, they completely confused me. The doctor did not even include an area code for the phone number. I thought that probably meant he did not catch the fact that we were in Mississippi. So I Googled his name and felt the familiar chill bumps start dancing when the results appeared. Dr. William lived in Jackson, Mississippi— less than one mile from Stephanie's home.

In short time, Dr. William worked Stephanie into his schedule. He helped her with her dentures and checked on previous scars from oral cancer. Dr. William then shared the hope of God with Stephanie and got her cheap, ongoing dental care.

Once again, God added to the wealth of His church.

THE WEALTH OF THE CHURCH

If I could follow the lead of Deacon Lawrence and round up a crowd, you would see mothers and children who are physically scarred and emotionally traumatized by trusted and loved hands. You would see the tenth grader who had no clothes that fit as she prepared to enter a new school year. Adults and children would stand whose lives were drowning in swampland of sexual transgressions. Couples staring over the cliff of divorce and foreclosure would be present. A family who lost significant income to an unexpected battle with epilepsy would be there. You would see a mom, dad, and two teenage children under the hardship of a yearlong battle with unemployment. You would see Ty, trying to survive in a world cold to felons. And if you take time to look closely enough, you would see the ribbon of God's glory flowing between, around, and among these people. After all, they are the adorning jewels of God's bride.

WHEN THINGS GO WRONG

> We can rejoice, too, when we run into prob-
> lems and trials, for we know that they help us
> develop endurance. And endurance develops
> strength of character, and character strengthens
> our confident hope of salvation.
>
> Romans 5:3-4 (NLT)

Relationships are messy. Thousands of self-help books
testify to the fact that it is not easy to deal with people.
We are a funny bunch. We know what we want to say
but often cannot express exactly what we are thinking.
We know what we want people to hear, but they seem

to conclude something different from what we intended. That is one reason the majority of marriages in the US now end in divorce. There is no simple formula for good relationships. They take commitment and a willingness to sort through the occasional mess.

When you add money to already tricky relationships, you begin a perilous journey. It is like walking through a cow pasture; you are almost guaranteed to step in something that smells.

The very first person that came to our church needing assistance was a young mother. She had four kids by two different men, and her current husband was abusing the entire family—physically and emotionally.

Through some personal connections, she found our church, and we found her a new place to live. Not only did she have a chance to start over, but we also found her a job at a partnering church's child development center.

Over the course of six months, we poured significant time and resources into this young family. We met with them regularly to check on her needs and to develop discipling relationships. We offered the mother a ready-made set of new friends. No one else in the church would know her situation, but we were confident they would love her and her children without hesitation. We invited them to the homes of church members for social gatherings and parties. We invited them to worship and offered to give them rides so that they would not feel uncomfortable coming alone.

During this six-month period, we invested well over five thousand dollars in this family and never saw any return. In fact, despite our continuous offerings, they never visited our church or any other church in our city. Although this mother had the offer of free counseling at her feet, she never once pursued help. The partnering church that offered her a childcare job eventually came to us and disclosed that she rarely showed up for work and often wanted to drop off her children, without paying. After five months of ongoing support, she moved her aunt, uncle, and their children into the rent-free home and tried to conceal their presence. Although her uncle was working, they never offered to pay any rent and never acknowledged their obvious presence in the home. When we finally pushed them out of the nest, she ran back to her abusive husband and severed ties with our people.

Only a couple of months into this relationship, we realized that our first attempt at missional giving was going to be an adventure. We knew that we had just stepped into a mess.

Thankfully, we were prepared for this situation. We knew beforehand that this would eventually come. It was just a matter of time until someone decided to enjoy a free ride on the money train. But scripture and a little common sense had already warned us that this would happen. The kindness of God is often received with an attitude of entitlement and contempt.

When you begin to give as freely as God gives, some of your gifts will be used inappropriately. Some people will take all that you offer and move on to the next potential giver. They are not worried about hurting your feelings. They are not bothered by stealing from a church. They are only concerned about the next handout.

These worst-case scenarios can cause bitterness and send us scrambling to conceal the perceived elephant in the room—missional failure. When you invest thousands of dollars and numerous personal hours for nothing in return, feelings of failure tend to hang on your shoulders like an overgrown pet snake.

So how can we avoid this type of failure? Or maybe a better question is, "How do we understand success?" When we have prayed, fasted, and sought the will of God, how do we define progress? In the midst of undesirable scenarios, how do we rationalize a lack of visible results?

DEFINING SUCCESS

In one sense, our church found that the worst-case scenarios served to shape us more into the image of Christ. Through this process, we became intensely aware that God's generosity is accompanied by patience. The kindness of God is typically adjoined to longsuffering for the sake of the gospel. This is the signature of the Divine. He is "patient with you, not wanting anyone to perish, but everyone to come to repentance" (2 Peter 3:9). And this early, worst-case scenario served to greatly humble us, reminding us how we also regularly and mechanically devour God's kindness.

In another sense, we realized that our definition of success was faulty. In Western, linear thinking, we rely on numbers to indicate success. Several years in one career are the equivalent of personal achievement; it may even earn you a Rolex watch. Numbers with commas in your bank account indicate your competence. The educational degrees attached to your name declare your intelligence. And a large worship gathering indicates a successful church.

We think of success in terms of numbers, but God explains success in a different manner. Throughout the Bible, God demonstrates success in stories.

You do not have to dig deep in order to find demonstrations of God-success in scripture: Abram triumphed in faith by breaking the traditions of his day and leaving his father's household; after sleeping with his daughter-in-law (thinking she was a prostitute), Judah became victorious by admitting his failures; Jacob became a success because he would not let go of God, and God would not let go of him; Joseph found God-success by believing the dreams God placed before him; David was a success when he revered the King of kings and honored Saul as he awaited his turn on the throne; Daniel was effective in life by defying the king and being sent to the lion's den.

In these biblical pictures, success is not measured in numbers but in the life of an individual. All of these success stories have two things in common: faith and a journey of discipleship. Each of these men trusted in the unseen God and over the course of their lives took steps (sometimes very small steps) toward imitating the character of God. In that light, it seems that God defines success in terms of discipleship and faith rather than statistical growth.

We struggle to define success in this manner because we cannot document it on stat sheets. We gravitate toward the words "go" and "baptize" of the Great Commission because we can place numbers behind those words. We can document how many missionaries we send out. We can note how many people we baptize. But how do you record discipleship (the heart of the Great Commission)? How do we report training people in the ways of Jesus when it is an ongoing, lifelong process? How do we measure faith?

Maybe we have become too bureaucratic when we cannot survive without reports. Based on the lives that are depicted in scripture, I do not think God will ask for a statistical report when we meet him face-to-face. At the judgment of believers, I trust that God will be more concerned with how we made disciples than "our" numerical accomplishments.

Incidentally, when Jesus speaks to the seven churches in the book of Revelation, he never mentions their sizes. We do not know if these churches are comprised of twenty people or twenty thousand people. All we know is how faithful they have been to the mission of God.

DISCIPLING AND FAITH

In the historical novel *Godric*, Fredrick Buechner invites us into the life of a sexually charged, overtly greedy, twelfth-century monk. Godric is a fascinating character who spends half of his adult life sailing the seas off the coast of England and defrauding unsuspecting travelers. Buechner says that Godric's "wealth piles up like dung"[17] during this time, and he buries his treasures on an essentially barren island.

Eventually, Godric's religious heritage catches up with him and he feels that he can no longer continue living in his sin. He vows to live the life of a monk and decides to get rid of his blood-stained money. So he journeys out to the island, unearths his buried treasure, and determines to leave it at the altar of a small church.

> I flung the sacks from off my neck and set them by the candle on the cloth. The priest would come at last and find them there. What he would do with [Godric's] wealth was God's to know. My only care was that it reach the poor that [Godric] wrung it from and thus God's will be done at last.[18]

When he finally starts walking in the ways of Jesus, Godric realizes that the results of his efforts are not his concern. He does not need a specific return on his wealth in order to successfully accomplish God's will. He only seeks two goals: the knowledge that he lived as a disciple and the faith that God would take care of the rest. To Godric, that was the epitome of success—discipling and faith.

As we pursue this definition of success, we may encounter worldly accomplishments. Hebrews 11 tells us that some people who walked in this path of faith "passed through the Red Sea as on dry land… conquered kingdoms, administered justice…shut the mouths of lions, quenched the fury of the flames, and escaped the edge of the sword…battle[d] and routed foreign armies" (Hebrews 11:29, 33-34). They were people that enjoyed the fruit of God's kingdom and also consumed the honey of the earth.

However, Hebrews 11 also tells us that some people who walked as disciples and lived by faith,

> were tortured and refused to be released, so that they might gain a better resurrection. Some faced jeers and flogging, while still others were chained and put in prison. They were stoned; they were sawed in two; they were put to death by the sword. They went about in sheepskins and goatskins, destitute, persecuted and mistreated—the world was not worthy of them. They wandered in deserts and mountains, and in caves and holes in the ground.
>
> Hebrews 11:35-38

It seems that God wants us to understand how little control we have over the outcome. He reminds us throughout scripture that although he allows us to plant and water, he controls the results. The sovereignty of God works with the freedom of humanity in order to establish the outcome.

When an abused mother exploits the kindness of a church, the mission is not aborted as a failure. When a homeless man mistreats the love of God, the missional work of the church is not thwarted. When a greedy person walks away with the money of the church community, failure is not assumed. The elephant in the room that we should be concerned with is not failure to achieve statistical results but failure to walk in the way of Jesus.

THE STORIES OF GOD

It is interesting to me that in the biblical depictions of heaven, our wounds are not necessarily healed. In Revelation 5:6, the apostle John sees Jesus as "a Lamb, looking as if it had been slain." And in Revelation 6:9, John recognizes the souls under the altar as those of the men and women "who had been slain because of the word of God and the testimony they had maintained."

In remarkable fashion, God remembers the wounds of those who have been mistreated as they followed him in faith. Part of the eternal glory of the saints is the evidence of obedience which resulted in suffering. Peter said that being harmed for following God is to our benefit and is to the glory of God. "But rejoice that you participate in the sufferings of Christ, so that you may be overjoyed when his glory is revealed" (1 Peter 4:13).

Even though things may not always turn out as we desire, our primary purpose is not to produce results.

> **"OUR PRIMARY PURPOSE IS NOT TO PRODUCE RESULTS. OUR PURPOSE IS TO FOLLOW THE FOOTSTEPS OF GOD IN LOVING OBEDIENCE."**

Our purpose is to follow the footsteps of God in loving obedience. So long as we have prayerfully approached the situation and followed in faith, there is no such thing as failure. All that remains are the stories of discipling—the good and the bad, the beautiful and the ugly. The stories are the only accurate measure of how well we are following the Jesus way.

Imagine what would happen if our churches started working with *discipling* and *faith* as our definition of success. Picture what this would look like with me. Business meetings would be called to order and reports would be produced chronicling the mission of God. Stories would be told to reflect the joys and sorrows of making disciples. Prayers would be recounted over individual lives, and church histories would be recorded in terms of breaking ground for families rather than breaking ground for facilities.

Maybe instead of producing statistical catalogues, we should begin producing books of stories. Instead of inflating our numbers for the good of our egos, we should recount the pleasures and hardships of walking in the ways of Jesus through pictures and narratives. Maybe our primary gauge for making disciples should be found in the art of life rather than the counting of heads.

There is one point in scripture where God is actually angry over the use of numbers. Do you remember what happens in 1 Chronicles 21? David orders Joab and the commanders of the troops to count the fighting men of Israel and Judah. Apparently, David did this because he wanted to know the size of the kingdom—*his* kingdom. He wanted to know how powerful his men had become. He was determined to count his fighting men for the sake of his pride.

There was obviously a major flaw in this plan. These men did not belong to David. He did not own any of them.

In Exodus, God made it clear to his leaders that they should only worry about counting what actually belonged to them. "When you take a census of the Israelites to count them, each one must pay the LORD a ransom for his life at the time he is counted. Then no plague will come on them when you number them" (Exodus 30:12). Each person counted had to pay a ransom for his life, acknowledging that his life was not his own. Every time a person was reduced to a statistic, God forced the leaders to remember that these people and these numbers belonged to him alone.

When David ignored this command and started counting the results of *his* work, the Lord sent a plague that killed seventy thousand Israeli men. The census numbers did not prove beneficial, but rather harmful to the children of God.

Statistics cannot tell the story of God. They are the quick alternative, the easy way out. And unfortunately, they often become the tipping point for ministerial self-esteem.

Maybe we should start paying attention to stories over numbers. Maybe we should follow God's lead as he draws out the real measures of success. After all, when God was wronged by humanity, he penned sixty-six books of stories that have proven highly beneficial to our faith.

HOPE PERSONIFIED

I wait in hope for your salvation, God.

Genesis 49:18 (MSG)

In 1940, Martin Luther King Jr. was a young student at David T. Howard Elementary School in Atlanta. It would be another twenty-plus years before he would write the "Letter from a Birmingham Jail" and deliver the famous "I Have a Dream" speech. As an eleven-year-old boy, King was still a long way from grabbing the reins of the Civil Rights Movement, but another African American man was championing the fight against racism.

Bigger Thomas was a twenty-year-old man in 1940, and by all accounts was not thought of as a great leader. He did not look or act the part. In fact, to all the South Chicago locals, Bigger was nothing more than an uneducated, "ape-like," petty criminal. He came from a poor family with no father around. He lived with his mother and siblings in a cramped, single-room flat. He was frustrated by life and was bound to live out a poor existence—until he murdered a wealthy white woman. That single act, which ensued because of fear, propelled Bigger into a spotlight and altered the way Americans looked at racial oppression.

Thankfully, Bigger Thomas was only a fictional character. Richard Wright created Bigger Thomas for his famous protest novel, *Native Son*. As a Mississippi-born African American, Wright was able to powerfully articulate the sentiments of the black community in his day. Within three weeks of the book's publication, *Native Son* sold over 250 thousand copies, and Americans were forced to look more closely at the flaws of racial arrogance. Possibly more than any literary character, Bigger Thomas opened our eyes to the lingering hopelessness of oppressed people across America.

At one point, Bigger summarized his life by saying,

> A guy gets tired of being told what he can do and can't do. You get a little job here and a little job there. You shine shoes, sweep streets; anything…You don't make enough to live on. You don't know when you going to get fired. Pretty soon you get so you can't hope for nothing. You just keep moving all the time, doing what other folks say. You ain't a man no more. You just work day in and day out so that the world can roll on and other people can live.[19]

For the majority of the novel, that is the way that Bigger felt—trapped, oppressed, and hopeless. And by the end of the novel, his hopelessness seems overwhelming. During the final section of the novel, Bigger sits on death row awaiting the day of his execution. Ironically, it is in this place of death that he recognizes hope for the first time. Of all the things that could potentially bring hope to his life—a governor's pardon, financial relief for his family, his mother's religion—his source of expectancy is ultimately found in a person. His mind is only relieved by a white, Jewish lawyer named Max. Even though Max never had a realistic chance to save Bigger, he risked his own life and reputation to genuinely understand the so-called "ape-like" man. It was only the compassion and empathy of an outsider that allowed Bigger to realize the possibilities of his life. For Bigger, Max was hope personified.

FAITH, HOPE, AND LOVE

I do not know if you have ever stopped to think about it, but hope is typically most powerful when it has a face. The most desperate moments of life are not often calmed by a report, a truth, or a handout. Hope that delivers typically comes in the form of a person. That is why your closest friends do not have to say a word at the death of your parent. They simply need to show up.

A person of hope is a remarkably beautiful thing. Isaiah poetically says, "How beautiful…are the feet of those who bring good news, who proclaim peace, who bring good tidings, who proclaim salvation" (Isaiah 52:7). When a doctor reports that the cancer is gone, hope flows delightfully. When a soldier returns safely from battle, the hope of a family shines brilliantly. When a Jesus follower offers provisions and a hug to the destitute, or when an infant is delivered from the womb, hope is artfully stunning. As was true for Bigger Thomas, personified hope changes the way we relate to the world.

Humanity cannot exist without this type of hope. It is indispensable. Those who mingle with suffering understand the gravity of personified hope. It is the food of the soul; it is the calm of the storm; it is the peace of the morning. Our relationship to the world, and to God, rests on hope which is embodied.

I think that is one reason that Paul ties hope so intimately to faith and love (1 Corinthians 13:13). It is only properly understood in community. It is only properly delivered face-to-face.

MISPLACED HOPE

Unfortunately, even personified hope does not always deliver what we need. As powerful as it is, hoping in the wrong person or community can lead to heart-wrenching results. In one of the most poignant stories in the Bible, Jacob runs away from his blood-thirsty brother and into the arms of his maternal uncle, Laban. In the process of this move, he meets and falls madly in love with Laban's daughter Rachel. After working seven years to receive her hand in marriage, he is deceived by Laban and ends up stuck with the older sister, Leah. According to Genesis 29:17, Jacob was furious over this deception because Leah was a girl with "weak eyes." In more blatant terms, she looked more like Popeye than Olive Oyl. Her personality far outweighed her physical traits. Unfortunately, the brunt of the joke was not on Jacob, but on his new bride, Leah.

After being pawned off by a dishonest father and being bound to a man who did not love her, Leah spent next several years in a *Big Love* family. Against her wishes and against all odds, Leah wrestled with her sister for the affections of her husband. It was during this polygamist debacle that God came near to Leah. In his typical fashion, God drew near to the one who was suffering. Mercifully, he opened her womb and allowed her to begin conceiving sons. Over time, Leah gave birth to six of Jacob's sons. And each time she gave birth, she looked at her new infant son as hope personified.

When Leah had her first son, she named him Reuben, which means "to see." She was honored that God had seen her misery and *hoped* that her son would cause Jacob to see her, to love her. As she continued to have sons, she gave them names to indicate the hope they represented in her marriage: "attached" (Levi), hoping that now her husband would be attached to her; "reward" (Issachar), anticipating blessings for the way she loved her husband; and "honor" (Zebulun), looking forward to the day when Jacob would treat her with honor.

Six sons, all received as gifts of hope, all representatives of increasing misery. Leah saw hope personified six times, and she never received the savior she anticipated. Even though hope became personified for her each time, Leah never realized the longings of her heart.

HOPE OF A SAVIOR

Almost 1700 years later (around 150 BCE), one particular man became hope personified for the entire Jewish race. Judah Maccabee was the son of a priest named Mattathias and by all accounts was the Alexander the Great of the Jews.

Judah became a military leader for Israel and fought against the Seleucid Empire (a remnant of Alexander's conquests for the Greeks). Using guerilla warfare, Judah remarkably drove the Greeks from Jerusalem and several other cities in Israel. As a result, he was praised and lauded as a forerunner of the Messiah. He stirred up thoughts of the long-awaited Savior. The book of First Maccabees proclaims his greatness:

> He extended the glory of his people.
> Like a giant he put on his breastplate;
> he girded on his armor of war and waged battles,
> protecting the host by his sword.
> He was like a lion in his deeds,
> like a lion's cub roaring for prey.
> He searched out and pursued the lawless;
> he burned those who troubled his people.
> Lawless men shrank back for fear of him;
> all the evildoers were confounded;
> and deliverance prospered by his hand...
> He was renowned to the ends of the earth;
> he gathered in those who were perishing.
>
> 1 Maccabees 3:3-6, 9 (RSV)

I don't know about you, but any man who can crush the lawless, gather the perishing, and gain worldwide renown sounds like a good candidate for Messiah to me. And the Jews thought so as well. Judah Maccabee inflamed the imaginations of the Israelites about the coming Messiah and established a precedent for Messianic glory. For the Jews, he was hope personified.

When God did step into humanity, not many people considered the infant child as comparable to Judah Maccabee. In fact, his neighbors probably looked at him as a symbol of misery. He was born to a poor teenage couple—out of wedlock—and was birthed in a common animal shelter. For the locals, he was certainly nothing to get excited about. They had been waiting patiently for a refined leader to take up the crown of Judah Maccabee, not another socially dependent child. They were hoping for nothing less than a powerful Messiah—a Savior. They wanted to touch the most powerful form of hope available. They wanted to ride the coattails of hope personified.

Ironically, that young, socially dependent child ended up being the hope of the entire world. Unlike Judah Maccabee, Jesus brought hope that had no end. It did not go to the grave. It was not limited to a single generation or isolated nation. When God wrapped himself in flesh and became a man, he infused the entire world with everyday, eternal optimism.

Normal human beings can provide hope for a few individuals directly around them. For example, parents can offer hope to the children they bear. Similarly, grandparents can be a source of hope to their grandchildren. A few trusted friends will have enough compassion and understanding to help conquer a devastating circumstance. That is normal. That is the way hope typically works.

Occasionally, one person can generate enough hope to spur on large groups of people. A few great leaders and visionaries have developed enough public personas to offer hope to the masses. President Franklin D. Roosevelt was hope personified for the United States during the Great Depression. His personal manner during his "fireside chats" reassured a nation and brought us through the worst economic downturn in US history. Because of his unique position and his friendly demeanor, Roosevelt was able to bear the weight of hope for a faltering nation.

Above those leaders, a miniscule few have been able to offer hope worldwide—at least to a generation of people. In 1940, Winston Churchill stepped in as Prime Minister to Great Britain during a volatile point of World War II. Much of the world watched in anticipation as Churchill rallied his seemingly overpowered nation to stand against Hitler and ultimately change the course of world history. Later, as a result of his heroic leadership, President John F. Kennedy would acknowledge the revolutionary hope offered by Churchill when he said, "He is the most honored and honorable man to walk the stage of human history in the time in which we live."[20] For a period of a few years, Churchill was hope personified to the entire Allied world.

As long as humanity has existed, we have looked to family, personal friends, and world leaders as our source of hope. We have looked desperately for hope personified. There are still women who get pregnant, like Leah, in a miserable attempt to win over the man of their desires. They are seeking hope personified. There are rebel groups across the Middle East today who are revolting against longtime dictators, hoping for a new leader and a new way of life—looking for hope personified. But throughout the course of history, only one man has been able to offer hope to all generations and all races of humanity—Jesus.

While family, friends, and great leaders can offer hope personified, only Jesus offers salvation personified. Only Jesus offers the hope of abundant life today through eternity. Only Jesus perfectly fulfilled all of the Messianic prophecies of scripture,[21] lived a perfect (sinless) life, died a perfect (substitutionary) death, and was raised to life again as the Savior. Only Jesus is *perfect* hope personified.

THE BODY OF CHRIST

Remarkably, when Jesus ascended to heaven, God appointed the church—even though he foreknew all of her flaws—to become a stand-in Jesus. He called us to physically represent Jesus to all the people on earth. He labeled us the body of Christ. For those who are the Church, that puts us in an extraordinarily unique position. We are potentially the greatest source of hope that our world will ever experience. We have been handed a unique mission from God to infuse *perfect* hope

> "REMARKABLY, WHEN JESUS ASCENDED TO HEAVEN, GOD APPOINTED THE CHURCH—EVEN THOUGH HE FOREKNEW ALL OF HER FLAWS—TO BECOME A STAND-IN JESUS."

into dying neighborhoods, communities, and nations across the world.

What if the Church really looked like Jesus to our neighborhoods? What if we took seriously the calling to be the body of Christ? What would our church look like if she focused on becoming the body rather than on perfecting services of worship? Is it possible that we are missing out on our greatest strengths because our ministry bull's-eye is off center?

In his book *Courageous Leadership*, Bill Hybels tells of what he experienced in the days after the September 11, 2001, attacks. As he stood near Ground Zero, he watched the rescuers working tirelessly and silently, listening for the sound of survivors. Later he passed by a designated area for families to post pictures of their missing loved ones on crudely constructed bulletin boards. According to Hybels, people were roaming the streets like zombies, hoping to hear some good news about their family, their friends, or their coworkers.

In the midst of that bleak agony, Hybels mind replayed something that he had long known to be true. "*The local church is the hope of the world.*"[22] He was reminded of the power of the church when it functions as God intended. Hybels goes on to say,

> There is nothing like the local church when it is working right. Its beauty is indescribable. Its power is breathtaking. Its potential is unlimited. It comforts the grieving and heals the broken in the context of community. It builds bridges to seekers and offers truth to the confused. It provides resources for those in need and opens

its arms to the forgotten, the downtrodden, the disillusioned. It breaks the chains of addictions, frees the oppressed, and offers belonging to the marginalized of this world. Whatever the capacity for human suffering, the church has a greater capacity for healing and wholeness.[23]

In an extraordinary, even illogical, move, God apparently positioned *us* as the only conduit for perfect hope in the world. He created us as the representation of Christ and sent us out with the Gospel of hope. He called us to do what no other person or organization can possibly accomplish.

REGIFTING HOPE

The decision to become a generous church is a decision to take up the mantel of perfect hope. It is *more* than a decision to hand out food and put families under affordable roofs. It is *more* than covering utility bills and running a clothes closet. It is *more* than the practice of financial regifting. Those arenas of hope are only windows to the magnitude of hope God offers through us. The decision to become a generous church is a decision to offer the communal presence of Jesus. It is the decision to offer salvation through Jesus. It is the decision to offer perfect hope face-to-face.

We can never replace the work of Jesus. But through the call of God and through the presence of the Holy Spirit, we can go with him to offer *perfect* hope to our neighborhoods. We can go with him to the slums of Honduras, the prisons of China, and even the boutiques of Hollywood. But first we need to go with him to the hopeless in our backyards. Those are the people we live among. Those are the people we can walk with and disciple. Those are the ones that Christ can speak to most organically through us as we do life together. And that is what it looks like to be the church.

Through the grace of God and the work of the Holy Spirit, we can become perfect hope personified. We can regift our source of hope. In fact, that is our mission.

In Chapter 5, I told you about a woman named Donna and her husband. They connected to our church through Donna's coworker, who is a member at Traceway. When I first met her, Donna's husband had recently resigned from his job because of cancer and other medical complications. Even though she was working a full-time job and an occasional part-time job, they were struggling to cover their basic needs. Through our ReGifting Project, we were able to help them until his disability income began.

When all of this happened, this couple was not part of any church. Years earlier, they had been involved with a church that left a sour taste in their mouths about organized religion. So, with some hesitation, Donna came to a Sunday gathering by herself. Her husband was still not so sure about church communities and did not want to rush into anything. Within a few weeks of that time, Donna's mother was hospitalized and they often spent extensive time by her hospital bedside. Our church people once again had a chance to regift, but this time we did not give financially. Instead, some church members sat with them in the hospital and gave them the gift of hope personified.

When I personally went to see them, I met Donna's mother and, maybe more importantly, I met her husband for the first time. We talked a little bit about work and a little bit about cancer, and more than anything else, we talked about fantasy football. I liked him immediately.

Today, that family is no longer hurting in isolation. They have a new family. They have a church community that loves them. On most Sundays, I can look out to the left side of our worship facility and see them. A few times they have even brought other people with them. They are now reconnected to faith, reconnected to love, and reconnected to the most powerful thing on this side of eternity—perfect hope personified.

There is no telling how wide the door of hope will swing once it is nudged open by the regifting of God's love and money.

PART THREE:
IN THE WAKE

REAPING THE REWARD

The kingdom of heaven is like treasure hidden in a field. When a man found it, he hid it again, and then in his joy went and sold all he had and bought that field.

Matthew 13:44

I am going to make an assumption. I am going to assume that most of us enjoy receiving rewards. I know I do. When I received a performance-based raise recently, I was pleased. Okay, I was downright excited. I needed that reward. American culture is driven by rewards. Good grades open the door to scholarships; good behavior leads to nice gifts from Santa Claus; loyal shoppers receive discounts and special offers; athletes

punish their bodies for fame and fortune; long-term employees receive extended vacations; intelligent leadership leads to greater responsibility. From potty training to retirement planning, rewards are central to our lives. Western culture hinges on the reward and punishment system. However, this is obviously not unique to our culture.

At one point in the gospels, a huge crowd gathers on a hillside to watch Jesus. Some of them had seen Jesus heal the sick and others had heard the rumors. For these bystanders, the miracles of Jesus probably produced curiosity similar to that of a county fair. They did not come out to see the world's smallest man, but they wanted to see the lame stand up and walk.

I am sure you remember the story. Jesus, in spite of their poor motives, was compassionate toward them. He accepted their presence, and beyond that he told his disciples to feed this crowd of rubberneckers. The disciples were dumbfounded at this request; even Peter was apparently at a loss for words. Finally, Andrew mentioned that one of the children sitting nearby had a few loaves of bread and couple of fish. It was little more than a Happy Meal, but it was enough. Jesus borrowed the food, blessed it, and returned it to the boy along with enough food for five thousand additional families.

The crowd was obviously amazed. They came out to determine whether or not these miracles were a hoax, and they all ended up with a free meal.

At that point, Jesus left the scene. He and the disciples made the ten-mile trip across the Sea of Galilee to Capernaum. Remarkably, the crowds did not go home.

They followed Jesus. Hopping into boats, they tracked behind the disciples and found Jesus on the other side. In all honesty, I would have been flattered if I were in Jesus's shoes. I would have assumed they followed me because they wanted to know more about the God who dictated the laws of nature. I would have assumed that I had them right where I wanted them, ready for the gospel. As a preacher, I would have been excited that the church was growing astronomically. Beyond that, since these people spent the night pursuing Jesus by boat, I would be proud that this was the ultimate "Sticky Church." These people really wanted to be with Jesus!

Evidently, Jesus did not feel the same way. He did not respond the way that I want him to respond. His instincts are not bent like mine. So instead of thanking the Father for vast church growth and remarkable commitment, Jesus said to the people, "I tell you the truth, you are looking for me, not because you saw miraculous signs but because you ate the loaves and had your fill" (John 6:26). In other words, they were just looking for another free meal. They were not following him to learn from his ways. It was no longer even about the miracles performed for other people. Now it was personal. They realized that there were a lot of potential rewards associated with following Jesus.

A GOD OF REWARDS

Two thousand years have not produced a great evolution in our intelligence. Christians across the world still salivate over the latest Mercedes and dream of better ways to fill their barns. The hope of material gain is still a major reason that people flock to certain churches. In many circles, God is not simply the provider of daily bread, but he is the supposed grantor of our latest desires. Jesus is pursued as a means to an end. Like those who received the miraculous bread and fish, these followers pursue God because at some point in time they have "had their fill."

The polar opposite theology, which is also flawed, worships at the altar of self-abasement. Unlike the boisterous prosperity gospel, the pursuit of lowliness is counter-cultural. It appeals to those who understand the radical ways of Jesus. It feels good to hold less so that others can have enough. For some, it feels right to display humility so that God can lift them up. "After all," they would argue, "didn't the early church sell their property and give to everyone as they had need? Didn't Jesus tell us not to be anxious for material possessions because God will take care of our needs? Wasn't Jesus essentially a homeless man? Doesn't that mean that God is not concerned with rewards here on earth?"

The danger in this line of thinking is that it is so close to being biblical. And it makes sense. The truth is only slightly twisted, almost to the point that you do not even notice it. God does honor humility. He cares deeply for the poor. But that does not mean that God is unconcerned with on-the-spot rewards.

In the self-abasement circles, it is hard to accept rewards as part of God's earthly mission. After all, they would say, the true and lasting rewards are eternal, not temporal. While we are walking on this earth, it is better to give than to receive.

Each theological camp can certainly find passages of scripture to defend their positions. But, taken as a whole, neither of these positions seems to match the heart of God. In coming to earth, Jesus displayed the selfless, humble character of God. He demonstrated that God is not overly concerned with rewards.

At the same time, the Bible is replete with men and women who received earthly rewards for their faith. Joseph was rewarded with a position of leadership in Egypt; Joshua and Caleb were allowed to enter the promised land; Hezekiah was given fifteen more years of life after Isaiah told him he would die and the apostles were entrusted with positions of remarkable influence. Hebrews eleven is not just a "hall of faith" but is also a record of their earthly rewards; they "conquered kingdoms, administered justice, and gained what was promised... became powerful in battle and routed foreign armies... received back their dead, raised to life again" (Hebrews 11:33-35).

C. S. Lewis offers some incredible insight into the theology of rewards and seems to be close to the heart of God when he says,

> The New Testament has lots to say about self-denial, but not about self-denial as an end in itself. We are told to take up our crosses in order that we may follow Christ; and nearly every description of what we shall ultimately find if we do so contains an appeal to the desire. If there lurks in most modern minds the notion

that to desire our own good and earnestly to hope for the enjoyment of it is a bad thing, I submit that this notion has crept in from Kant and the Stoics and is no part of the Christian faith. Indeed, if we consider the unblushing promises of reward and the staggering nature of the rewards promised in the Gospels, it would seem that Our Lord finds our desire, not too strong, but too weak. We are half-hearted creatures, fooling about with drink and sex and ambition when infinite joy is offered us, like an ignorant child who wants to go on making mud pies in a slum because he cannot imagine what is meant by the offer of a holiday at the sea. We are far too easily pleased. We must not be troubled by the unbelievers when they say that this promise of rewards makes the Christian life a mercenary affair. There are different kinds of rewards... The proper rewards are not simply tacked on to the activity for which they are given, but are the activity itself in consummation.[24]

REWARD FOR THE CHURCH

So what is the proper reward for community faithfulness? What, if anything, would be the reward for radically trusting God with the finances of the church? If the letters to the churches in Revelation make it clear that communities can receive rewards, what type of reward will the church receive for administering God's resources faithfully?

At Traceway, we noted a few rewards that were inherent with this work. The first was the most natural reward and possibly the most valuable—faith.

It only makes sense that when you step into the unknown, you begin to walk in faith. I was proud of our staff for embracing this challenge from the beginning. It would have been very easy to find some sort of compromise to giving everything away. It would have been natural to look for a way to help the community without putting their paychecks on the line. But instead of shrinking back, our staff members stepped up and began to model the faith that they had taught so many times. And this amazing faith was not limited to the staff. As our church community saw the staff modeling faith, they became more and more willing to walk in faith themselves. Some began to model faith in the way they helped the hurting in their lives. Others began to live out their faith by sharing the joy of regifting with unchurched friends. Beyond that, many began sharing the good news of the gospel with people in a new, positive way. As we sought to follow God without hesitation, faith became the basis for our entire ministry. We did not just learn faith with regard to our finances; faith permeated every purpose and ministry of the church.

Second, we were rewarded with increased responsibilities. We were often reminded of the statement of Jesus to the faithful: "You have been faithful with a few things; I will put you in charge of many things. Come and share your master's happiness!" (Matthew 25:23).

For a young church with under a hundred members, we have been amazed at the amount of responsibility that has been entrusted to us. There have been a couple of local newspaper articles about ReGifting, and we have been featured on the nightly news as well. People in our city and in our neighboring city have begun to look to Traceway for direction in community assistance.

When a tornado hit our city (destroying the neighborhood behind our building) we tried to move in and help our neighbors as soon as possible. A few hours after the tornado hit, we were able to walk through the neighborhood and talk to those who were hurting. Since power was out around the majority of the city and since people did not have a way to prepare food, we set up a makeshift buffet in our parking lot. We brought out grills and walked the neighborhoods (you could not drive through because the roads were littered with trees) and told the victims that free food was available. We used ReGifting funds to buy hamburgers, hotdogs, drinks, and chips. That night we served over two hundred meals, but maybe more importantly, we became a church of influence in our own neighborhood.

One day later, as I was walking back through the destruction, multiple people told me that they recognized me from newspaper articles and TV coverage. A couple of people specifically stated, "I want to be a part of a church like Traceway. You guys really care for people, and you are making a difference."

For an entire year, we did not have any money designated for a marketing budget and during that time God increased our reach and influence far beyond what we could have imagined. Over the previous two years, we used every marketing scheme available—billboards,

Internet, e-mail marketing, handing out doughnuts at local businesses, personalized direct mail, radio spots, and word of mouth. While those things helped people become familiar with our church, they paled in comparison to the influence that God afforded us when we stopped marketing ourselves.

Finally, we assumed that we would be rewarded with additional wealth in the church—not in terms of dollars but in terms of people. And this happened. We honestly have not had a huge increase in financial offerings during or immediately after this year of regifting. However, as a direct result of this work, we have been able to connect a number of new people to our church community. Some of these people started attending our gatherings because they were hurting and needed help. Others started attending because they were looking for a place to serve in a missional community.

As a result of our faithfulness to this mission, God has blessed us with wealth—not the wealth of gold and silver but the wealth of community.

THE REWARD OF ABRAHAM

It is hard for me to imagine what life was like for Abraham. He never owned a computer. He never wore a pair of Nikes. He never dealt with big banks or had a mortgage payment. But he was the father of faith. In a culture that worshiped a different god for every occasion, Abraham was called to walk with one God alone—the Living God. He was called out, to show the world an entirely new culture. And as he was called to this life of faith, he was promised a reward of biblical proportions.

> The word of the LORD came to Abram in a vision:
>
> "Do not be afraid, Abram.
>
> I am your shield,
>
> your very great reward."
>
> But Abram said, "Sovereign LORD, what can you give me since I remain childless"... And [God] said, "Look up at the heavens and count the stars—if indeed you can count them." Then he said to him, "So shall your offspring be."
>
> Genesis 15:1-2, 5

I love God's promise. First of all, he told Abram, "If you follow me in faith, you will receive more of me." He told Abram, "I am your very great reward." To be frank, there is no greater reward. How can you top an offer to gain God (who will never be destroyed, who can never be overpowered, who will never be unfaithful, who created all, who owns all, who is all)? The offer of intimacy with the Sovereign is truthfully so great that we cannot even wrap our minds around it. It is more than we can fathom.

Apparently, Abram did not comprehend the audacity of this reward, either. So he asked for an additional reward. He asked God to make good on his earlier promise—"I will make you into a great nation and I will bless you" (Genesis 12:2). God always intended to follow through with his earlier promise. There is no reason to doubt God's intent. So, Abram became a father. After his wife had passed childbearing years, she gave birth to Isaac. And the rest is history, literally.

One thing that always strikes me about Abraham's story is that he only saw the beginning of his reward. He only witnessed the tip of the iceberg. The vast majority of his reward was reaped on the earth long after he was gone. Although nations today still look to Abraham as their father, he only laid eyes on one or two generations, at best.

I am starting to believe that when churches decide to become generous and when churches decide to walk by faith rather than logic, they will be rewarded in a fashion similar to that of Abraham. Their responsibilities will increase, the church will expand, and the current membership may only see the tip of the inter-generational rewards. The staff may be long gone before the significance of their work is fully appreciated.

> **"STARTING THE DAY THAT WE BEGIN WALKING IN FAITH... WE WILL RECEIVE GOD HIMSELF AS '[OUR] SHIELD, [OUR] VERY GREAT REWARD.'"**

Maybe more significantly, we are assured to receive one chief reward, starting the day that we begin walking in faith. We will certainly reap the reward of God that is so profound Abram could not comprehend it. We will receive God Himself as "[our] shield, [our] very great reward."

What higher aspiration is there for a community of Jesus followers?

SUSTAINING THE MISSION

Take on an entirely new way of life—a God-fashioned life, a life renewed from the inside and working itself into your conduct as God accurately reproduces his character in you.

Ephesians 4:24

Do you remember what it was like to be twelve? Can I remind you of something? Twelve is a hard age.

At twelve, I had braces and was the new kid in school. I was one of the tallest kids in my seventh-grade class. I am pretty sure I was twelve when I started to learn how to shave my face. A razor blade in the hands of a pre-teen is always scary.

Twelve was also the point where *awkward* was the defining word in my life: my newly deep voice did not match my one-hundred-pound frame, my face was starting to sprout clumps of peach fuzz, and I was not sure if it was still cool to watch WWF wrestling. Some adult men are still not sure if it is cool to watch entertainment wrestling, but that was a particularly gut-wrenching decision as a seventh grader. Twelve was hard.

Twelve is an age that is dripping with social challenges. But for one twelve-year-old in Clinton, the social challenges of being a tween are exponentially greater than those of his peers.

Brandon was born into a life of hardships. His mother was a drug addict; his father was nowhere to be found. Additionally, because of a disease that he was born with, he is bound to a wheelchair for life. While his friends are thinking about playing football, Brandon is thinking about the implications of a life sitting down. While his peers are talking about dating, he is talking about how to get on and off the bus without making a scene.

Around the age of ten, a judge finally acknowledged that his mother could not care for him, and Brandon was placed in the custody of his aunt and uncle. While that decision would guarantee him a life of being properly loved, it did not do much to change his economic status.

Brandon's aunt and uncle live in an eight-hundred-square-foot home in one of the poorest areas of Clinton. The house was built in 1950, and it doesn't look like there have any improvements made since its original construction. But the worst part is that the house is built on a conventional foundation. There are three and a half feet worth of stairs stretching from the grass to the porch. Three and a half feet is a nice jump for an adult, but it may as well be a leap to the moon for a kid in a wheelchair. That distance is virtually impossible to surmount without help.

For two years, Brandon's uncle (who breathes through a tracheostomy tube) and his cousins have hoisted him over that three and a half foot span from the porch to the ground. Each time Brandon wanted to go outside, it took a family effort to get him out of the house. Any time he wanted to hang out with a friend, he had to gather a small army of volunteers. And when he got home from school each day, it would take two men to get him back in the house—maybe more if it was raining.

Toward the end of the ReGifting Project, Brandon's family was nominated for assistance. As a result, our church came together and designed a city-approved plan for a wheelchair ramp. Some men showed up with hammers and power tools. Others showed up with shovels and gloves. As the assistant to the assistant, I had the option of standing in the way or sitting on the porch with Brandon. I often chose to sit and talk.

In many ways, Brandon is like all other kids his age. He likes to hang out with his friends. He like to act goofy. And while he may never impress anyone on a football field, he can perform tricks in a wheelchair that would even impress Simon Cowell.

He did not need us to give him a life. He just needed more freedom to come and go from his home. He also needed to see that the Heavenly Father does not look a whole lot like his biological father. And through the work of a few selfless men, Brandon received both.

As we completed Brandon's ramp, our regifting efforts were coming to a close, and we were beginning to wrestle with an incredibly important question. We did not want to miss out on meeting the "Brandons" of our community when this year was over. We did not want to look at our city and say, "It's been an incredible year. Good luck going forward." Instead, we wanted to know how we could make regifting a sustainable ministry.

FUNDING GENEROSITY

In Genesis 18, God is on his way to destroy Sodom and Gomorrah. For some reason, instead of going directly to the scene, God decides to stroll through a nearby neighborhood and make a pit stop at Abraham and Sarah's tent.

After being accepted at their home with reverence and honor, God decides to unveil his intention to destroy the cities. Apparently, Abraham was in the "need to know" group because of his place in God's plans.

As God confirms that he is going to tell Abraham of the coming destruction, he says, "Yes, I've settled on [Abraham] as the one to train his children and future family to observe God's way of life" (Genesis 18:19, MSG). In other words, God is saying that Abraham will be the man to start the family of faith. He will be "generation one" in a line of people who follow the ways of God.

As part of that statement, God goes on to tell us exactly how Abraham should train his children. He makes it clear that there are certain things that are fundamental to walking in the ways of God. Specifically, he says Abraham should teach his children to live lives that are "kind and generous and fair" (Genesis 18:19, MSG).

For Abraham, his kids, and anyone else who would follow in the ways of God, generosity was designed to be a lifestyle. It is a basic building block for God-style living. There was nothing temporary about this assignment.

Understanding that, we were forced to ask the question, "How can this be the way of life for our church? How can regifting Your love and money be a tenured characteristic of our congregation? How can this type of generosity be sustained?"

As we prayerfully sought an answer to this question, we were struck by the unique stewardship patterns in scripture. For example, God commands us to be good stewards of our bodies. In order to help us remember and carry out this commandment of rest, he gives us the Sabbath.

On a trip to Israel a few years ago, I was deeply impressed by the way the Jews observe the Sabbath. Each Friday evening, large groups of Jews gather at hotels and begin a family celebration of rest. They do not prepare any food; the hotel staff has all of the food prepared for them. They dance, they sing and they celebrate the time of rest. Even the hotel electronics are programmed to provide complete rest on these special days. One elevator in each hotel is designated as a "Shabbat elevator." This particular elevator is constantly in motion during Sabbath. It travels up and down, stopping on each floor of the hotel. That way, the people observing the Sabbath never even have to press a button to go up or down. They simply walk on this elevator and wait for it to stop on their floor. Once they enter their hotel rooms on the Sabbath, the motion sensors turn on all of the lights for them.

While these things can (and have) become legalistic, they also allow the Jews to bask in the luxury of God's rest for one day each week. In all honesty, I should learn from the Jews. I break the command of the Sabbath regularly. Working as a bi-vocational pastor and keeping up with the demands of a family have pushed me toward a seven-day work week. However, the more I understand God's reasoning for the Sabbath, the more I want to join him in this rest. When I fail to follow this command, I am being a poor steward of my body. I deserve better; God deserves better from me.

In much the same manner, God tells the people of Israel that they are to be good stewards of the land. Every seventh year is a Sabbath year of rest for the land (Leviticus 25:1-7). During this time, they are not to plow or to plant anything. They are not to have their annual times of harvest, either. The land is to rest.

During this land-rest, God allows the people to eat whatever grows naturally during that year. He makes provisions for the land-owners, the servants, and even the wild animals to eat whatever springs up from the ground. But in order to be good stewards of the God's property, they are to let the land rest.

In both of these examples, the number seven is important in the process of stewardship. So, at Traceway, we have decided to follow this God-pattern. As we move forward, we are reorienting our budget to make every seventh year a regifting year. For six years, we are intentionally limiting our operational budget. In addition to assigning a percentage of our annual budget to helping the hurting in our community (our current number is 10 percent), we set aside 15 percent of the budget for a separate savings account. Therefore, after six years, our savings account will cover approximately 90 percent of the seventh year's (the regifting year's) budget.

Because of increases and decreases in the annual budget, this savings account may not cover an entire year's worth of expenses. We fully anticipate that in the regifting years, we may be forced to cut our budget. Or we may be required to raise some additional funds. Either way, the majority of our seventh year budget is covered by the funds we have saved during the previous six years.

So our budget will looks similar to the following example:

Years 1-6

Operations—60%

(including building funds/expenses)

Agency Donations—15%

(including denominational support and outside missions agencies)

ReGifting Stewardship Funds—15%

Missional Giving (or Annual ReGifting)—10%

Year 7

ReGifting Year – 100% Missional Giving

Our desire is to get to the point that 50 percent of our budget is designated for our neighbors (loving them as much as we love ourselves). That means that over time, we will need to move our operational expenses down to 50 percent of the total budget.

"IF WE ARE GOING TO MAKE A SUSTAINABLE IMPACT ON OUR COMMUNITY, WE ARE GOING TO HAVE TO ... LET GO OF THE AMERICAN CHURCH DREAM MENTALITY."

While this may take some time, we believe it will be well worth the effort.

We want to invest in eternity—not possessions that will eventually rust and decay. We want to be good stewards of all that God has entrusted to us. We want to regularly regift the love and kindness that God extends toward us...for the good of our community and for the glory of God.

If we are going to make a sustainable impact on our community, we are going to have to rethink our long-term budgeting practices. We are going to have to let go of the American Church Dream mentality.

Alan Hirsch and others have aptly noted that the importance of the church budget goes well beyond healthy collections and accurate reporting. In fact, for the church community, the budget is really our theology in practice. We can sit in meetings all day with our elders and staff and church council to exegetically map out our statement of faith. But what we really believe is always seen in our financial statements. What we really value is more accurately noted by our financial secretaries than it is by our most eloquent sermons. Our financial practices define us.

POSITIONAL FAITH

When I think of the great faith chapters in the Bible, I almost always think of Hebrews eleven. But recently, as I was reading in Matthew, I noticed something about chapter seventeen that I had never seen before. Matthew seventeen is a faith chapter. It begins by telling about Jesus's mountaintop transfiguration and a pact with Peter, James, and John to keep their mouths closed. That took some faith. It probably took more faith to keep their mouths shut than it did to believe what their eyes saw.

After telling us about the transfiguration, Matthew relates the story of a demon-possessed boy. The demon would threaten the boy's life by causing him to fall into fires and stumble into bodies of water. No one had an answer for the problem—except Jesus.

After rebuking the demon and healing the child, Jesus rebuked the disciples. They had failed to take care of this problem. So, he told them that their downfall was not in their access to God's power, but in their pitifully small faith. "I tell you the truth, if you have faith as small as a mustard seed, you can say to this mountain, 'Move from here to there' and it will move. Nothing will be impossible for you" (Matthew 17:20).

Finally, Matthew closes this section by telling an odd story that connects money and faith. He tells us that while Jesus was in Capernaum, a local tax collector approached Peter and, with an apparently accusatory tone, asked why Jesus had not paid the temple tax.

Specifically, he wanted to know why Jesus had not paid the two-drachma tax (which was enough money for about two sheep).

Interestingly, when Peter encountered Jesus again, Jesus was the one to bring up this subject. He said, "What do you think, Simon? ... From whom do the kings of the earth collect duty and taxes—from their own sons or from others?" (Matthew 17:25).

Peter was pretty sure that the king's sons did not have to pay taxes. And that is how he answered.

Jesus affirmed his response by saying, "Then the sons are exempt" (Matthew 17:26).

If I am Peter, I am thinking this means that Jesus is not going to pay the tax. He is exempt. After all, he is the Son of the King (which Peter previously acknowledged in Matthew 16). But Jesus did not stop with that statement. He went on to say, "Go to the lake and throw out your line. Take the first fish you catch; open its mouth and you will find a four-drachma coin. Take it and give it to them for my tax and yours" (Matthew 17:27).

I do not know if it sank in right away, but when Peter stopped to think about that statement, he must have been stunned. *The sons are exempt... you'll find a four-drachma coin for my tax and yours? Did Jesus just pay my tax and call me a son?*

I do not know how long it took to sink in, but Peter eventually got the point. Money is not the big concern here. Paying the tax was not the real issue. Faith and proper relation to the Father are what really matters. Money is the peep-hole through which we stoop down and view what we really believe. Our relation to money exposes our relationship to God.

Interestingly, as far as I can tell, this is the only miracle of Jesus that does not have a conclusion. We never get the rest of the story. We never witness Peter's fishing trip.

Matthew's motivations for leaving this story open-ended are unclear. Take your best guess. As for me, I tend to think he left it unfinished because the miracle is not the important part of the story. The way of life is what really matters. Jesus showed Peter a new way of relating to financial concerns. In some sense, he was saying, "Your financial dealings should not look the same as those of the world. You don't approach money from the viewpoint of a taxed peasant, because you are no longer in that class. You are now a child of the King."

Jesus took the financial chains off of Peter and told him to live with confidence in his Father's standing.

Starting with the God/Abraham relationship, weaving through the God/Peter relationship and today in the God/Church relationship, things have not changed. God's message is still the same: "Join me by faith in a lifestyle of kindness and generosity."

As long as we are called children of God, the one thing that will really matter is how we follow God in faith. The long-term money practices may change over time. Our standards for who we help and how we extend that assistance may evolve, but the driving force behind them will remain constant.

Because of our Father, we no longer have to be shackled by financial concerns. We are free to run the race of faith.

GETTING PERSONAL

The Lord God placed the man in the Garden
of Eden to tend and watch over it.

Genesis 2:15 (NLT)

I do not know if this has really hit you yet, but *you* are the church. God never chose a building. He chose you. In scripture, God does not marry an institution; he takes his people as a bride. He does not identify weekly rituals as his body, but he clearly says you are the body of Christ. You are God's plan to strengthen relationships. You are God's vessel for influencing your community. You are God's plan for your neighbors and your coworkers. You are God's choice for making disciples. You are the church.

I do not know about you, but that is an intimidating task to me. Some days I do not know if I am capable of fulfilling that calling. Some days I do not know if I am cut out to really love my neighbor in the same way that I love myself. I do not know how often I am up for making disciples. I mean, even on a bad day I can stand in front of a crowd, smile for an hour, and help people understand that God speaks through the Bible. But that is not the biblical definition of the church. That is not the core of God's plan for us. Many men and women have been called to work in a "Christian" environment, but it is another level of calling to stand as God's hope for your neighbors. Many people have been happy to volunteer for an event, but few have realized the need to volunteer their dining room table for an intimate meal. It is easy to go to a church building, but it is an intimidating call to *be* the church.

In some ways, our ideas about the institutional church today are in direct opposition to the actions of Jesus. He rarely sought out crowds. In fact, there are multiple occasions in scripture where Jesus fled from crowds. He was not an "attractional" Messiah. In one of his biographical descriptions, he is called "despised and rejected by men, a man of sorrows, and familiar with suffering" (Isaiah 53:3). How many leaders do you know that desire to emulate those characteristics?

By the end of his time in the flesh, Jesus left the world with a church of eleven confused disciples, and approximately one hundred other followers (Acts 1:15). No senior pastor, no education minister, no children's director, no worship leader, no elders, no deacons, no teaching pastors, no worship services, no outreach events, no marketing plan, just a few former fishermen and tax collectors. Just a few scared individuals with the promise of the Holy Spirit. They were the church. They were God's "A-game." They were not a contingency plan; they were God's predetermined, calculated plan to reconcile the world to himself. And today, you and I stand in a very similar place. You are a movement of God. You are the church.*

I wonder what it was like for those early believers to navigate what it meant to be the church. I wonder if they were aware of the way they were changing the world. I do not know exactly how they felt, but I do know how history records them—as radically generous people. Have you ever wondered why they sold their fields, their homes, their extra furniture and clothes? Have you ever questioned their motivations and considered why they gave this money to the people around them?

I have my suspicions that it was more than an attempt to look radical. I do not think it was a community outreach program. It was not a way to gain publicity. It had nothing to do with liberal or conservative political statements. In fact, I would bet that they were just being the church. They were leveraging what they had for the purpose of the kingdom. They loved their neighbors as themselves. They realized that everything

---

*As the church grew and developed, God would later appoint people to these positions (minister, evangelist, deacon, etc.), but they were born out of necessity. As the church grew, so did the need for organization. However, in its infancy, at its core, the church was not developed around positions–it was developed around people.

147

they had gained to this point in their lives—the accomplishments, the savings, the prestige, the opportunities—was all rubbish compared to the surpassing greatness of knowing and following Christ. They were more enamored with the idea of living as the King's bride than they were with holding on to the possessions of a slave. So it was only natural to be generous. It was the innate response of those who realized they had been given more than they could ever ask for or imagine. Therefore, the early church became defined by generosity.

BY THE NUMBERS

As God began to lead our local church to become radically generous, my wife and I realized that this call was not an impersonal prompting. God was not just speaking to an institution; he was speaking to our family, his bride.* He was not just calling us to a new way of thinking about church budgets; he was calling us to a new way of thinking about everyday life. He was calling us to think seriously about our family budget and to stop worrying about hoarding the possessions of a slave.

You may have heard the global statistics before, but we do not often stop to think about how much wealth God has really entrusted to us. According to a 2009 report, 80 percent of the people in the world live on

---

*"You are the church. You are the body and bride of Christ." As much as I understand the truth of those statements, they are still hard for me to internalize. Even when we comprehend that the church is not a building or a place, it is still hard to make this personal. As I write that my family is the Bride of Christ, it feels and sounds funny. Additionally, it is not completely accurate. We are only part of the body. I get that. But I also know that our family will never learn to live as the church until we take this personally.

less than ten US dollars per day. So, if you make more than $3,650 a year, you are among the top 20 percent of the wealthiest people in the world. Additionally, 50 percent of the world lives on less than two US dollars per day ($730 a year).[25] Conversely, in the United States, people who are considered "low-income" are eligible for enough Medicaid benefits to be considered among the wealthiest people alive. In 2001, over forty-seven million Americans received an average of $3,965 in healthcare benefits alone.[26]

I do not know what those statistics say to you, but they are humbling to me. My children have more money in their piggy banks than some people earn over several months of work. We do not tend to think of ourselves as wealthy. Our family lives at approximately the median income for families in the United States. Some relatives and close friends look at us with pity because we do not often have extra cash. And in all honesty, sometimes I look at myself with this same pity.

I do not consider myself wealthy. Chances are, regardless of your income level, you do not feel wealthy either. Comparatively speaking, though, you and I have been entrusted by God with a staggering number of resources.

Early on in this ReGifting Project, God began to speak to our family about how well we use the resources that we have been given. We began to think that the money that we spend on TV, entertainment, and eating out could be better invested in the Kingdom. Maybe we do not need 150 channels or the unlimited phone plans. Maybe we do not need the fastest Internet service, and maybe the money that we spend vainly at restaurants could be better allocated. Maybe the mortgage payment is keeping us from what we are really supposed to be accomplishing. As crazy as it sounds, we started thinking that we might find more fulfillment in life by intentionally getting rid of our "wealth" and investing more in the things of God.

In his book *Crazy Love*, Francis Chan suggests that, as God leads us, it would be a good idea to "aspire to the median." In other words, we should consider family budgets that allow us to live at the median level of US income ($46,000 according to 2006 statistics) so that we can give everything else away.[27] This has nothing to do with political beliefs and is not a suggestion that everyone should be financially equal. Instead it is a suggestion that everyone should live in constant obedience, including financial obedience, to the promptings of the Holy Spirit. And it is a suggestion that our family wants to take seriously, regardless of the resources that God sends toward or distributes from us.

Chan also points out that it is in this kind of living that we really find deep intimacy with God. He says,

> Jesus refers to the Holy Spirit as the "Helper" or "Comforter." Let me ask you a simple question: Why would we need to experience the Comforter if our lives are already comfortable? It is those who put their (comfort) at risk and suffer for the gospel who will most often experience His being "with you always, even to the end of the age."[28]

Ultimately, our goal in life is not resources but intimacy with God and the ability to equip others for that same intimacy. Missional generosity allows our family to walk on that playing field. It allows us to actively participate in God's kingdom rather than building my personal kingdom.

On a larger scale, the organized church in the United States is easily one of the wealthiest organizations in the world. In terms of revenue, the churches of our nation receive about one hundred billion dollars per year.[29] That is more annual income than 70 percent of the all of the countries in the world.[30]

If our local churches today were defined by radical generosity, what type of influence would we have in our communities? How far would forty or fifty billion dollars go toward serving the people in our neighborhoods? On the local level, how far can one senior pastor's salary go toward impacting his neighborhood? If some of our pastors decided to stay with their congregations but serve bi-vocationally for one year (in order to increase their missional giving), how many families would become engaged? How many people would become generous givers as a result of their pastor's leadership? How many individuals would look at their local church communities in a whole new light? How many people, inspired by this faith in action, would start taking discipling seriously?

> **"IT IS TIME TO START HEEDING THE CHALLENGE OF JESUS; EITHER WE SERVE GOD OR WE SERVE MONEY, BUT WE DO NOT CAMP OUT ON THE MIDDLE GROUND."**

It is time to start heeding the challenge of Jesus; either we serve God or we serve money, but we do not camp out on the middle ground.

ONE LITTLE LADY

Have you ever noticed how generosity is inspirational? Radical giving moves people. It takes two totally separate worlds and conjoins them emotionally. That is the whole premise behind television shows like *Extreme Makeover: Home Edition*. Someone in need receives a radical gift of love, and half of our nation sits teary-eyed in observance.

We have seen the inspiration generated by financial generosity, but have you ever recognized that generosity is also contagious? You are probably aware that many of the people in the early church wanted to be more like Christ because of Barnabas's sacrificial giving. His giving was so contagious that people lied so that they could be associated with this generosity. Although they did not all apply it appropriately, they caught the generosity bug.

Interestingly, I do not think Barnabas's act was the origin of generosity in the early church. I have no way of proving this, but I think this movement started well before Acts chapter two. I tend to think that one little lady encouraged the early church to depend solely on God rather than on their possessions.

When Jesus entered Jerusalem for the last time, he led the disciples to the temple. He knew he would be crucified within a week, and now he was doing everything he could to ingrain his teachings into the lives of the disciples.

Just as he had done many times before, Jesus took his disciples through the Court of the Gentiles and then ascended the fourteen steps leading into the Court of Women. They may have dropped something in the temple treasury before Jesus sat down to watch.

It is a little bit odd to me that Jesus would sit and watch the "collection plate." The Jews coming through that place would have been paying a tax, as well as surrendering an offering. Either way, for someone to sit and watch seems weird. And this is the guy who taught his followers to give in secret. But apparently, he knew what he was doing.

As is often the case with Jesus, when he sat down, he was not just resting; he was preparing to teach. He sat down to direct their attention. Before long, the disciples were all peering at the individuals gathering around the treasury. Men and women were coming and going, dropping in their offerings and moving on to other stages of worship.

As people passed by, some dropped in a few dollars and others gave more substantial gifts. Then a frail little widow walked through and dropped in

> two very small copper coins, worth only a fraction of a penny. Calling his disciples to him, Jesus said, "I tell you the truth, this poor widow has put more into the treasury than all the others. They all gave out of their wealth; but she, out of her poverty, put in everything—all she had to live on."
>
> Mark 12:42-44

153

Apparently, this end-of-life lesson from Jesus did not fall flat. Her radical generosity was about to become contagious. Although she did not know it at the time, this little widow was giving missionally. She was investing in the future of the church. She was teaching the future teachers. She was just doing what she would have done on any other given day, and God was using it to shape the lives of those present. Without making any type of blatant statement, she taught the disciples what it meant to live life without worrying about possessions. She apparently knew that "the pagans run after all these things, and your heavenly Father knows that you need them" (Matthew 6:32).

Only a few short months after observing this woman, the newly gathered group of believers began selling their fields and sharing everything they owned. The generosity of a frail widow sparked a movement of God.

CONTAGIOUS GENEROSITY

Throughout history, we have seen this pattern of contagious generosity periodically spring up around the world. Leo Tolstoy was a Russian novelist in the nineteenth century. He is considered by many as the greatest writer of all time. His epic work *War and Peace* sold over thirty-six million copies[31] (compared to the two or three thousand that most books sell). He was born into wealth and always had plenty as a result of his writings. But by the end of his life, Tolstoy was so convicted by the teachings of Jesus that he decided to give away the rights to his books and develop a lifestyle of radical generosity. It is said that by the time of his death, he was so loved by the peasants, that in spite of police presence, thousands of them lined the street for his funeral.[32]

To this day, there are Tolstoian communities organized across Europe, Africa, and North America that are shaped by the generous spirit of Tolstoy. These people share many of their possessions and hold their land in common. They live ascetic and simple lives with generosity permeating their way of life. They are generous because someone else's lifestyle inspired them toward giving.

Bob Pierce was an all-American guy. He was born in Iowa and spent much of his childhood in California. In 1947 he was working as a traveling evangelist with Youth for Christ. On a trip to Asia, Pierce met a teacher named Tena Hoelkedoer. She introduced him to a battered and abandoned child named White Jade. Unable to care for the child herself, Hoelkedoer asked Pierce, "What are you going to do about her?" Pierce gave the woman his last five dollars and vowed to send the same amount each month to help her care for the child. This simple act of generosity was the beginning of the Christian relief agency World Vision.[33]

Today, that act of generosity has become so viral that over two hundred million dollars are given annually to World Vision for child sponsorship.[34]

In the ancient Middle-East, a man lived who was not wealthy by any cultural standard. He never owned land; he never bought a house. Some would even say that he did not have a bed of his own. However, everything he did have was invested in the lives of the people around him. When his life was coming to an end, he even offered his (substantial) inheritance to his friends.

Since that time, people throughout the world have devoted themselves to becoming generous as Jesus was generous.

Generosity is contagious.

REALITY CHECK

I have to admit something. I have an obsession. Every day, I receive notices in my e-mail inbox that I am among an elite group of people who may be chosen to win millions of dollars from Publishers Clearing House. Even though these messages are always filtered into the spam box, I seek them out, complete the necessary forms, and review the newest sales offers. Two or three times a day, I spend about thirty seconds letting the Publishers Clearing House know that I am interested in winning the money. Currently, I am expecting that the Prize Patrol should roll into my driveway on August 31 to announce that I have won five thousand dollars a week for life.

In our less sane moments, my wife and I talk about what life would be like if we won millions of dollars. We talk about paying off the house, and how we could invest that money for the Kingdom. We dream about what could be done for our church community and laugh at the possibilities.

In reality, I have read that the odds of winning these huge prizes are about five hundred million to one.[35] That means there are about two entries for every person in the United States. That means that even if I enter a few times every day for the rest of my life, the only thing I will likely gain is a few insane—and somewhat funny—daydreams.

In reality, I have already been entrusted with everything I need to be radically generous toward the kingdom of God. I may never bring home thousands of dollars a week, but what I do have can go a long, long way toward extending God's influence. What I already have in my possession is comparable to winning a sweepstakes to some families. And God has entrusted this to me for the development of his kingdom.

Paradigm shifts and world movements generally do not start with excited crowds. They do not start with lottery collections or prize winnings. They start with the vision of a passionate few. They start with a handout to a peasant or a donation to an orphan. They start with an investment in a coworker. They start with a friend who sticks closer than a brother and individuals who love their neighbors as themselves. They start with missional generosity and perfect hope personified.

We are the church. Let's be the catalysts to redefine our Community as radically generous—just as God is generous to us.

APPENDIX: REGIFTING PROJECT PLANNING GUIDE

Walking through this process helped Traceway understand that faith is a dynamic blend of spontaneity and planning. Following God in faith sometimes means turning over every rock and examining every avenue. After all, God is the king of organization. When he created the heavens and the earth, he knit cells together, creating species and sub-species that were all interdependent. He created life and planned some remarkable ways to sustain it all.

Hopefully this planning guide will assist you as you begin to organize your missional giving. It is my prayer that the questions will uncover potential pitfalls and built-in opportunities for you to celebrate the work that God is accomplishing through your community.

At the same time, let me encourage you to keep your ears open to God throughout this work. Faith is not possible apart from some spontaneity.

I am often amazed at some of the overlooked details of our most cherished faith stories. Everyone who grew up around the church has heard the story of Jesus walking on the water countless times. We know about the swelling storm. We can visualize Peter stepping over the hull of the boat. But recently I have been amazed at another part of the story.

Do you remember how this all started? Jesus fed the five thousand and told the disciples to get in the boat to head to the other side of the sea. I am guessing that there were a few boats docked around this place as Jesus told them to go ahead. Then, Matthew and Mark tell us that Jesus dismissed the crowds and went up on the mountain to pray.

When Jesus came back down the hillside, apparently all of the boats were gone. No one was left to reconnect him with his disciples. No one was around to transport him across the water. As he stood at the edge of the sea, he and the Father were all alone.

Just in case you have forgotten, people do not walk on water. I do not know of any instances prior to this where a man decided to wander out onto the sea. But as Jesus stood there conversing with the Father, he apparently asked how he was supposed to get to the other side. And the Father said, "Go ahead. Step on top of the rising tide and walk."

So Jesus said, "Okay" and stepped out.

That is a moment of spontaneous faith. Regardless of how and when the Father actually directed Jesus onto the water, stepping into the rippling waves was a moment of spontaneous faith. We like to analyze the faith of Peter, but in reality his small amount of faith was spawned by the faith of Jesus. Jesus was the one who gave him the idea. And Jesus did not have any prior example to follow. He just had a directive from the Father.

As you and your community leaders work through the process of becoming radically generous, I pray that this guide will help you to plan in faith and also free you to follow the Father spontaneously.

STAGE ONE: LISTENING

Just as the thought of walking on the water was initiated by a prayer/conversation, the process of radical generosity must begin in the presence of the Father. God has already spoken about certain forms of generosity. He has instructed us to give faithfully to our churches. There is no need to agonize over this in prayer because he has already answered. However, until you hear a directive from God about radical generosity, I would encourage you to be still and keep listening to him. Trust his timing and wisdom. As you pray, listen for the answer to these questions:

1. How can I/we become more like you today?

    _____

    _____

2. What does it really mean to be the body of Christ in this neighborhood?

    _____

    _____

3. How do you want your resources invested in this community?

    _____

    _____

4. Do you want me/us to follow you in radical generosity at this time?

    _____

STAGE TWO: INITIATING THE CONVERSATION

Spiritual leadership does not mean enforcing your will. It means equipping people to join God as he works. Whether you are going through this process with a leadership team or with a spouse, you probably need to begin thinking communally.

When the Russian novelist Leo Tolstoy decided to start giving everything away, his wife never shared his enthusiasm. As a result, their interests were divided, and it ended up hurting both his mission and their family.

The last thing that God wants you to do is use this to start a family dispute over money. Our "God is not a God of disorder but of peace" (1 Corinthians 14:33). If you and those around you are genuinely seeking his leadership, he will eventually get you all on his path. So as you follow God into radical generosity, serve as a spiritual leader and intentionally bring others into this conversation with you. You may want to work through questions like these:

1. Has more than one person felt led to this mission?

    _____

2. What spiritual mentors—outside of our immediate community—should be praying with us in this process?

    _____

3. Is our community currently equipped to live missionally? (Mimicking government handouts will not transform lives.)

    _____

    _____

4. How much additional teaching/training is needed to equip people to make disciples in their workplaces and backyards before we take on this project?

    _____

    _____

5. What will be the duration of this project?

    _____

6. In the end, what needs to be accomplished for this work to be considered a success?

_____

_____

7. How are the community leaders going to model this to the rest of the congregation?

_____

_____

STAGE THREE: BUDGETING

The budgeting phase may be the defining point of this whole process. This is the summit. It is at this point that you will determine if you are really compelled to follow in faith or if you have simply been tossing around another new idea.

When you are at this point, remember that you would not even be here if you—*and others*—had not been moved here by God. There are incredibly difficult decisions at this stage, but if you can successfully navigate the budgeting questions, you will begin a downhill journey toward missional giving.

1. What steps need to be taken to transition our budget to one of faith rather than numbers?

_____

_____

2. Is there any obvious "fat" in our budget that can be trimmed immediately?

_____

_____

3. Are we really going to consider allowing our staff to temporarily work as bi-vocational ministers? (Not only to reduce the budget, but to place us in environments with the unchurched?)

_____

4. Are we going to need to raise funds to make this work?

_____

5. If we consider raising funds, how should we approach this process and who all should be involved?

_____

_____

STAGE FOUR: HELPING THE HURTING

Helping the hurting is an enviable goal, but it also presents perilous problems. You are certain to encounter people who only want your resources and not your relationships. Therefore, how you answer these questions will move you past several pitfalls and define the parameters of your giving. While it is tempting to answer these questions purely with logic, make sure you spend time as a community praying through each of these items. Remember that God's thoughts and ways are not like our thoughts and ways.

1. With this project, do we assist those outside our local neighborhoods or limit ourselves to those that we can truly engage missionally?

   _____

   _____

2. How do we spread the word about our mission to our community?

   _____

   _____

3. What is our process for selecting the recipients?

   _____

   _____

4. Do we need references for those receiving help, and how do we verify the references?

   _____

   _____

5. Do we give priority to any one particular area of need in our city/community?

   _____

   _____

6. Do we conduct entrance/exit interviews with those that we help?

   _____

   _____

7. What do we require in return from the people receiving assistance?

    _____

    _____

8. How can we get resources to the hurting quickly and efficiently?

    _____

    _____

9. How do we handle male interactions with single females and female interactions with hurting men?

    _____

    _____

10. How do we protect our host families from inappropriate and dangerous situations?

    _____

    _____

11. When do we limit the assistance or redirect the assistance for families who are not cooperating or progressing?

    _____

    _____

12. Where do we direct people whose needs are beyond our scope of help?

    _____

    _____

STAGE FIVE: BECOMING MISSIONAL

You are the church. However, if you do not dwell in this "Becoming Missional" stage, you will end up simply handing out checks.

1. What is it about the character of God that we are trying to emulate?

   _____

   _____

2. How well do our people understand their role as the church outside of the walls of our building?

   _____

   _____

3. How can we engage as many of our members as possible in this project?

   _____

   _____

4. How do we move from handing out a check to engaging a family/individual?

   _____

   _____

5. How do we move the hurting beyond their host families to a small group setting?

   _____

   _____

6. How do we protect the dignity of the participants as they become incorporated into our church community?

7. How much training is needed for our host families (those who regularly interact with people receiving assistance)?

8. How do we involve other local churches?

9. What other partnerships do we need to form in the community to make this most effective?

STAGE SIX: TRACKING

1. How do we regularly track our efficiency and progress?

2. How do we efficiently connect our budgeting team to our decision makers (those who

determine which cases receive help) and our host families?

_____

_____

3. How do we celebrate our successes?

_____

_____

4. How do we keep everyone informed about the work?

_____

_____

STAGE SEVEN: LOOKING AHEAD

1. What steps need to be taken at the end of the project to ensure that we continue promoting generous living?

_____

_____

2. Do we want to take Matthew 22:39 literally? Going forward, should we find a way to set aside as many resources for our neighbors as we do for ourselves?

_____

_____

3. How can we encourage other congregations to become radically generous?

_____

_____

THANK YOU

I do not know how to say thank you for following God in faith and engaging your community other than to pray for you. I want to end by voicing a prayer for you now, and please feel free to contact me as you move through this process. My contact information is on the following page.

> Father,
>
> Thank you for allowing us to be a part of this process. I am amazed that you take us as your bride and trust us with your name. I am humbled that, in spite of our faults, you would pursue us and call us your own.
>
> Right now, I pray specifically for the communities and individuals that you call to live generously. Father, give them the faith to walk step-by-step behind you. Speak clearly to all who are involved and involve them personally in your acts of missional giving. Deepen their walk with you during this process. Strengthen their faith if it wavers.
>
> Even now, at this very moment, begin instilling your wisdom in those who are following this path. Help them to know how you want to relate to the people in their neighborhoods and allow them to be amazed by your sovereignty. Enable them to live under your wing and as they are going about life each day enable them to be disciple makers. Help them to encounter you in a new way as they attempt to become generous, in the likeness of your character.

Even now, at this very moment, begin preparing the hurting who will be engaged by your church. Open their lives to your people. Open their hearts to your word. And lead them to abundant, eternal life with you.

Advance your kingdom and your glory in our neighborhoods, at our jobs, and in our families.

I pray this in the name of Jesus. Amen.

Send me a note. You can find me online at:

Twitter: @RichardsonJohnD

Facebook: www.facebook.com/RichardsonJohnD

And next time you're online, review *Giving Away the Collection Plate* at Amazon.com. Good or bad, let us know what you think.

NOTES

1   See *Church 3.0* by Neil Cole

2   The popular 1990s sitcom *Seinfeld* was known for creating short catch phrases to describe unique situations. In one particular episode, a character named Elaine gives a label maker as a gift. Eventually the gift ends up back in their circle of friends as people keep rewrapping the gift and trying to get rid of it.

3   American Red Cross. Accessed in July, 2010.   http://www.redcross.org/www-files/Documents/pdf/corppubs/2006Annual_Report.pdf

4   "Bypassing the Plate" Leadership Journal (Summer 2009), 13.

5   Philip Yancey, *Finding God in Unexpected Places* (Waterbrook Press, 2005), 197.

6   Shane Claiborne, *The Irresistible Revolution: Living as an Ordinary Radical* (Zondervan, 2006), 113.

7   F. Scott Fitzgerald, *The Great Gatsby* (Wordsworth Editions Limited, 1993), 114.

8   John Ortberg. *Giving: Unlocking the Heart of Good Stewardship* (Zondervan, 2000), 106.

9   Philip Yancey. *Money: Confronting the Power of a Modern Idol* (Multnomah, 1985), 3.

10 Since first trying this with our children, we have discovered that the older they get, the more they have a propensity toward hoarding. I am not sure if that is a result of our traumatic giving experiment or if it is just part of growing up. Either way, we still look for creative ways to give our best as a family.

11 MSN. Today Show, "Tricked: Husband says Wife faked Cancer for free Goodies" Accessed on September 8, 2010. http://today.msnbc.msn.com/id/39041806/ns/today-relationships/?Gt1=43001

12 Emma Lazarus. "The New Colossus"

13 Andy Stanley. "Be Rich: Confessions of a Fixer" (October 2008)

14 For more detailed information on the biblical feasts, see Dr. Richard Booker's book, *Celebrating Jesus in the Biblical Feasts* (Destiny Image, 2009)

15 Jeremiah 27:1-2

16 Sr. M. Clement Eagan–translator. *The Poems of Prudentius,* C.C.V.I. *The Fathers of the Church,*

Vol. 43 (The Catholic University of America Press, 1962)

17 Fredrick Buechner, *Godric* (HarperCollins, 1983), 48.

18 Buechner. *Godric*, 107.

19 Richard Wright. *Native Son* (Harper Perennial Modern Classics 1993), 353.

20 Wikisource. "Honourary Award for Winston Churchill," Accessed on April 4, 2011. http://en.wikisource.org/wiki/Honourary_ Citizenship_Award_for_Winston_Churchill

21 In his book *The Case for Christ*, Lee Strobel documents the improbability of any one man fulfilling all forty eight prophecies about the Messiah in the Hebrew scriptures. He states that the mathematical probability is approximately one in one trillion to the thirteenth power. That number is millions of times greater than all of the people who have ever lived on the earth (*The Case for Christ*, pg. 183). Further, if you tend to question statistical science, studying the prophetic nature of the biblical feasts will open your eyes to God's prophetic "story." The feasts of Leviticus 23 paint a detailed picture of the Messiah and the course of human history. For more information, see Dr. Richard Booker's book, *Celebrating Jesus in the Biblical Feasts*.

22 Bill Hybels. *Courageous Leadership* (Zondervan, 2002), 15.

23 Hybels. *Courageous Leadership*, 23.

24 C. S. Lewis. *The Weight of Glory and Other Addresses* (William B. Eerdmans Publishing Company, 1979), 1-2.

25 Wikipedia. "International Inequality," Accessed in March 2011. http://en.wikipedia.org/wiki/International_inequality

26 Work World. "Medicaid Data and Trends," Access in March 2011. http://www.work-world.org/wwwebhelp/medicaid_data_summary_and_trends.htm

27 Francis Chan. *Crazy Love:Overwhelmed by a Relentless God* (David C. Cook, 2008), 122.

28 Francis Chan. *Forgotten God: Reversing Our Tragic Neglect of the Holy Spirit* (David C. Cook, 2009), 107.

29 National Center For Charitable Statistics. "Quick Facts About Non-Profits," Access in March 2011. http://nccs.urban.org/statistics/quickfacts.cfm

30 World's Richest Countries. Accessed in March 2011. http://www.worldsrichestcountries.com

31 Wikipedia. "List of Best-Selling Books," Accessed in April 2011. http://en.wikipedia.org/wiki/List_of_best-selling_books

32 Wikipedia. "Leo Tolstoy," Accessed in April 2011. http://en.wikipedia.org/wiki/Leo_Tolstoy

33 World Vision Canada. "History," Accessed in June 2011. http://www.worldvision.ca/About-Us/History/Pages/History.aspx

34 World Vision Canada. "Financial Statements of World Vision Canada, Year Ended September 30, 2010," Accessed in June 2011. http://www.worldvision.ca/About-Us/financial-information/Scripts/FinancialStatementsFY10.PDF

35 About.com. "Contests and Sweepstakes," Accessed in June 2011. http://contests.about.com/od/sweepstakes101/tp/publishersclearinghousefaq.htm

LORD, SEND REVIVAL

LORD, SEND REVIVAL

Richard Lee

BROADMAN PRESS
NASHVILLE, TENNESSEE

© Copyright 1991 • Broadman Press
All rights reserved
4260-50
0-8054-6050-0
Dewey Decimal Classification: 248.4
Subject Headings: CHRISTIAN LIFE / SPIRITUAL LIFE / REVIVAL
Library of Congress Catalog Card Number: 91-16064
Printed in the United States of America

Unless otherwise noted, all Scripture quotations are from
the *King James Version of the Holy Bible*.

Scripture quotations marked (NASB) are from the *New American Standard Bible*.
Copyright © The Lockman Foundation, 1960, 1962, 1963, 1968,
1971, 1972, 1973, 1975, 1977. Used by permission.

Scripture quotations marked (TLB) are from the *The Living Bible*.
Copyright © Tyndale House Publishers, Wheaton, Illinois, 1971. Used by permission.

Dedicated to the members of

REHOBOTH BAPTIST CHURCH

Atlanta, Georgia

who honor me greatly by affording me
the privilege of being their pastor

Preface

Perhaps you are thinking, "Another book on revival? We need to hear more about evangelism and soul-winning!"

The fact is: if Christians don't experience heaven-sent, Holy Spirit revival, the stream of evangelism will virtually trickle to a standstill. Revival, after all of these years, is still one of the most misunderstood terms in Christianity.

Many Christians believe revival can come only during a "revival meeting," and when the meeting is conducted, the church members often think of it as an evangelistic, soul-winning crusade. It is magnificent when people are saved—that is the number-one mission of the church of the Lord Jesus Christ, but salvation of the lost is not revival.

Of course, salvation of souls results when born-again believers first experience revival and then move out to share Jesus Christ with the lost. You have heard many messages about the dire necessity for revival—but the problem is, so many of us have become "revival hardened." We have heard so much about revival, and we have nodded our heads and shouted "Amen" (some of us anyway), but so many haven't experienced revival.

Revival happens when God awakens a few believers to understand the urgent need for His moving. Revival begins with a few and grows to many. Genuine revival is accompanied by seasons of unrelenting prayer and a renewed desire for holiness and righteousness—then will ensue the harvest of souls born into the kingdom of God.

You may well be one of those chosen to spark revival. That has to start in your heart, and it will spread to your home, then to your church . . . yes, and throughout this nation!

I'm tired of the doomsayers who claim we cannot have revival. We can have it if only a remnant of God's people earnestly desire the fire of God to fall, not in judgment, but in power. Pray with me in the lyrics of B. B. McKinney:

> Lord, send a revival,
> Lord, send a revival,
> Lord, send a revival,
> And let it begin in me!*

> *Richard Lee*
> Rehoboth Baptist Church
> Atlanta, Georgia

Acknowledgments

There are many people who contribute to a man's ministry—his family, his church, his staff, and his denomination. I want to thank all those who have helped make my ministry possible as pastor, author, and in my continued involvement in the broadcast ministry through radio and television.

I also deeply appreciate the confidence of my Southern Baptist brethren who have elected me president of the Southern Baptist Convention Pastors' Conference for 1990-1991.

And finally, special thanks to Broadman Press of the Sunday School Board of the Southern Baptist Convention for their help in publishing this book, and to my secretary, Emily Boothe, for her help in typing the manuscript.

Contents

LORD, SEND REVIVAL

Part I

Lord, Send Revival

. . . in Our Hearts

1

How to Have
a Personal Revival

For thus saith the high and lofty One that inhabiteth eternity,
whose name *is* Holy; I dwell in the high and holy place, with him
also that is of a contrite and humble spirit, to revive the spirit of
the humble, and to revive the heart of the contrite ones (Isa.
57:15).

Let me ask you a pertinent question: Are you at the point in
your life where you can candidly, openly admit, "I'm going to die
if I don't have more of God"? Are you desperate to know God?
Can you go on for the rest of your spiritual life precisely as you are
now? Or have you come to the place where you feel you cannot
go on unless God, in His power and might, does a special work—
fresh, new, deeper, fuller, and more powerful in your heart?

If you are seeking God in such a way as that, I have good
news for you. That good news is: as much as you want to know
God, God wants you to know Him more! As much as you desire
to have the fullness of God in your life, God in turn desires to fill
you with that fullness, love, power, and might. Are you hungry
for that? If so, then *personal revival* is available for you.

There's an intriguing Scripture in Isaiah 57. The prophet

17

Isaiah, in verse 15, teaches us about God's desire. First, he introduces God to us. "For thus saith the high and lofty one that inhabits eternity, whose name is holy. . . ." The prophet wants us to meet God. What an introduction! God is high and lofty. His name is holy, and He inhabits eternity.

He continues by reporting God's words: "I dwell in the high and lofty places with him also that is of a contrite and humble spirit, to revive the spirit of the humble, and to revive the heart of the contrite ones." What an introduction and what a promise! As much as I yearn for personal revival in my life, I am enthralled by this truth: God says the reason He is in heaven is not only that He might be high and uplifted, but that He might grant personal revival to those on earth who have a contrite and humble spirit.

Recall Jesus' beatitude. "Blessed are they that hunger and thirst after righteousness, for they shall be filled" (Matt. 5:6). What's the key to being filled? You have to hunger and thirst before you can be filled. All of us have been thirsty and hungry, haven't we? You know how it is to get a dry mouth, and you must have a drink of water. When that happens, you realize that more than all else in your being, you have to have water. Christ made it plain, "When you become hungry and thirsty for Me like that, seeking My presence, then you are going to be filled." With the psalmist, we should testify: "As the hart [young deer] panteth after the water brooks, so panteth my soul after thee, O God" (Ps. 42:1).

The fact is evident that God is always willing to do His part, if we're willing to do ours. That's the way it is in the spiritual life. With that in mind, I want to share with you what I believe must happen in our lives if we're ever going to have personal revival.

First, I believe if personal revival is to come:

We Must Be Discontented with Things As They Are

In other words, the status quo won't do anymore. We are not content with laissez-faire. We become sick with "as is." That may not mean you're unhappy in your church. That doesn't imply you don't worship in the hymns and spiritual songs. Neither does it mean you're not a joy-filled Christian. But you have come to the place where you are ready to cry out, "Lord, I must have more of You, more of You, O God!"

God's inerrant Word declares that when we look at our spiritual experience and are aware the status quo will no longer do, and we must have the fullness of God, God is going to notice that we no longer accept the "as is."

Years ago a writer named Gordon Graham observed about discontent: "There are two kinds of discontent in this world; the discontent that works, and the discontent that wrings its hands. The first gets what it wants, and the second loses what it has. There's no cure for the first but success; and there's no cure at all for the second."

Sometime ago I was in a department store and came across a table with a banner above it. "As Is Items—Get Yours Cheap Today." Naturally I was interested, so I strolled over to see what was so cheap. As I began to rummage through all the merchandise, I came across a super-looking radio. It had no scratches—it wasn't damaged or dented. It looked brand new, so I picked it up from the "As Is" table, carried it to the salesman, and remarked, "Sir, this looks like a great radio. Is there anything wrong with it?"

The salesman replied, "Well, not much."

"What do you mean, not much?"

He said, "There's only one minor problem. The tuner is broken, and it's stuck on one station. But if you like that station, it's a great deal!" As I put it back and walked away, I thought about his explanation, "It's stuck on one station, but if you like that station, it's a good deal!" That is exactly how Satan operates. He thinks if he can get your spiritual life stuck on one station, that's a good deal.

Many people are positioned on the other side of salvation, and there they remain—stuck, mired, immobile. Now, there can be nothing more wonderful and glorious than salvation, but many people are right on the other side of the mountain of salvation, and there they stay. But God insists, "I want you to have more. I want you to know Me so intimately that I am in complete control of your life day in and day out. Moment by moment I want to draw you closer and closer to Me. I want you to know me more fully and more intimately."

I want that kind of relationship with God in my life. But I am all too aware I will never have it if I look at my life and claim everything is OK like it is. I can't have it just "as is." We have too many "as-is" churches and "as-is" preachers who preach "as-is" sermons to "as-is" Christians, who go out into a world that desperately needs a saving knowledge of Jesus Christ, as they act "as is."

"W. H. Griffith Thomas used to say: 'The Christian life is like a bicycle; if you do not go on, you go off.' There is a very truthful sentence in *Through the Looking-Glass* to the effect that 'it takes all the running you can do, to keep in the same place.' An anecdote is that of the little boy who fell out of bed. As his mother tucked him in again she asked him how he came to fall out. 'I don't know, Mother,' he replied, 'unless I went to sleep too near to where I got in.' This is the tragedy of many a Christian life— falling asleep soon after uniting with the church."[1]

You must become discontented. You must petition, "God, I *must* have more!"

Second, I believe if we are going to have personal revival:

We Must Be Willing to Seek God's Presence Desperately

We must be holy fanatics about seeking God's presence. We must become serious with God in an urgent, desperate manner. The "magnificent obsession" of our lives must be God.

We know what obsessions are. Have you ever known an obsessed fisherman, a guy who ate, talked, and walked fishing? One who read all the fishing magazines, owned his own boat filled with all the lures, baits, and rods and reels. It seemed he had to fish every day, obsessed with fishing and hoping he can fish in heaven.

Or have you ever known a fellow obsessed with golf? If you haven't, I can introduce you to several. They have the little caps and hats, even the cute knickers and shorts—registered clubs— and all the trappings of golf. Obsessed with golf! Why, believe it or not, some won't even take their wives on vacation unless there is a golf course nearby. It seems ridiculous, but they are absolutely obsessed with it.

I'm stepping on toes now. Have you ever seen a lady obsessed with shopping? Every day they go to the mall and shop. I saw a bumper sticker on a lady's car that read, "A woman's place is in the mall!" That's all right—but they're obsessed.

Perhaps we need to learn a lesson spiritually. We will never have a deep knowledge of a holy, eternal God until we become obsessed with Him. When we arise in the mornings we'll have to think about knowing God more. All through the day we must be obsessed with knowing Him more. When we lay our heads on our pillows at night, we must look to the Lord and pray, "God, I must know You more, not because a pastor has told me to, not because someone has forced me, but because I love You, and I'm desperate to know You more."

Allegedly, a young man once came to his pastor and enquired, "Pastor, how can I know when I get desperate for God?" The pastor tried to describe the yearnings of the heart that is desperate for God, but the young man didn't understand. After a while, the preacher saw he wasn't getting to first base with the young man so he suggested, "Come on, I want to take you into the baptistry." He took the man down into the baptistry, put him below the water, and left him there. In a short while bubbles began to come up. The fellow began to kick his heels, choke, and gag. Finally, the preacher pulled him up, and as the young man was spitting water and gasping for air, he cried out, "Preacher, why did you do that? You almost drowned me!"

The elderly pastor replied, "Son, I wanted to teach you a lesson, and it is this: 'You'll know when you want personal revival when you want God as much as you just wanted air.'" When we want God as much as we want air, as much as we want our toys and games, as much as we want our positions in society, as much as we want our business to prosper, as much as we want that new car or new house, when we want God with a holy obsession, He will show up on the scene ready to reveal Himself to our hearts.

Also, if we want personal revival:

We Must Come to the Place of a Deep, Deep Repentance

I'm not talking about repentance of only the overt, outward sins. We are rather well acquainted with these sins. We know when we lie, steal, and cheat. Most of us know the Ten Commandments. No one needs to tell us those things. I'm referring to those deep sins—when God takes His searchlight and shines it into the deep closets of our hearts and shows us sins we didn't even know we have.

The Bible assures us: if we will seek God, through the light of His Holy Spirit, He will shine His searchlight into the depths of our souls. We'll see sin like we've never seen it before. The main reason we no longer have altars overflowing with tears is that Christians in our nation have forgotten what sin really is. We've become accustomed to our sin. It sounds like a song—a funeral dirge, so much sin that we often don't even know it's there.

Sin reminds me of going into a darkened restaurant. You go in and sit at the table. From the shadows someone gives you a menu and says, "I'll be your waiter."

You ask, "Where is that voice?" You can't see a thing! There you sit in near darkness, trying to see the menu in front of you. Finally, after a few minutes of adjustment, the menu becomes readable. Why? Because your eyes have become accustomed to the darkness. That's why believers are not full of repentance any-more. So many Christians are not weeping their way to close fel-lowship with God because they've become so accustomed to a world darkened by sin they don't even see the darkness of sin within their own hearts.

When we reach the point of deep repentance, when we start to plumb the depths of our souls, and God begins to open this closet and that compartment we have hidden and shut off from Him, He says, "Here's a sin, there's iniquity, and there's a trans-gression." When we start to confess those sins, then God's Spirit will begin to be poured out upon us, and we will feel the refresh-ing winds of personal revival.

Then, if we're going to have personal revival:

We Must Go to Those We've Wronged and Make It Right

Most people don't care for this step. Do you know why? The flesh never cares for that. It's easy to pray, "Lord, I want some-thing to happen in my heart, I want to be different within, but let's keep this matter of repentance personal, just between You and me." But it's not easy to seek pardon and restitution.

The Bible talks about Zacchaeus. When Zacchaeus met Jesus, he said (Luke 19:8), "Lord, I'm going to give half of my goods to the poor, and if I've robbed from any man, I'll go and restore him fourfold." Zaccheus had revival. Why? Because the *inward look* had caused an *outward action*. Not only was Zacchaeus re-pentant, but Zacchaeus acted upon it. He immediately sought forgiveness and restoration with others.

When revival comes, you will have to pay the debts you owe. When revival comes, you will seek that person you may have of-fended or slandered or talked against, and done wrong, and you will ask their forgiveness, so in turn God may give you forgive-ness. You must turn your life around, not merely by lip service, not just by saying, "Lord, I want Your Spirit," but also by seeking forgiveness from others. You must make the wrong, right. Go back and mend fences. Go back and apologize. Go back and admit, "I was wrong. Please forgive me."

You argue, "That's tough." Yes, it is awfully tough. I don't know anything in my life that's tougher than that. Do you know how tough it is to go to someone who has wronged you and put your arm around them and say, "I'm sorry. I was wrong, and for my part in this, I want to ask your forgiveness"? Rough. But that's necessary. The Bible stresses that God will not forgive our trespasses if we don't forgive those who trespass against us.

The master painter Leonardo da Vinci supposedly painted the face of Judas in "The Last Supper" to favor a personal enemy. But then the great painter had terrible trouble painting the face of Jesus and succeeded only after he had painted out the face of Judas and reconciled himself with his enemy. None of us can truly paint the face of Jesus for an evil world, either literally or symbolically, unless we have repented and made restitution.

Another factor necessary for revival is:

We Must Position Ourselves in the Place Where Revival Comes

I am not thinking about a physical place but rather about a position, a place in our lives, certain places before God where we must be as an individual, as a church, as a denomination—a place we must be if revival is going to ensue.

First, *it's a place of constant prayer.* The Bible says we must pray without ceasing (see 1 Thess. 5:17). That's determined prayer that doesn't give up. In Genesis 32:24-32, the Bible records Jacob's wrestling with an angel. I like Jacob because he was a man who wouldn't quit. He locked hold of this angel and wrestled all night long. He was determined not to let go until the angel blessed him. Morning came, and the angel asked, "What is your name? I've never known a wrestler like you."

Jacob replied, "I am Jacob." Do you remember what the angel said?

"And he said, Thy name shall be called no more Jacob, but Israel: for as a prince hast thou power with God and with men, and hast prevailed" (v. 28). Jacob was constant. He refused to let go until he was blessed.

The problem with some praying is that it is only repeated before a meal, and that's all. Others pray only when they're in trouble, or when it's convenient in their religious life. But, we are never going to have revival with that kind of praying. We must pray, "God, we must have revival, and we're going to lock horns on the altar of prayer, and not cease until revival comes." This is unceasing, unswaying, prevailing prayer.

But there's another place—*the place of love for the Word of God*. You must love the Book. You must love what's in the Book. This Book must come alive in you.

I recall the story of two men walking down the street who passed by a taxidermist's shop. They glanced in the window and one remarked, "Look at that sorry job of taxidermy. There's a bird sitting in there, and that's the lousiest taxidermy job I've ever seen." About that time the bird flew away. The problem was they weren't aware of what they were looking at. That bird was alive!

The skeptic will look at the Bible and scoff, "It's not really true. That never happened! There's no power in that Book." The difficulty is, he doesn't know what he's looking at. The Bible is alive. If you're going to have revival you must get into a Bible-teaching church under a Bible-preaching pastor who believes the Bible is alive. Common sense indicates you're never going to feel the breeze until you go where the wind is blowing. You must be where the wind of faith is blowing.

Last, we must come to: *the place of total obedience*. God's Word is not just a guidebook of suggestions. It's God's mandate for our lives. Although we can parrot, "God, I love you," although we can pray and do what we think we must do for revival to come, if we don't obey God, He will never pour out His power and Spirit upon us. We must reach the point where we will request, "God, anything you want. Any time you want. Any way you want, God, I'm going to do it. God, I don't care if it embarrasses the flesh, I don't care if it is exactly the opposite of what my flesh wants me to do, that doesn't matter. Desperately in my heart I want to know You and experience Your power." That and that alone is the place of total obedience.

Do you really want personal revival? If you do, it's available for you. Make sure your heart is right with God, start obeying that Word. Then God promises, "I will pour out my spirit upon all flesh." And when He pours out His Spirit upon your family, your church, your personal life, it will never be the same again. You have God's unfailing Word on it!

> Holy Spirit, breathe on me, Until my heart is clean;
> Let sunshine fill its inmost part, With not a cloud
>   between.
>
> Holy Spirit, breathe on me, My stubborn will subdue;
> Teach me in words of living flame What Christ would
>   have me do.
>
> Holy Spirit, breathe on me, Fill me with power divine;
> Kindle a flame of love and zeal Within this heart of mine.
>
> Holy Spirit, breathe on me, Till I am all Thine own,
> Until my will is lost in Thine, To live for Thee alone.
>
> Breathe on me, breathe on me, Holy Spirit, breathe on
>   me;
> Take thou my heart, cleanse every part, Holy Spirit,
>   breathe on me.
>
> —Edwin Hatch

Note

1. Paul E. Holdcraft, Comp., *Encyclopedia of Bible Illustrations* (New York and Nashville: Abingdon Press, 1947), 19.

2

Confessions of a Struggling Soul

Because the church that I pastor has a rather large media ministry, I often receive heavy amounts of mail. Many of these letters are from distraught, struggling souls. Recently I read what just such a person wrote many years ago: "It seems to me to be a fact of life that when I want to do what is right, I inevitably do what is wrong. I love to do God's will so far as my new nature is concerned, but there is something else deep within me in my lower nature that is at war with my mind, and wins the fight, and makes me a slave to sin that is still within me. In my mind I want to be God's willing servant, but instead I find myself enslaved to sin. You see how it is. My new life tells me to do right, but the old nature that is still inside me loves to sin." In closing he confessed, "Oh, what a terrible predicament I'm in!"

Do you ever feel like that? Have you ever reached the painful plateau where, in a moment-by-moment struggle, where you talk to yourself and say, *I want to do what is right. I know what's right, but somehow, I just blow it. I love God, and I want to keep His commandments. I love the Lord Jesus, and I love the Holy Spirit. And the greatest desire of my heart is to be obedient to*

27

God and obey Him, but somehow, sometimes, I just fall flat on my face.

If those are your sentiments, you're probably just being honest with yourself. All of us who know Christ, who are plagued by our own mistakes, can testify, "Yes, I can identify with what that man wrote," but who was this man? Who is this man who sounds like us, who says, "Sometimes I do what I should do, and sometimes I don't do what I should do. I'm in a terrible predicament." When we search a while we will understand that these words are from none other than Paul the apostle in Romans 7:21-25 (TLB).

When you are first confronted with these words, you might exclaim: "This couldn't be the Apostle Paul. He was the greatest apostle who ever lived. After all, he was beaten, shipwrecked, and thrown into prison for Christ. No other mere human could compare to the magnificent life of the apostle. Reflect on his life. He stood before kings and potentates, fearlessly standing for the Gospel of Christ—and oh how he was persecuted. He wrote all those letters in the New Testament. Of all people, it couldn't be Paul."

Yet, it was Paul, and in the middle of Romans 7 he is confronted with a time of personal and public confession. There he pours out the frustration of his heart in a torrent of "true confessions." "I am a struggling man," he cries.

What about you? Are you also struggling right now? No doubt you want to do what's right. You do love Jesus, but somehow nothing seems to go right. From this amazing confession we can understand Paul and ourselves better. We can also grasp what to do during those times when we're struggling with sin and really don't want to sin at all. Bear in mind the words of William Penn, as he thought of the trials and triumphs of the Christian life: "No pain, no palm; no thorns, no throne; no cross, no crown!"

Notice that:

On His Own He Is a Slave to Sin

Look with me in verse 14, "For we know that the law is spiritual, but I am carnal, sold unto sin." He says three things there.

First, the law is spiritual, but second and most importantly, Paul confesses his carnality. What is carnal? It means "flesh" with the reference to the struggle with human nature which is not done away with at conversion. Paul is keenly aware that he is still flesh and bones, and as long as he lives on earth in a fleshly body he will be carnal—he will have a fleshly nature.

Then he continues by declaring that:

He Was Sold into Sin

That means on his own, without any help from God, he was a captive, enslaved to his sin. The carnal man has desires. What are those desires? They are the desires of the flesh. It means that all you do in life is still wrapped up in the senses—what you can see, hear, smell, taste, and feel. You live an entire life based upon what you can do to gratify your sight, taste, smell, hearing, and feeling. All the carnal man wants to do is to live to satisfy his sensual, fleshly being. Paul wrote that without Christ, he was sold unto sin. In other words, he was captive—a slave—to sin.

We who are believers must understand that any person without Christ is a slave to sin. They live only for their sensual being. When we as Christians look at magazines and television, and see clips from R-rated (or worse) movies that are coming to our town, and hear some of the ungodly music going on we may exclaim, "I don't understand that. Why would anyone want to fool with that garbage?" In your "piousness," you might ask, "How could anybody want to do that?" But you must recognize that a person without Christ lives basically to gratify his senses. That's why they do what they do—because they have a huge "natural man" (see 1 Cor. 2:14) within them that demands, "Feed me, feed me." They live in a carnal atmosphere, thinking the more they feed the flesh the better off they are.

Let me give you an example. Why does an alcoholic drink alcohol? Does he want bloodshot eyes? I don't believe so. Does he want to smell bad? No. Does he want to wreck his mind and body, family and home? No. So why does an alcoholic put that awful-tasting stuff into his mouth? Because the flesh says, "Give me, give me, give me." When you comprehend he is dominated by the fleshly man, you can better understand why he does what he does.

Why does a cocaine addict snort cocaine? Does she want to fry her brain cells, that she can't have logic or reason and can't think straight for the rest of her life? Is that why she does that? No. Does she want to destroy relationships with family, husband, and friends? No. She continues to sniff or free base cocaine because this massive, carnal man inside is demanding, "Feed me, feed me, feed me." She is feeding the sensual nature, and she is ensnared.

> This is the debt I pay
> Just for one riotous day,
> Years of regret and grief,
> Sorrow without relief.
>
> Slight was the thing I bought,
> Small was the debt I thought,
> Poor was the loan at best—
> God! but the interest![1]

Ephesians 4:18 speaks of this. "Having their understanding darkened; being alienated from the life of God through the ignorance that is in them because of the blindness of their heart." They're blind in heart, because they're one-dimensional beings. They live only for their carnal flesh.

Paul confided, "Without God, I'm hopeless. Without God, I'm just a carnal man. Without God, I simply live for one thing—

what I can get out of life to satisfy the old, sensual, fleshly nature within me."

You may think that you don't have that within your being, but the Bible declares, "There is none righteous, no not one" (Rom. 3:10). The Bible makes it plain: "All have sinned and come short of the glory of God" (Rom. 3:23). I wonder if there is a person among us who can say they've never yielded to temptation. They've never lied, stolen, cheated, envied, lusted, been jealous, or done any of those things. If you claim you haven't you have proven that you did, because you just told a lie. Outside of the Lord Jesus Christ, no one has ever been without sin. David cried out, "In sin did my mother conceive me."

Paul is merely confessing, "Look, world, without leaning on God I have a problem, because I have this carnal man within me and I am enslaved to sin."

Look at his second confession in verse 15. He confesses that:

Although He Desires to Do Good, He Doesn't Always Do It

"For that which I do, I allow not; for what I would, that do I not, but what I hate, that do I." To paraphrase, Paul says, "Look, I know I have a problem. Sometimes the things I want to do, I don't do. Sometimes the things I don't want to do, I do." Like all of us Paul was torn between the carnal and the spiritual, two worlds—this one and heaven. Many times he wanted to escape his predicament, praying that God would call him home.

Perhaps there is a man who attends church every Sunday. He is a good, honest, and upright man. In fact, he loves Jesus. He arises every Sunday morning, dresses, and puts his Bible under his arm. He drives his family to church. He sits in a worship service, and he is excited to hear the singers and the choir. When the pastor preaches, the fellow takes his Bible and follows along as the preacher exegetes the Word of God. The guy just loves the study of the Word of God, but he still has a habit in his life, a bad habit, what Paul called a "stronghold" (see 2 Cor. 10:5). Every week he commits this sin, and each Sunday morning he becomes convicted in the worship service. He prays to God, "God, I know what my sin is, and I promise *by my strength* I won't commit that sin this week."

He goes out the back door reminding himself, *I am not going to sin that sin this week.* Sunday passes by—Monday, Tuesday, Wednesday, Thursday, and then Friday. Day by day he has weakened in the flesh, saying, *I'm not going to do it; I'm not going to do it. Maybe I might do it. No, I really shouldn't do it* Then along comes Friday, and he commits that sin. The old pattern is repeated.

The man returns to church next Sunday, and he is cowed down and defeated. He mumbles to himself, *Why should I even try to be a Christian? I can't do it. I have that inescapable urge to sin that particular habit against God.* Now let's just look at that man and ask several questions.

"Does he want to sin?"

No, he doesn't.

"Does he want to harm the body of Christ?"

No, he doesn't.

"Does he want to bring a reproach upon the church of the Lord Jesus Christian?"

No, he doesn't.

"Does he want to hurt Christ Himself, or perhaps his wife or his family?"

No, he doesn't.

So, why does he do this? Because he's trying to live the believer's life according *to his own ability.* He's repeating to himself, and then to God, *I'm going to do it in my own strength.* "God, I'm not going to sin because I've made up my mind I'm not going to do it."

On the other side in this man's life is this fleshly, carnal "old man" (nature) who is saying, "You can't whip me. You may have determination for a while, but you see, I rule your life!" By human efforts there's no way that fleshly man is going to over-come. That old nature is going to cause you to sin because it looms larger within you if you are alone in your battle. So Paul wrote, "I must confess. Why do I do the things that I do?"

Next, Paul confesses:

There's a Battle of Two Natures Within Him

"Something is going on—there's a war within my heart." Let's understand what he's talking about. It's confusing, isn't it? First, *remember that when a person comes to Christ, something happens in his life.* Not only is he forgiven of his sins and brought into the family of God, but he has a new heart—a new nature—within him. Here's the carnal nature the man has had all his life, but suddenly he is saved. He is regenerated, born again into the family of God. What happens? God puts a new heart, a new nature within.

In Ezekiel 11:19, God said, "And I will put a new spirit within you. . . ." Now God has taken over this carnal man and put a new spirit within him. But as much as that new spirit is within that man, the remnant of that carnal nature is still there. I have heard it expressed: "At conversion the 'old man' is struck a death blow, but all the rest of our days he is still kicking." In Jeremiah 17:9 it declares: "The heart is deceitful above all things, and desperately wicked: who can know it?"

A born-again believer has within him two natures. He has a new heart which wants righteousness. It wants to do right. The new man loves God and tries in every way to be pleasing unto God. But on the other side there is a carnal nature which lives for the senses. There is a war going on.

Paul continued to talk about this war in Galatians 5:17, "The flesh lusteth against the Spirit, and the Spirit against the flesh: and these are contrary one to the other. . . ." The flesh is battling the spirit and the spirit, the flesh. The flesh whispers, "Yield to sin," when the spirit urges, "No, stand and resist."

This is vividly seen throughout the Bible. Joseph was in Egypt living in Potiphar's house. Potiphar was the captain of Pharaoh's guard. Potiphar's wife lusted after Joseph so she came and tempted him to sleep with her. I can almost see Joseph as he was standing before Potiphar's wife—no doubt she was tempting—and the flesh was saying, "Joseph, take this beautiful woman for yourself. After all, who would ever know it? Potiphar is gone. She wants you, so why don't you accept her advances and fulfill the lust of the flesh?"

Then along came Joseph's spiritual nature—the greater man within him—and warned, "No, Joseph, you are chosen by God. Resist and flee." The Bible reports that Joseph listened to the spiritual man within him and fled. Potiphar's wife was left with Joseph's garment hanging in her hands (see Gen. 39).

In contrast we note another account in the Bible of a prominent leader whose name was David. David, king of Israel, walked upon his porch one night and viewed a woman by the name of Bathsheba, bathing herself. She also was a beautiful woman, and as he looked upon her, I can almost hear the flesh calling out, "David, take her. After all, you're a king, and who's going to deny the king? Her husband is one of your soldiers, and you should not even care about him. Take her for your own pleasure."

But the spiritual man pled, "No, David, you're chosen by God to rule Israel." What did David do? He did not listen to the new man as Joseph did. He yielded to the flesh and had sex with Bathsheba. Not only that, he sent her husband, Uriah, to the front lines of battle, where he was killed. David was sorry for the rest of the days of his life for what he did. He sinned against God and man. Why did he sin? Because he listened to the fleshly man (see 2 Sam. 11).

Repeatedly in the Scriptures we read of this raging battle between the spirit and the flesh. Paul wrote in Romans 7:23, "But I see another law in my members, warring against the law of my mind and bringing me into captivity, into the law of sin which is in my members." Paul was admitting, "All right, on my own I'm under the domination of sin. By myself, I'm a slave to sin." Second, he had to confess, "Not only am I a slave to sin, but there are times when I do what I don't want to do."

Herschel H. Hobbs wrote: "A military tactician said that battles are won before they are fought. That was his way of saying that victory depends on prior preparation. One general called it 'Making a good ready.' The same principles apply in spiritual warfare. God in Christ has made all necessary prior preparation in effecting His eternal purpose of redemption to give us victory over sin."[2]

His last confession is found in verses 24 and 25. He cannot win this battle alone:

He Needs a Savior

Verse 24, "Oh wretched man that I am! Who shall deliver me from the body of this death? I thank God through Jesus Christ, our Lord. . . ." How is this struggling soul ever going to find victory? Through Christ and Christ alone! And that's true with all of us.

Another translation puts it, "Thank God, it has been done by Jesus Christ the Lord, for He has set me free." Understand the situation. Paul confessed that on his own he was merely a sinful man who did things on his own to the extent that he really didn't want to do. He realized there was a fierce battle going on he couldn't win on his own, but thanks be to God, Christ had set him free.

What did Christ do for Paul? He did what he'll also do for you and for me. Number one: *Christ Took Away Paul's Guilt.*

Christ called Paul forgiven. Have you ever deeply thought about the guilt Paul carried on him? He was not always the Apostle Paul. Once he was Saul, the hater and persecutor of the church. Acts 9 spoke of the fact, "He went about with threatenings and slaughter, persecuting the Christians." That means when he was Saul he went about supervising the slaughter of the believers. Can you imagine in his mind and heart the memories? How he must have thought time and time again of the man he tore from his wife's arms and shipped to prison, the woman he had executed because she professed to be a believer, the parents he had snatched from children, and all the sordid sins involved in his persecution of the New Testament church. What a heavy load of guilt!

But when Paul met Christ, there was a terrific change. Christ took away his guilt. All the pain and guilt were gone because of the forgiving power of Christ.

No wonder Isaac Watts could exult:

> Was it for crimes that I have done He groaned upon the tree?
> Amazing pity, grace unknown, And love beyond degree!
> At the cross, at the cross where I first saw the light,
> And the burden of my heart rolled away, It was there by faith
> I received my sight, And now I am happy all the day!

Second: *Christ Enlightened Him.* Jesus Christ is not only the Light of the world, He is the Light of the soul as well. Christ helped him to understand what was happening within him. That's what's wrong with believers who have fallen into sin. They don't know what's going on within their hearts. They hear a sermon that sin is wrong, and they know it's wrong, because every time they do it they get into trouble. They live in guilt and fear, looking over their shoulders. They alibi, "Yes, I know it's wrong, and I don't want to do it. I don't want to yield to temptation—to lust, jealousy, envy, or gossip. I don't know what's happening within me, because sometimes I do what I don't want to do."

The believer who is struggling with that has never come to the full comprehension about the nature of the battle going on within him. There's a spiritual man, and there's a carnal man. Whichever is greater is the one who will win. The question is, which one will win? We know by which is greater, larger, and dominant in our lives in the hour of temptation. What we do then tells us who we are and what we are, or who we are not and what we are not.

Jesus illuminated Paul's mind and said, "Not only are you forgiven, but there's a battle going on within you between the spirit and flesh." And not only did Jesus remove his guilt and enlighten him, but: *Christ Empowered Him by the Power of the Holy Spirit.* There is the key. Paul confessed. He admitted that on his own he couldn't do it; on his own he was a slave to sin, in bondage to sin. On his own he committed sins he didn't want to do. He sinned, and he didn't want to do that. On his own he felt hopeless and helpless. Along came Christ and He consoled Paul with: "I'm going to empower you by the presence of the Holy Spirit so you can win that battle within your heart."

The Bible promises, as Paul expressed it in Galatians 5:16, "Walk in the Spirit, and ye shall not fulfill the lust of the flesh." Paul gave this encouragement, "There hath no temptation taken you, but such as is common to man: but God is faithful, who will not suffer [let] you to be tempted above that ye are able; but will with the temptation also make a way to escape, that ye may be able to bear it" (1 Cor. 10:13). The Apostle John wrote, "Greater is he that is in you than he that is in the world" (1 John 4:4).

Paul said that we don't have to sin. We don't have to give in to the forces of the world, the flesh, and the devil. Once you've been enlightened and endued by the power of the Holy Spirit—no matter what your temptation—"Greater is he that is in you than he that is in the world."

Notes

1. From *A Treasury of Sermon Illustrations,* Edited by Charles L. Wallis (New York and Nashville: Abingdon Press, 1945), 262.

2. From *My Favorite Illustrations,* Herschel H. Hobbs, Ronald K. Brown, Comp. (Nashville: Broadman Press, 1990), 264.

3

Understanding Christian Conviction

Did not our hearts burn within us when he walked with us in the way? (Luke 24:32).

If you are involved with a Christian fellowship, more than likely you have heard of Christian conviction. When I speak of conviction, I refer to that feeling, that tugging at your heart, that comes when the Holy Spirit places His hand upon you when you have sinned—when He points out to you the sin in your life, and also the necessity of dealing with it.

How do you handle conviction? You can in one of three ways. Number one:

You Can Ignore It

We can rebel and say, "OK, I'm not convicted. I know I've sinned, but I'm going to ignore this conviction in my life."
Or:

You Can Reject It

Rejection is when we don't ignore it. We know it's there, but we don't admit it. We simply say, "I'm just going to push this feeling of guilt out. I'm going to reject it."

Or:

The Best Way to Handle Conviction Is to Understand It

We can determine to know what God is up to in our lives. We can say, "All right, I know I've sinned. I know what that sin is. I know what I am to do about it. I know why this conviction has come, and I am going to handle it the way God wants me to handle it so it can be used as a tool to draw me nearer to Him."

This is crucial. The way you handle and understand conviction will determine your success or failure in the Christian life. We were convicted before we were saved. We are still being convicted. Why? Because all of us who are believers and have the Holy Spirit living in our hearts are subject to conviction. I'm glad we are, aren't you? All of us from time to time have the Holy Spirit convict us. But when that conviction comes, how do you handle it? Of course, the answer to that question is of great importance.

William H. Bathurst aptly summed it up in "Holy Spirit, from on High":

> Light up every dark recess Of our heart's ungodliness;
> Show us ev'ry devious way Where our steps have gone
> astray.
>
> Teach us, with repentant grief, Humbly to implore relief;
> Then the Saviour's blood reveal, And our broken spirits
> heal.

The Role of Conviction

What is conviction in our lives? I would define it as, "God moving upon the heart of one of His children, calling him/her from sin to repentance and to forgiveness."

In Luke 24, there is a marvelous post-resurrection story of two men who were walking with Jesus on the road to Emmaus. As they strode along, Jesus began to teach them the Scriptures—in fact, truths about the Scriptures they had never heard before. The text expresses it: "Their hearts burned within them" (see v. 32).

What is this burning sensation? What is this that makes one feel heavy, and when one sins it makes one feel guilty? The Bible calls it *conviction*. It's the power of God's Holy Spirit moving on your heart, pointing out barriers between you and God. More than all else God loves you and wants to have fellowship with you. But the Bible says, "But your iniquities have separated between you and your God" (Isa. 59:2). God cannot reach you—He cannot have harmony with you and fellowship with you—when there is sin in your life. "If I regard iniquity in my heart, the Lord will not hear me" (Ps. 66:18).

The Bible says God sent His only begotten Son to die on a cross that you might be restored to fellowship. Here you are, saved and born again, in right standing and fellowship with God. But once again there is turmoil in your life. You're not perfect. You're not sinless. We all mess up. "Prone to wander, Lord I feel it, prone to leave the God I love!" We all make errors and mistakes. Many times there are overt or covert sins in our lives. What does that sin do? It separates us from fellowship with God.

Thus, God devised a beautiful plan to overcome this separation. The plan is called conviction. You fall under conviction, and when you do, your mind and heart are stimulated to realize there is a gap, a breach between you and God. So God gives us this fantastic gift called Christian conviction that comes upon our hearts so we will confess our sins and have restored fellowship with Him. That's the role—the meaning—of conviction. God reveals our sin so we can confess it, go back to Him, and have full fellowship with Him.

Second, I want you to think about:

The Revelation of Conviction

This is how it is revealed in our lives. How does it come? It comes along many avenues, but I want to point out three distinct ways conviction comes.

1. Conviction Can Come from the Word of God

That's why it is so important that we always, consistently believe the Word of God. The Bible reveals human nature in all its ugliness, even in the lives of its greatest heroes—men like Abraham, Moses, Joseph, David, Paul, and Peter.

This marvelous road map, this guide, this instrument of truth, this document of the laws, precepts, and principles of God—the Bible—must be relevant and vital in our lives, that we might always have the source on which we can depend to bring us into conviction and help us to recognize our sin. Perhaps the most telltale sign that might indicate a backslidden heart is when a person disregards the Word of God, when a person starts laying the Word of God aside. That should show all of us that there is something wrong in one's spirit. The Word of God opens our eyes to the truth and helps us to understand our lives in the light of the words of God Himself.

> I know the Bible was sent from God, The Old, as well as
>   the New;
> Inspired and holy, the Living Word, I know the Bible is
>   true.
>
> I know the story of Christ is true, His virgin, glorious birth,
> His life, His death, and the open tomb, And His return
>   to the earth

I know the Bible is wholly true, For peace it gives me
within;

It finds me, comforts me day by day, and gives me vict'ry
o'er sin.

Tho' foes deny with a spirit bold The message old. but still
new,

Its truth is sweeter each time 'tis told, I know the Bible is
true

I know, I know, I know the Bible is true;

Divinely inspired the whole way thro', I know the Bible is
true. [1]

In Hebrews 4:12 we read, "For the word of God is quick, and powerful and sharper than any two-edged sword; it pierces even to the dividing asunder of soul and spirit and of the joints and the marrow; and is a discerner of the thoughts and intents of the heart." When others can't discern our thoughts and intents, when husbands and wives don't even know what each one is thinking, when our friends and neighbors don't know, when we ourselves don't really grasp what's going on in our lives, the Word of God shares that with us. It opens the eyes of our understanding and it is sharper—it pierces our hearts—than any two-edged sword. God reveals our condition through His anointed Word.

But not only does conviction come from the Word of God:

2. Conviction Can Come from the Witness of Men

That's why God gives us pastors, Sunday School teachers, godly husbands and wives, mothers and fathers. Others are given to us by God to help us recognize sin—those who are willing to share with us, not in a self-righteous, judgmental way, but in a spirit of love, the area of our lives that needs correction.

We view this facet in the life of David. In our previous chapter we referred to his sin with Bathsheba. He committed a triple transgression—adultery, murder, and hypocrisy. The Bible indicates he went on living in that sin for about a year. One day a friend of his arrived. Actually the man was a prophet but also a friend who loved David.

"Then the Lord sent Nathan to David" (2 Sam. 12:1ff.). Nathan related a parable about a rich man who stole a ewe lamb from a poor man, cooked the man's treasured lamb, and served it to a guest. David shook his head. You know how many people do when they hear about *other people's sins*. "Oh, that's terrible. How could a person ever do that? I just can't imagine a person ever sinning like that." In fact, David said: "As the Lord lives, that man deserves to die" (v. 5b). Nathan then pointed to David and indicted him with, "David, thou art the man."

Nathan was spelling out David's heinous sin, his transgression. In Psalms 51:3b David, with broken heart, cried, "And my sin is ever before me." He recognized it. He was painfully aware of it and acknowledged his transgression, confessed it, repented of it, and God cleansed his life. Sometimes conviction comes from the witness of men and women.

And then lastly,

3. It Always Comes Through the Work of the Holy Spirit

It may come through the Word of God and through the witness of people, but it always emerges through the work of the Holy Spirit. That is one of the major attributes of God's Spirit. One of the main purposes of the Holy Spirit on earth is to reveal to our hearts the sin in our lives.

In John 16:8, Jesus prophesied, "And when he is come he will reprove the world of sin, and of righteousness, and of judgment." The Holy Spirit will reprove (convict) us and awaken our consciences to the sin in our lives. Wouldn't it be a dreadful situation if I, as a saved, blood-washed believer who loves Jesus, was walking through this life and piling up all these sins. Here is a sin of anger, of malice, of bitterness, or harbored ill feelings, and I am stacking up all these sins against me. Then I wouldn't know why I couldn't talk to God. I would pray, and He wouldn't hear me. I would carry out all the actions of a Christian, but I wouldn't have any joy or abundance. I would know something was wrong, but I wouldn't know what it was. Because of the lack of the Holy Spirit working in my life, I would be flying blind.

But praise God He gave us the Holy Spirit that we might *know*. He is the Revelator. He enters our lives when we are born again, and He controls and guides us.

Regardless of where we are—in a worship service, reading the Word of God at home, in a Sunday School class, you name it—when we feel the power of the Holy Spirit begin to convict us and convince us of our sin, that's the greatest blessing God could ever give us, the deep-down knowledge that there is something radically wrong. He is saying, "Look, you have a sickness here, a need here; you must confess it and repent of it that that sin might be blotted out and wiped away, that you might enjoy restored fellowship with God the Father."

Conviction may come through the Word of God and the witness of men, but it *always* comes through the work of the Holy Spirit.

Next, I want to focus on:

The Reason for Conviction

What produces it? Sin calls for conviction. But I believe Christians follow a distinct pattern of sin. In my ministry as a pastor, I have found this to be true in the lives of many. When you feel cold and indifferent, when you sense yourself straying from God, you must gaze at your life in the example I am going to share with you.

I have detected a lucid, unmistakable pattern in believers' lives as they backslide and stray from God. There are three steps. Number one, *it begins when they start living with distractions*. Their minds and hearts become distracted from God and from His things. Their faculties start going to people, places, and things of the world. The lost world begins to look a mite better to them than the things of God, the people of God, or the place of God. Why is that? Because they were not fully committed, because they have a short spiritual attention span, because they became bored, and because they have never grown up within their hearts. They just wanted to play.

In 1 John 2:15, we are warned, "Love not the world, neither the things that are in the world. If any man love the world, the love of the Father is not in him." That is plainly cautioning, "Be careful. Don't get distracted and sidetracked onto the things of the world." In 2 Timothy 4:10, Paul wrote of a disciple who had traveled with him for quite some time. The disciple Demas had been his companion. He had been a faithful ally of the gospel of Jesus Christ. But there was an unfortunate change in Demas's life. He started looking at the things of the world, and he was distracted. Paul wrote of Demas, "Demas hath forsaken me, having loved this present world."

Demas loved the present world. I ask you, "Have you been distracted, having loved the world, the wicked world system, around us? Do you seem to love the world more than you love Jesus? Do you seem to love the world more than you love the church, His bride? Do you seem to love the world more than you love the things of God? We can actually become so tempted with the things of the world, that we have an absolute forgetfulness, loss of memory, concerning the things of God Himself.

I heard of a wealthy man who was going to hire a driver. He interviewed three men and then together led them down the road to a cliff that went about one hundred feet down. He informed the men he was going to hire one of them before they left.

He looked at candidate number one and asked, "Sir, how close could you drive my limousine to that cliff without going off?"

"Oh, I could drive it five feet without going off."

"You could?"

"Yes sir, I could drive it five feet without going off."

He stared at the second candidate and asked, "How close could you get to that cliff?"

"Oh, Sir, I could drive this limo about five inches from this cliff and still not go off."

"Is that right?"

Then there was number three. "How about you? How close could you drive this limousine to this cliff?"

"Let me tell you something, Sir, I wouldn't get within a mile of this cliff!"

Then this rich man shouted, "Sir, you're hired!" Guess what the boss wanted. He wanted a driver who wouldn't play with temptation. Don't flirt with the things of the world. You'll lose every single time.

The progression of sin begins with distraction. But *it continues with spiritual separation.* Suddenly the things of God seem to drift away from you. They don't hold your interest any longer. You used to read the Word of God daily because you loved it. The principles and concepts you learned there were so exciting to you. Perhaps you would carry your Bible to work with you, and at breaks and lunches you would read it and hide it in your heart. Now you hardly think about the Word. You let it lie around and maybe pick it up on Sunday morning—when you attend Sunday School and church (if you still do).

It's tragic, but you don't love your church like you used to. Earlier in your Christian life, nothing came between you and your church. Every Sunday morning, every Sunday night, and every Wednesday night you would be there. Whenever the doors were open, they could count on you. But now, you may go every now and then. What's happened? First, you've been distracted by the things of the world. Second, you've begun to be separated from God because of the things of the world.

The last digression is *we move from distraction to separation to rebellion.* Rebellion snorts, "All right, I won't have anything to do with this religious stuff anymore. It was good at that particular time in my life. I needed it, but now I just don't need God messing in my affairs." Your heart has become hardened. Sins you used to blush about, you do now. You've become "liberal" now. You've let the gate down. You're sort of "broadminded." Things you used to abhor you now like to be involved with. Those things of the world you used to despise, you now love.

I suppose the most glaring sign that a person is living in spiritual rebellion is their attitude about sin. You can discern in your heart of hearts your relationship with God by your relationship with sin. Do you despise and hate sin? The Bible teaches that the sanctified believer cannot stand sin. It makes him nauseous. Sin is a stench in the nostrils of God. Sin nailed Jesus to the tree, and God abhors sin. The closer we come to God, the more we become like Him, and the more we hate sin.

Sin in a believer's life is an abomination to God. When you become close to the Lord, you're not drawn to sin like you used to be. Do you understand me? Those sins which used to tempt you no longer seem to do so because your nature has changed. You have new desires, new goals, and new aspirations, because you have a new name. The closer you approach God, the more of God's nature you have—and as much as God hates sin, you will hate it equally.

Evangelist J. Wilbur Chapman, who was a strong influence on Billy Sunday, related this true story. After a preacher had cried out against sin, one of his members complained: "We don't want you to talk so plainly about sin because if our boys and girls hear you preaching so much about it, they will more easily sin. Call it a mistake if you will, but don't call it sin."

The preacher went to the medicine chest and returned with a small bottle of strychnine marked "Poison." He said: "I see what you want me to do. You want me to change the label. Suppose I remove this label 'Poison' and put on some mild label, such as 'Essence of Peppermint.' Can't you see what would happen? The milder you make the label, the more dangerous you make the poison!" Sin is poison no matter how one tries to package and label it.

People can descend all the way from living close to God to distraction; to separation; and finally, rebellion in their hearts. What does God do? If we're living in distraction, separation, and rebellion, does God kick us out? That's not our God. Does God turn His back on us? No. That's not what God does. God's precious, indwelling Holy Spirit brings conviction into our lives. The Holy Spirit begins to perform His work of reclamation, and He does that through His glorious ministry of conviction.

Finally, I want to single out:

The Results of Conviction

We react to it in different ways. We can ignore it, reject it, push it away. But, "whom the Lord loveth he chasteneth" (see Heb. 12:6). Do you know what chastening is? It's whatever God must do to bring you back to Him. Think of God's prophet Jonah. God loved Jonah, as He loves us, but Jonah disobeyed God. He was going to Tarshish (Spain) to flee from the presence of the Lord. The Bible records that God, through His powerful hand of conviction, put Jonah into the belly of the fish. Then Jonah was ready to repent. You can reject conviction and let God put you into the depths of trouble, and He'll do it if necessary to lead you to repentance (see Jonah 1:1—2:9).

Or, you can accept conviction and let God put it to work in your life. There are steps you must take and understand when conviction enters your life. Here you are, your heart is heavy and you feel conviction. What are you going to do with it?

Recognize it. You reply, "OK, I recognize that God is moving in my soul. God is working within my heart, convicting me. Lord, show me what it is that is separating us, and I'll repent of it and return to You." God will do it. The problem with recognition is not with God—it's with us. When we put on our blinders we shut up our hearts. If you're under conviction, and you'll pray to the Holy Spirit, He will spell out your sins.

Repent of it. That's not simply saying, "I'm so sorry I did this."

it. I turn my back on it and am going to walk in a totally different direction."

Receive the joy that comes from repentance. Do you know what that means? It signals that once you have been convicted, and have repented of your sin, just go on about your business. David said, "Restore unto me the joy of thy salvation." We can live the most joyful life anyone could possibly live. If you're a believer, and you're irritable, grouchy, and hard to live with; if you're not enjoying abundant life, it may be because you're under conviction and won't repent of the sins that block your fellowship with God.

Conviction is God whispering into your heart, "My Child, you have strayed. Confess your sin, and let me pour out from the windows of heaven a 'joy unspeakable and full of glory.'"

Note

1. © Copyright 1926. Renewal 1953, Broadman Press. Words and Music by B. B. McKinney. Used by permission.

4

Walking Together with God

Can two walk together except they be agreed? (Amos 3:3).

"Can two walk together," Amos asked, "except they be agreed?" The Prophet Amos was addressing the children of Israel, but more than that, he was giving a message to you and me.

What was Amos talking about, "Can two walk together unless they be agreed?" He was *talking* about *walking* with God. If you don't have Jesus Christ as your personal Savior, and you don't walk with God, life is too long, and the road is too tough to walk it without Him.

Perhaps you're a believer, and you're missing the joy and abundance Christ promised in His Word. If so, let me suggest that maybe it's because you have never learned to walk with God.

May we learn to pray with William Cowper:

> O for a closer walk with God,
> A calm and heavenly frame,
> A light to shine upon the road
> That leads me to the Lamb.

. . . .

51

The dearest idol I have known,
Whate'er that idol be,
Help me to tear it from Thy throne,
And worship only Thee.
So shall my walk be close with God,
Calm and serene my frame;
So purer light shall mark the road
That leads me to the Lamb.

It's almost mind-boggling to think about the fact that we can actually walk with God, the Creator, the Sovereign God of the universe. The Bible makes it plain that God wants to walk with us. He allowed His Son, the Lord Jesus, to enter this earth to be scorned, spit upon, and crucified on a cross, so we might walk hand in hand with Him.

And the Bible speaks at length about God's companionship and our walking with Him. The written Word assures us that we can walk before and with God. What does walking with Him mean? It is recorded, for instance, that "Enoch walked with God; and he was not, for God took him." Enoch was one of two saints who were translated straight to heaven without tasting of death (the other being Elijah). It means God is watching our lives, looking over us as a parent would a child, or a friend would another friend. He is watching over us day by day.

The Psalmist plumbed deeply into the matter. In fact, you will read in the Psalms as David writes about how God presided over his life. It is almost beyond our ability to understand how God watches over all of us, but He does. How? *Because He is God.* The Bible reveals He knows all about us. He numbers the very hairs of our heads.

God is aware of every act we do day by day. He knows the thoughts of our minds and the intents of our hearts, our burdens, our cares, our needs, even our wants. He knows them all.

In Psalm 139 David sings of this. "Oh Lord, thou hast searched me and known me; thou knowest my downsitting and mine uprising; Thou understandeth my thoughts afar off." I like that. The psalmist says, "God, you understand my thoughts even while they're afar off" (vv. 1-2).

> Such knowledge is too wonderful for me. It is high. I cannot attain unto it. Whither shall I go from thy spirit? And whither shall I flee from thy presence? If I ascend up into heaven, thou art there. If I make my bed in hell, behold thou art there. If I take the wings of the morning and dwell in the uttermost parts of the sea, even there shall thy hand lead me, and thy right hand shall hold me (vv. 6-10).

Then he concludes the chapter in verses 23-24 with, "Search me, O God, and know my heart. Try me and know my thoughts. See if there be any wicked way in me, and lead me in the way everlasting."

David is exulting in the divine providence of God, how God tends to us day by day. I remember hearing about the little girl who was praying by her bed, and her father would come in and pray with her. He noticed one night she would always begin her prayers by reciting the Lord's Prayer. She started off like this, "Our Father, who art in heaven, how does He know my name?"

That is so true. God does know one's name. He tenderly cares for us. That's what it means when we speak about walking *before* God. The Bible also refers to our walking *after* God. This means in obedience to His laws, His commandments, and His precepts, we walk after the way in which He has fashioned and shaped us. How do we discover that way? The Bible affirms we will hear a voice behind us saying, "This is the way, walk ye in it" (Isa. 30:21).

What does it mean, "a voice walking behind us"? In other words, God is going to speak to our hearts. You remark, "God doesn't speak to my heart." Yes, He does. If you're a believer, living in harmony with Him, God speaks to your heart. The problem is, sometimes you're not listening. You may not hear Him.

He has demonstrated in His word, "I will speak a word. I will say this is the way. I will guide you with my eyes. I will speak."

The problem with many believers is not God's silence. God is indeed speaking. The dilemma is we are simply not slowing down enough to hear Him. When a little girl had finished her bedtime prayers, she remained on her knees at the bed. Her mother impatiently instructed her to crawl into bed. The girl replied, "I was just waiting to see if God had anything to say to me."

I heard about a naturalist, a man of science who studies nature, walking with a friend along a busy street. Near a street corner he stopped, and asked his friend, "Do you hear that cricket?"

The friend looked at him and said, "What?"

The naturalist repeated, "I hear a cricket. Do you hear it?"

The friend protested, "There's no way you could hear a cricket with all the traffic and all the noise."

With that the naturalist walked over to the curbside and spied a rock. He picked up the rock, and there was the cricket. Off it hopped.

The friend was astounded. "That's amazing," he said. "How in the world did you hear that cricket?"

The naturalist replied, "I am trained to hear the cricket. Let me show you something."

Then the naturalist reached into his pocket, pulled out a silver dollar, and threw it onto the sidewalk. It jingled loudly. A dozen people stopped and looked around. The man then explained to his friend, "See, we hear what we're listening for."

The difficulty with many believers is they're not listening for God. They're listening at work to their boss, at home they're listening to television, the radio, cassettes, CD, and the like. They are absorbed in newspapers, books, magazines, some of them questionable. But they're not listening to God. What did and does God say? "I will cause you to walk in my statutes and commandments. You will hear a voice behind you saying, 'This is the way.' Don't turn to the right hand or the left, walk ye in it."

How do we do that? We walk after God. But the greatest thing is not only walking *before* God, and walking *after* God, but the Bible spells it out that we can actually *walk with* God. That leaves no doubt that day by day, no matter where we are or what we are doing, if our hearts are right before Him, God, the Sovereign Creator who made it all and knows it all, will walk with us.

C. Austin Miles caught the ecstasy of walking with God in his old song:

> I come to the garden alone, While the dew is still
> on the roses,
> And the voice I hear, Falling on my ear, the Son
> of God discloses.
>
> And He walks with me, and He talks with me,
> and He tells me I am His own;
> And the joy we share as we tarry there, None
> other has ever known.

Jesus loved to teach this truth. In John 16 He was about to be forsaken by His disciples, and He predicted in verses 32-33, "Behold the hour cometh, yea is now come, that ye shall be scattered, every man to his own and shall leave me alone." In other words, "Now, fellows, you have traveled with Me a long way, but the time has come that you're going to leave Me alone, and yet I am not alone, because the Father is with Me." In spite of His grief and pain, in spite of His disciples' dereliction, in spite of Judas's betrayal, in spite of the bloody ordeal before Him, He promised: "These things I have spoken unto you that in me ye might have peace. In the world you shall have tribulation. But be of good cheer, for I have overcome the world" (John 16:33).

Yes, the disciples would be gone in a short time, but He wouldn't be alone because the Father was with Him, and He was relating these spiritual matters because He would be with them to the end of the world. Yes, they would have horrible tribulation and dread circumstances, but they could be of good cheer, because He would be with them. He was also saying He would never leave us or forsake us. Not only can we know God, but God can walk with us day by day.

When we're driving the car, sitting in the classroom, processing our work, washing the dishes—wherever—God consoles us, "Because you love Me, I'm going to be with you. I'll never leave you or forsake you. I'll be with you to the very end of the world." We shake our heads in awe and exclaim, "Oh, what a glorious truth, but why don't all Christians walk with God?"

Number one:

Some People Don't Want God's Company

Yes, they want to be sure they're going to heaven. They walk down to an altar one day and get saved. They accept Christ by a public profession of faith in Him, they're baptized, but they seem to indicate after that, "God, leave me alone. I want to have life like I want it." They have never arrived at an awareness of what a sacrificed life is all about.

If you are coming to Christ now, or you already have, you must consider all that is involved. Every person who is going to follow Christ must *deny himself,* take up his cross, and follow Him. Then Jesus said to His disciples, "If anyone wishes to come after me, let him deny himself, and follow me" (Matt. 16:24). The Bible further commands that we are to "present your [our] bodies [everything] a living sacrifice, holy, acceptable unto God which is your [our] reasonable service" (Rom. 12:1). In other words, when you come to Christ, you come all the way. Everything you have ever had or ever will must be laid upon the altar of sacrifice to God. It is all there. He owns it all anyway—your finances, your hopes, your dreams. Admit it or not, some of us may be thinking, *I don't want to because I'm afraid God's not going to do what I want Him to do.*

Let me specify what God is going to do. He is going to do the very best for your life. Do you think He is uncaring and unfeeling when He has given His all for you? "Yea, I have loved with an everlasting love, and in lovingkindness have I drawn thee" (Jer. 31:3). When you come to the moment and understanding of what happens at salvation, and what the lordship of Christ is, when you lay down your life, you lay it *all* down in sacrifice to Him. Oh, what God will do for and in you and through you! Not only will He walk with you, He will be with you without fail. In love He will meet your needs. You will understand what the Christian experience is all about only when you live that sacrificed life.

A preacher from the past, Brother Hanna, spoke of the "Christ life," the life on the altar: "Jesus says, 'Take up My yoke: throw off the yoke of pride, of covetousness, of sensuality, of worldliness, of ambition, of self-indulgence; take on that yoke which consists in devotedness to Me and to duty, in a life of self-restraint, in a struggle with all that is evil, a cultivation of all that is beautiful and good and holy.'"

I remember reading the touching story about a young lady from Australia. Because of a terrible disease, surgeons had to operate on her and remove her arms and legs; all she had left was the trunk of her body! She was angry with God because of her disease and calamity. One day she was listening to the radio and heard an evangelist preaching on the love of God. This was the first time she had ever heard about the love of God, how God loved her and cared about her. The evangelist stated that if anyone would give their life to God, they could change the world for the cause of Christ.

As she listened about the love of God, she cried, "I want to feel the love of God. I want to know this Jesus the preacher is talking about. I want to be that one person he has challenged to give their life to God. I don't have much—only the trunk of a body—but I'm dedicating the trunk of my body to God!"

It wasn't long before an inventor devised an apparatus that she could strap to her body. In that unusual appliance was placed a pen. As months passed by she learned to write with that pen in the apparatus. Each day she would enter a room, take out pieces of paper, and write. She wrote letter after letter all day long to people around the world who had not accepted Jesus Christ. Thus, she shared the testimony of her faith in Christ. She lived twelve years after her conversion, and it was estimated that over 1,500 people received her Christ as their Savior, because of the trunk of one woman's body that was dedicated to the Lord!

I ask you, "What are *you* doing for Christ?" It is no surprise God is not walking with us. We have our own agenda. We have our own things and "do our own thing." Don't you dislike that selfish phrase? Often we don't present anything to God as a living sacrifice, but God emphasizes, "Present it all, and if you do, I'll walk with you."

Some claim, "No, I don't want God's company," but:

Others Don't Walk with God Because They Don't Agree with His Truth

You have to agree with the truth of God. Let me reiterate Amos's question: "Can two walk together except they be agreed?" The Bible answers *no!* God cannot walk with you until you agree. With what? What He speaks in His Bible. You must agree with what God says about Christ. Jesus Himself said, "I am the way, the truth, and the life. No man cometh unto the Father but by me" (John 14:6). The Bible says: "He that hath the Son hath life; and he that hath not the Son of God hath not life" (1 John 5:12).

The Word further asserts: "He who believes in the Son of God has eternal life, but he who does not obey the Son shall not see life, but the wrath of God abides on him" (John 3:36).

You have to come to agreement with this. You have to agree that Jesus Christ is the only entrance into heaven. The only one, "Neither is there salvation in any other, for there is none other name under heaven, given among men, whereby we must be saved" (Acts 4:12). Not religion, not denomination, not baptism, not good works, not your giving—none of these will save you. It is Christ and Christ alone.

You must come to an awareness of sin. Agree with God about it. What's the question? "Can two walk together except they be agreed?" No. You must agree with God about Christ. You must agree with Him *about sin*. Romans 6:23 says, "The wages of sin is death, but the gift of God is eternal life through Jesus Christ our Lord." Sin pays in spiritual death. Ezekiel wrote, "The soul that sinneth, it shall die" (18:4). The Bible is the text on sin and salvation. Sin is not a misdemeanor. Sin is a monstrous felony. Sin is not just a little something we don't want to do. It's what nailed Jesus Christ to the cross of Calvary. We have to agree with what the Bible puts forth about sin.

We must go on to understand God's Word and agree with Him on the Word. Do you agree with God that the Bible is the infallible, inerrant Word of God? Do you believe that every jot and tittle is breathed upon with the very breath of God, and there is no portion of Scripture, absolutely none, that is not for men, women, boys and girls today, that it is all true and applicable for our lives? This is *The* Word of God. It has no mixture of error within it. If you do not agree with that, you cannot walk with God, because you're not in agreement with Him. You must agree with what the Word of God says. Amos questions, "Can two walk together except they be agreed?" God emphatically answers, "No."

John Greenleaf Whittier aptly expressed the efficacy of God's inerrant Word:

> We search the world for truth, we cull
> The good, the pure, the beautiful
> From graven stone and written scroll,
> From all old flower fields of the soul;
> And, weary seekers of the best,
> We come back laden from our quest

> To find that all the sage said
> Is in the Book our mothers read.

Do you want God with you? Not only must you invite Him into your life, but you must agree with Him concerning His truth. Also,

Some Are Not Willing to Walk with God Because They're Not on the Same Road with Him

That's so obvious. You have to be on the same road to walk together, Here is God's plan for their life, His way for their life. He has laid it out through the Holy Spirit, convicting their hearts. God wants this or that to go His way, but they don't want to go His way. Oh, they have a "better idea." They want to control their careers, their aspirations, their involvement with other people. They insist on going their own way. They forget the Bible perception, "There is a way that seemeth right unto a man, but the end thereof are the ways of death" (Prov. 14:12).

Yes, there are many reasons people don't walk with God. But there is *a plan for God's companionship*. It is two-fold, and most simple. It is desire and agreement. You must *desire* God in your life. God is a gentleman. He will not force Himself on any man or woman, boy or girl. He will not knock down the door of one's heart. You must want Him in your life. You must desire Him more than water to drink or food to eat. Only in that desire will He ever loom large on the scene of your life.

Do you remember what Jesus guaranteed about those "who hunger and thirst after righteousness"? "They shall be filled." God put it like this, "You shall find me when you search for me with all your heart" (Deut. 4:29). I want to ask you a simple question. Are you willing to seek God now? Are you willing to lay down a sacrificed life? Is there anything you haven't given to God? Your body, your mind, your home, your finances, your will, your career, your desires, your relationships—are they all sacrificed to God?

Only when you reach an agreement with God will you ever walk with Him. When you do, life changes. Be riveted to His words, "Draw nigh unto God, and he will draw nigh unto you" (Jas. 4:8).

Part II

Lord, Send Revival

. . . in Our Homes

5

How to Have
a Happy Home

And these words which I command thee this day shall be in thine heart: And thou shalt teach them diligently unto thy children, and shalt talk of them when thou sittest in thine house, and when thou walkest by the way and when thou liest down, and when thou riseth up (Deut. 6:6-7).

Do you have a happy home, a home where the members are loved, honored, and respected; a home in which each family member feels they are worthy, they count for something, they are special; a home where trust, love, peace, and joy exist? Do you have a home like you deserve?

Every person deserves to have a happy home. God knew that, and God, the very Founder and Builder of the home, has given us a plan, a formula, whereby we might have a happy home.

You ask, "Why must I rely on God for a happy home? Why must I look to the Bible? Why must I follow God's formula and plan?" You really want to know? The home is God's idea. Man didn't think of the home. Man didn't create the home. Again, it's God's idea.

Psalm 127:1 says, "Except the Lord build the house, they labor in vain that build it." Because God is the Builder. He sets forth the foundations by which we build our homes.

May I share with you some of those foundations? I want to guarantee you (not according to my ideas, but according to the Word of God, which is not only on the printed page, but can be experienced right now): If you follow His plan you can have a happy home. No two ways about it.

What is a happy home? First of all:

A Happy Home Is Where Love Is Both Shown and Known

Love—shown and known, not merely talked about but demonstrated. The Bible makes it manifest that God's chief characteristic is love. "He that loveth not knoweth not God, for God is love" (1 John 4:8). Certainly He is a God of righteousness and holiness and justice—all of these attributes make up the character of God, but the primary characteristic of God is love.

Doesn't it stand to reason if you have God, who is love incarnate—the ultimate love—as the Center of your home, then around that Center will flow love, and love will fill your home? In our society, there are many people who don't know what it is to have love in their homes. I counsel with people time and again who grew up in a home where dad was a grouch and mom was a bitter pill. Mr. Grouch and Mrs. Bitter Pill had a child come along, and they expected that little child to be a veritable angel. How can that child be an angel when it grew up in a home where people act like the devil? That child can never be an "angel" under those conditions.

All homes are not like that, thank God, but many are. As I counsel with people, a man will confess, "I don't know how to love my wife. I don't know how to love my children."

I'll ask, "Why?"

They'll reply, "Because in my home I never saw my dad love

my mother. I never saw my dad caress my mother. I never heard my dad tell my mother he loved her. I never saw my dad kiss my mother. My dad never took me, put me on his knee, hugged me, and held me close, and said, 'I love you.' Therefore, I don't know how to love my family."

That's a tragedy. It breaks my heart to hear the admission that there are actually men who claim to be fathers who do not show love in their homes. They do not demonstrate to their children who are growing up, and will someday have spouses and children of their own, how to love and have love in the home.

It has been rightly said that the greatest thing a father can do for his children is to love their mother and demonstrate he loves them. That's a remarkable truth. Love is not something we just talk about, but love is demonstrated.

But there are homes where God is the center, and love is constantly shown. The dad comes in from work, and the children happily meet him. He's not going to push them aside, but he is going to embrace them and tell them "I love you, and I'm glad I'm your Daddy." The kids will see mom and dad embrace. That gives a sense of security to the children and to the parents. Why? Because love ensures security.

Love is not only a foundational character of God, it is also a foundational need of our lives. When we sense love between parents, love among brothers and sisters, and between parents and children, it fortifies the foundations and spreads the warmth of acceptance. That's a happy home. A happy home is a secure home where love is both shown and known.

Second, notice

A Happy Home Is Where the Bible Is Taught and Practiced

When Moses was teaching the children of Israel the fundamentals of a happy home (Deut. 6:6-7) he emphasized:

> And these words which I command thee this day shall be
> in thine heart: And thou shalt teach them diligently unto thy
> children, and shalt talk of them when thou sittest in thine
> house, and when thou walkest by the way and when thou
> liest down, and when thou riseth up.

The core of Moses' message is to make the teaching of God's principles a normal practice in the home, not merely what the children learn in Sunday School, or Vacation Bible School, or in preaching. But make sure that the principles of God, in His infallible Word, are taught daily in your home.

Be natural (really *supernatural*) about teaching your children the truths about God. Moses laid out unfailing, unchanging precepts that are just as valid in the A.D. 1990s as they were in 1440 B.C. After you have hidden the Word in your *heart*, teach your children.

When and where? At home, when you sit down, when you walk (or ride today), by the way (on the way to the grocery store, on the way to the office, on the way to church or community events), teach your children the bedrock principles of the Scripture. Many young people today don't know where they are, who they are, or where they're headed. They don't understand what's going on in the world and why. Thousands of them are falling for false cults and weird philosophies. What they're really looking for—and often can't even find in their churches—are answers, and they deserve honest, solid answers to life's questions.

The Bible is the Book of life. When we don't teach our children The Book, we're cheating and robbing them. We're withholding from them the very answers of life. You may teach your children many subjects—English, mathematics, geography, geometry, or psychology. You mothers may teach your girls how to cook and sew. You dads may instruct your boys about how to hunt and fish and play ball.

But in all your teachings, if you've never taught them the basics of God's Word, you've hardly taught them at all. A child doesn't really learn how to live by cooking and sewing, by fishing and hunting, or by geometry or geology or mathematics or languages. The principles that work are the concepts of the living Word of God. The psalmist sang, "Thy word is a lamp unto my feet and a light unto my path" (Ps. 119:105). That's what life is all about, and the practical answers are found only in the Word of God.

Children—in fact, all of us—need *a creed to live by,* a set of guiding principles. They need to know what they believe and why they believe it, not simply because mom and dad or the preacher say so. They should personally know from the Word of God what they believe and why they believe it. A creed to live by.

Children need to have *a cause to live for.* That cause is the cause of Jesus Christ. That makes for a family where, since early childhood, the children have been diligently taught the principles of the written Word. Those children know the Word of God, the answers for life, why events in the world are happening as they are. Nail it down. A home founded upon God's Word is a happy home.

But

A Happy Home Is Where Prayer Is
a Regular Activity

How true that "The family that prays together stays together." As I see really close families, they almost always will be families who pray together—not merely a prayer over a meal, but a family that has a family altar, and they seek the face of God together. As I write this I wonder how many readers can say they are Christian parents who have a family altar.

Is there a place in your home where your children and you (or you and your spouse, if you have no children at home) kneel down and pray? Maybe you have a single-parent home or even a home where you are the only one. Do you set aside that time where you call on God? Do you have a time and a place where you teach your children to pray? Do you spend prayer time with your spouse? Nothing in all the world will substitute for those precious periods of prayer.

How often I have heard, "Preacher, that's such a private thing." Certainly it is, but it is surely not too private for your family! Is there anything so private in your personal life that you would alienate your family from it? If you are living for Christ, nothing should be that private.

Vicious cycles are perpetuated in some families. The reason many Christians are not having family altars, where they teach their children to pray, is that mom and dad never had a family to teach them the things of God. Or maybe mom and dad had that kind of Christian encouragement, but they have grown cold and backslidden. Listen parents, it's going to require all God and you can do to raise your children in this sin-cursed society in which you live.

If you do not have a prayer home, what are you going to do when your daughter reports, "Mom, I've fallen in love with a non-Christian boy"? She claims to love him. They are thinking about living together—maybe marrying later. What are you going to do then, Mom, if you haven't hidden the Word of God in her heart and prayed for her? Or she may even confess, "Mom, I'm pregnant." What will you do?

What about you, Dad, when your son lays down the law, "Dad, I'm not going to church anymore because I've chosen my own way. I'm going out into the world and live like I want to. I'm going to do things my own way." You know what most parents say, don't you? "If my daughter comes in like that, or if my son gives me trouble, I'm just going to reason with them." No, you're not. Do you know why? Because in all our lives there are times when we are unreasonable.

Has there even been a time when you were unreasonable? There are periods in our lives, no matter who we are, no matter what religious facades we wear, when we are hard headed as we can be, and we're not going to let anybody or anything tell us what to do. And there were times in our formative years when we were hard to reason with. You may not be able to reason with that son or daughter. All you can do is trust in the Word of God you have hidden in their hearts. If you haven't done that, you are in for aggravation and sleepless nights.

What a marvelous assurance it is when you are assured that, if that son or daughter begins to go astray, you have invested the kingdom of God in their lives, and the Bible is so true: "Train up a child in the way he should go; and when he is old, he will not depart from it" (Ps. 22:6). *A home where prayer is a regular activity.*

Notice also that:

A Happy Home Is Where Jesus Is Honored as Lord

The name of Jesus is used in this kind of home on a frequent basis, not like in many households where His name is uttered in vain. Why? Because Jesus is part of the family. In fact, He sits upon the throne of the family. The family in that home belongs to Christ. When the family considers what they're going to do, where they're going to go, they ask themselves, *What would Jesus have us do?* When the family considers where it's going to invest their time and monies they ask, "What would Jesus have us do?"

When the family members think about how they're going to treat one another, they inquire, "Now, what would Jesus do?" Why? Because Jesus Christ has first place in that home—the preeminence. The home belongs to Christ, and that offers parents and kids a deep-down security.

Through the years I have noticed that God takes care of those persons and things which belong to Him. When you present God your home, to whom does it belong? You pray, "Jesus, I want to thank You for entrusting my son or daughter into my hands, but Jesus, in reality they belong to You. I dedicate them to You." Then, "God, I thank You for my mate. We have a wonderful marriage, but I want You to know, God, that I give my mate to You."

"This house is perhaps the greatest investment of our physical lives, but, God, it doesn't really matter because it's only brick, mortar, stone, and wood. It will pass away one day. But, Jesus, I give it to You."

"I give You my job, my car—everything I have." If I dedicate it all to Christ and say, "Lord, it belongs to You," then whose responsibility is it? . . . not only mine, but it is God's. Why? Because you have, with a Spirit-controlled will, given it to Him.

What a consolation, what a stabilizing influence. That which God owns, God takes care of. We don't have to wring our hands and worry, crying, "What in the world is going to happen to my marriage—to my children?" I don't have to fret and strain about whether the world is going to blow itself apart, or whether there is any hope for the future. I just say, "Jesus, You're Lord. Father, I know You can take care of it all. You can provide for this home," a home where Jesus Christ sits upon the throne and is Lord.

A happy home is:

A Home Where Regular Worship Is
Expected and Desired

I repeat the great Scripture of promise: "Train up a child in the way that he should go; and when he is old, he will not depart from it." Hebrews reminds us that part of that training is, "Not forsaking the assembling of ourselves together, as the manner of some is" (10:25a). Magnify the assembling of yourselves together in a time of worship. In other words, a happy family is a churchgoing family. They go to the house of God; they worship in the sanctuary of God, and they enjoy doing it.

You may alibi, "You don't understand my church. My church is dead, dry, and dull. The service is listless, cold. I have to force my kids and mate to go." Someone else may critique, "When my pastor stands to preach, he preaches over our heads. We don't understand what he says. It's just some theological jargon, and the choir sings in another language. When we go in and go out we receive nothing to support a Christian life-style. Well, that's my church. No wonder I don't want to go to church."

No wonder you don't want to go to church. But I have another question. "Why are you still going there? Why do you bother to go to a church where you are not receiving spiritual food?" Some parents carry their children to some of these churches that are dead, liberal, and do not teach the Word of God, and there's no life, no joy, no thrill, and the atmosphere is absolutely contrary from what Christ taught about the church. These poor children have to sit there and listen to music no one understands, and they hear messages they can't apply to their lives. At about the age of 12 they realize they don't have to go through that torture all their lives. At 12, 13, 14, or 15, they breathe a sigh of relief, "Only a few more years, and I'll be out of here!"

At the age of 16 they start saying, "Mom, I don't feel like going to church today."

Mom replies, "Oh yes, you're going to go." So they drag them to church. At 17 and 18 they've made up their minds that they're not going. Neither words of encouragement nor condemnation can induce them to attend. In many instances, I simply cannot blame those kids. Why? Because in 2 Timothy 3:5 such anemic, godless churches are spoken of: "Having a form of godliness, but denying the power thereof: from such turn away." If you are going to a dead church that doesn't teach and preach the Word of God, where souls are not being saved, and people are not being baptized, either help change that church or make your own exodus. Get out and align yourself with a Bible-believing, gospel-preaching church.

There are thousands of churches in this land where the Spirit of God is flowing. People are meeting Christ there, and those churches are alive and are exponents of Jesus' words, "I have come that they might have life, and that they might have it more abundantly" (John 10:10). Get your family into a church where God is moving.

It is thrilling when kids get up and exclaim, "Mom, Dad, let's get dressed and go to Sunday School and church." They want to go. Parents often show interest with, "I wonder what we're going to sing today. I can hardly wait to hear the preacher. He'll give us the Word, and I'll be able to apply the truth to my life during the week. What truths will be shared with us that will enhance our lives?" You need a place where worship is not only expected but is fervently desired.

Last of all:

A Happy Home Is Where the Family's Eternal Salvation Is a Priority

The greatest goal in your home should be to win your husband/wife, son/daughter to Christ. Many homes make plans in life. Men and women have money that has been set aside for their retirement. Some of you have designated funds for the graduation and education of your children and/or grandchildren. You have laid all these plans in preparation for that day when "My children will need that security."

What is tragic about that is, many have made no preparation at all for their family's eternal security. I want to ask you, "Doesn't it stand to reason that more important than the education of your child, or the automobile your child drives, or the house your child lives in, or the furniture in your child's room, is the eternal destiny of your child, of your son/daughter, husband/wife?

Now I have another heavy question. How is heaven going to be heaven for you when your loved one is in hell because you never told them how to be saved? I have often wondered about how those who are mute about salvation—those who are alibing, "Well, I don't want to tread upon their personal decision"—account for the fact that if they belong to your family, their personal decisions belong to you as well. Your loved ones should be the interest of every beat of your heart!

Moms and dads, sons and daughters, in your home the most important factor is: Are you going to serve the Lord? Joshua challenged the Israelites, "But as for me and my house, we will serve the Lord" (24:15). When you bring a newborn baby home and put the baby into the crib, I pray you look at him and think, *One day, because I am going to teach this child the things of God, one day the Holy Spirit will grip this child's heart, and he's going to accept Jesus Christ as his eternal Savior and Lord."* That's what a happy home is all about.

Is your home happy and joyful in the Lord? Is your home a place where love is shown, where the Bible is taught, where prayer is a natural exercise from your hearts to God? Is your home one where Jesus Christ is Lord, where you go out to worship at an exciting church fellowship? Is your home a home where eternal salvation is the main objective?

You may reply, "No, that's not my kind of home. My home is one of confusion, turmoil, strife, and tension. What can I do?" First of all, you must personally know Christ as your Savior, and you must make Him Lord. Start where you are. You don't have to go back twenty years, five years, six months, or even a day . . . start where you are. Have a coronation of Jesus Christ as King upon the throne of your home, and your home will experience revival.

Then, as He is crowned, He will usher in peace, love, joy, and abundance. Then you will truly know what it is to have a happy, happy home!

6

Keys to a Maximum Marriage

. . . For this cause shall a man leave father and mother, and shall cleave to his wife: and they twain shall be one flesh? Wherefore they are no more twain, but one flesh. What therefore God hath joined together, let not man put asunder (Matt. 19:5-6).

When God created man and woman in the garden of Eden, He started the greatest intimate institution in our world. We call that marriage. I suppose of all the blessings God has in His kingdom, of all the wonderful experiences between believers, God's ultimate is that union called marriage. For within Christian marriage, He has gifted us with all the joys, expressions of love and acceptance, we could possibly stand on planet earth.

But it is heartbreaking to realize there are countless believers who are not living maximum marriages. Separation and divorce are epidemic even among believers. I believe this often contributes to difficulty in our churches.

The other day I came upon a statement by the late Dr. M. R. DeHaan, founder of "The Radio Bible Class." "The nearest thing to heaven on earth is the Christian family—the home where the husband and wife and the parents and the children live in love

77

and peace together for the Lord and for each other. But the nearest thing to hell on earth is an ungodly home, broken by sin and iniquity, where parents bicker and quarrel and separate and the children are abandoned to the devil, and all the forces of the wickedness of this world."

He was right on target. Marriage can be heaven or hell. What is your marriage today? It is amazing, but the Christian has the resources to make it either way. Which is your marriage, and what are you making of it presently?

In the Word of God there are "Keys to Maximum Marriage." If used, these keys can guarantee your marriage being the best it can possibly be.

There are not many guarantees in this sin-benighted world. There are not many things that will absolutely work. But I believe, according to God's Word, these keys will work. They are practical, workable, pragmatic. No matter what your marriage is facing now, no matter your situation, if you will enter these keys into your marriage, your relationship will be even better. You will have the most maximum marriage any couple can possibly experience.

The first key is:

The Key Called Commitment

Jesus spoke of this in Matthew 19:5-6:

> For this cause shall a man leave father and mother, and shall cleave to his wife, and they twain shall be one flesh. Wherefore they are no more twain, but one flesh. What therefore God hath joined together, let not man put asunder (see also Mark 10:9).

The divorce rate for first marriages is now near 50 percent. For second marriages it is 65 percent. And I believe the reason many Christians do not abhor divorce like they should and once did is because they simply do not understand how seriously God views marriage.

Since God instituted marriage, He looks at it specifically and definitely. Why? Have you understood what transpired when you came to the marriage altar? As a Christian, you didn't merely come with your spouse to be. You came with God. When you stood before the marriage altar and vowed, "I promise to love, honor, and cherish until death do us part," you weren't making promises to that lovely lady alone; you weren't making vows to that handsome groom alone. You were making vows to Almighty God! That is serious business.

You ask, "Why is the church so adamant against divorce? Why are gospel preachers so against divorce?" Why? Because you not only break the vow to the partner you married, you violate a solemn promise to Almighty God, and God takes your vows very seriously. If two Christians join together and they break those bonds of marriage, God deems it an aberration of His plan and purpose.

You may protest, "Well, how am I going to stay married to somebody I don't love? How can I possibly remain with somebody I don't have affection for?" Think about this. You have control over your affections and your love. Love is not simply a raw emotion. Love is an emotion and response that can be learned. Love is a matter that can be decided. Love is a choice of commitment. You can choose to love. That is the difference between real love and mere infatuation.

The Bible says: "Set your affections on things above, not on things on the earth" (Col. 3:2). You can determine to love. You can set your affections.

I have an alarm clock by the side of my bed. I can't control many situations in the world, but I control that alarm clock. Every now and then I'll turn those digits and watch them spin by rapidly, knowing I have control, and I can stop it when I want to. I can turn that clock on and can turn it off. It is mine.

It never talks back to me and commands, "Quit turning me on."

It never argues, "Quit turning me off."

It never says, "I don't want to stop at 8:30." It does exactly what I want it to. I have total control over that alarm clock, and I can set it.

"Set your affections." You have control over them. You can gauge your feelings, your likes and dislikes. The other day I was watching a "National Geographic" special, which I like quite a lot. One came on the screen about a lady who had a special pet in her home. I thought that would be interesting, and I guessed it would be a playful little puppy or maybe a soft, furry cat. This lady had, in her home as a special pet, a possum. Can you believe that? An old, ugly, ring-tailed possum. They asked her, "How can you allow this possum to live in your home?"

She replied, "Well, I must be honest with you. When my husband first brought it home from a hunting trip, I didn't like it around the house. It is rather ugly, but after a while, I sort of got used to it. I set my affections on it, and now I think it's a great pet to have."

I can understand a cute raccoon with black circles around his eyes—I might even in some weird way understand a snake, a goldfish, and the like. But a possum that looks like a giant rat (I'll make an exception for Pogo)! Nevertheless, she had an affection for an ugly old possum. Why? *Because she wanted to.*

You reply, "I can't set my affections." Oh, yes, you can. Have you ever wondered why some teenagers adore grotesque, gross rock or rap stars? They shave their heads on one side, let their hair grow on the other side, and dye it different colors. They literally belch into a microphone, and they sweat over their bare chests. They scream and murder their musical instruments. They jump across the stage as though their feet were on fire, and the kids think they're fantastic! These kids have "set their affections." That's the only reasonable answer. If anybody can love some of these rock groups, you can love whatever and whomever you choose to.

Setting your affections merely means choosing what you are going to like or love. If somebody can like a possum or a rock singer, then two believers who are married can love each other. You ask, "How?" It's called commitment, biblical, godly commitment.

The second key is:

The Key Called Selflessness

May I give you an illustration to help you understand selflessness? Let's think of two people we'll call Billy and Mary. Here is Billy who grew up in a home where he was the only child. Billy was a "mama's boy." Have you ever seen a mama's boy? Jacob was. When Billy was small all he had to do to get what he wanted was cry, and mama would let him have his wishes. When he became a teenager and wanted a new automobile, he didn't have any idea how he was going to get it. So he decided to threaten his mama, "I'm going to run away from home if I don't get a new car." There was a 17-year-old baby, going to run away from home.

Mama rushed out and bought him that new car. All during his growing years, his mother had told him he was "the most special boy in the world." Her whole life was wrapped up in Billy, and Billy thought everything in the world revolved around him. He was the king, the center of the universe.

Over here we have Mary, who was born into a family with four brothers. Those brothers thought Mary was everything a little girl should be. Also, Mary was "daddy's little girl." He had all those little boys running around the house, but there was sweet little Mary dressed in her pink dress with ribbons in her hair.

Daddy loved Mary. She didn't even have to ask for a car. Daddy bought it for her sixteenth birthday. His entire existence was built around that girl. He often put her on his knee and bragged, "Mary, you're the most beautiful little girl who has ever been born. You're so special. There's never been anybody like you. In fact, Mary, you're the only little girl in the world to me. There's no one like you in all creation."

Mary grew up through her childhood years, her teenage years, thinking all the world belonged to her, that everybody was there to please her.

We have Billy, the center of his world, and Mary, also the center of her world. Everything in their lives is wrapped around them. The only relationships they have cultivated is for the purpose of using others. They think the whole world revolves around each of them.

Then one day Billy met Mary, and they "fell in love" and came together in marriage. Now we have a crucial question. Whose world is it going to be? With the mentality of this world, our children are often reared to think everything in the world is for one purpose—what they can squeeze out of life.

"To see what you can get out of it" is humanistic teaching. "What's in it for me?" is the worldly slant. So humanistic Billy and humanistic Mary come together in marriage, so whose world is it going to be?

For all the Marys, let me share with you whose world it's going to be. Wives, submit yourselves unto your own husbands, as unto the Lord" (Eph. 5:22). Then to all the Billys, Paul wrote, "Husbands, love your wives, even as Christ also loved the church, and gave himself for it. So ought men to love their wives as their own bodies" (Eph. 5:25). Whose world is it? It's your partner's world. We call this selflessness, which is really l-o-v-e, preferring one another in love.

How are we to treat our partners? The Word emphasizes that wives are to look to your husbands as "unto the Lord." Women, what happened when you came to the Lord? You gave Him your all. There's nothing in your past, present, or future you haven't yielded to the Lord Jesus Christ. Spiritually, you have submitted everything.

When you came to the marriage altar, what did you present your husband? *All*. When you slipped the ring on his finger you promised, "With all my worldly goods I thee endow." All with nothing withheld.

Then the Word instructs husbands to ". . . love your wives, even as Christ also loved the church, and gave himself for it." How much did He give to His church? His very life—His all. You husbands no less should be willing to lay down your life for your wives.

Frankly, I have never met a truly Christian wife—if her husband was a man who loved the Lord and was willing to lay down his life for her—who wouldn't submit herself unto that husband as unto the Lord. It's a relationship we call selflessness. It is patterned after Jesus. It's no longer I, no longer me, no longer just myself; it's you, I give myself to you in love. You're the center of my world underneath the umbrella of the Lord Jesus. Selflessness, lack of self-seeking, have that in your marriage, and your marriage just cannot fail.

Third, there is:

The Key Called Communication

That's merely being able to express your honest heart to each other. To communicate is extremely important. I want to share with you seven basic questions which will help you ascertain if you are communicating well.

1. *Is my partner my closest confidante?* Do you express yourself and your feelings to your partner more than the neighbor next door, your mom and dad, your friends, or children?

2. *Do I always tell my partner the plain truth?*

3. *Do I avoid sarcasm, harmful remarks, and public criticism of my husband/wife?* Whether in private or public, do I avoid such sarcasm, remarks, and criticism of my husband or wife?

4. *Do I regularly compliment my husband/wife and tell them*

I love them? Do you ever praise your wife with: "You have a beautiful dress on"?

You reply, "No, I don't tell her that. She doesn't have that kind of dress." Then why don't you go out and buy her a beautiful dress? Do you ever brag on your husband, "You surely do look great today. That's a handsome tie you have on"? Do you regularly compliment your spouse?

5. *Do you listen attentively when your spouse speaks to you?* Do you listen when they're talking to you?

6. *Do you value your partner's opinion?* In the affairs of life, do you ask your partner opinions on matters of importance?

7. *Do you discipline yourself not to interrupt or contradict when your partner is talking?* I realize that's not easy. I have often been visiting in homes when the husband would be talking, and the wife would chime in, "That's not exactly right." Or the lady would be talking, and all of a sudden her husband would butt in, "You know that's not the way it happened. Hey, get the facts right." It requires discipline not to interrupt or contradict when your partner is talking, and you think, your valuable information—they used to call it your "two cents' worth"—needs to be added to the conversation.

These are very important aspects in communication. Communication can be godly. The Gospel is communicated through the teaching and preaching of God's inspired Word. God designed it that we might know the heart, the intent, the feelings, the emotions, the hurts, and the joys of one another. That's why we should communicate with each other.

Fourth:

There Is the Key Called Purity

What does that mean? It means keeping yourself unspotted and undefiled in a world that is basing life on everything but purity. The Bible says in Ephesians 5:3, "But fornication, and all uncleanness, or covetousness, let it not be once named among you, as becometh saints." Why? Why does the Bible put this so strongly? "Let it not be once named among you"? There's no marriage that can stand the forces of sexual immorality. If immorality is injected into a believer's marriage and not dealt with, it is doubtful that the marriage can last.

We live in a society that is bent on dragging Christian marriages into the gutter. Have you ever noticed the theme of most movies at the theaters? Have you ever looked at the target of all the tabloids, the soap operas, the magazines? What are they? They emphasize fornication and adultery (they call them "affairs"). They include homosexuality and other perverted sexual sins. These put a horrible strain on marriages.

Beautiful, precious, and marvelous is the marriage that is undefiled, and it is rare in the eyes of the world, but it is special indeed. Proverbs 31 deals with a godly woman—a wife—and a mate. "Who can find a virtuous woman? for her price is far above rubies. . . . Her children arise up, and call her blessed; her husband also, and he praiseth her" (vv. 10,28). Sir, let me remind you, if you have a wife who is pure and loves you, if you have a faithful wife, you have a precious jewel of valuable price. Likewise, if a wife has a husband who is honorable and true to her, she has a tremendous treasure.

The last key is:

The Key Called Forgiveness

Forgiveness must permeate our marriages. Years ago there was a movie based on a novel, *Love Story*. Its main phrase was, "Love is never having to say you're sorry." That's insane and ridiculous. The Book of Ephesians says, "Be ye kind one to another, tenderhearted, forgiving one another, even as God for Christ's sake hath forgiven you" (4:32). If forgiveness rules and reigns in your marriage, there's going to be peace and harmony in your home. It is a blood-bought guarantee. You may have made all the mistakes. You may have "blown it" all over the place, but if you have biblical forgiveness in your marriage, your marriage is going to make it!

In New York there is a cemetery with a most unusual head-stone. Tourists walk by and look at this unusual headstone for there is no person's name, no date of birth, no date of death, no eulogy, no epitaph. There's only one word inscribed on the head-stone of that grave, "Forgiven." No name, no date of birth or death, no epitaph, no eulogy—one simple word, "Forgiven." My friend, that's the greatest tribute that could be paid to anyone—forgiven. When forgiveness fills your home, hatred, anger, jeal-ousy, and malice cannot coexist. As love and forgiveness reign in your home, a taste of heaven can be yours, and you will ex-perience the maximum marriage that God intended for you to have!

7

The Kind of Homes Our Children Deserve

Except the Lord build the house, they labour in vain that build it: except the Lord keep the city, the watchman waketh but in vain. It is vain for you to rise up early, to sit up late, to eat the bread of sorrows: for so he giveth his beloved sleep. Lo, the children are an heritage of the Lord: and the fruit of the womb is his reward. As arrows are in the hand of a mighty man, so are children of the youth. Happy is the man that hath his quiver full of them: they shall not be ashamed, but they shall speak with the enemies in the gate (Ps. 127).

A recent survey indicated that nationwide there were over a million youth who ran away from home last year. One third of all major crimes committed in the United States were carried out by people under the age of twenty. Seventy percent of all babies born out of wedlock were brought into the world to teenaged mothers, and the average age of those mothers was sixteen years old. Suicide is the second-leading killer of our youth, and alcoholism is the number-one problem among youth in America.

When I read that recent report I was startled. I'm sure you feel the same as you consider these statistics about today's children.

As we ask, "What's happening with our children?" we look for many places to lay the blame. We examine our society. We feel that society is wicked and godless. Our society does not teach the things of God. It's a society that, for the most part, endorses immorality and godlessness.

We examine our education system, and we feel the education systems of America are rife with either agnostics or atheists. To a degree that's true. But the Bible teaches us it's not the public educational system that is responsible for our children. Neither is it the federal, state or local government which bears the responsibility. The Bible emphasizes that we, who are parents, are responsible for our children.

Clearly it is manifested that the home has the responsibility for the children. Before we criticize our children and teenagers today, before we start to put them down, we must look at our lives as parents. Look through the eyes of God's Holy Word, and find out if we're really giving our children the homes they deserve.

Psalm 127:3 affirms, "Lo, children are an heritage of the Lord." That means there is nothing more marvelous you can have or imagine to have, than what God gives you in your home through children. Children are your heritage. They are a genuine blessing.

Let me ask you, "Are you passing on to your children the heritage they deserve? Are you giving them the home they deserve?" You might ask, "What kind of homes do they deserve?" Let me share with you the kinds of homes our children deserve.

Our Children Deserve a Home
Where Love Is Outwardly Demonstrated

They deserve a home where love is not covered up. I spoke of this in an earlier chapter, but it bears repeating. You must look for ways to love your children. You inquire, "How can I love my children? Give them games, toys, automobiles?" The best way to let your children know you love them is to tell them so. Spell it out. I don't understand why we've forgotten that. Why in American society and in the home, have we forgotten how to honestly and from a sincere heart confess, "I love you"?

Many people remark, "I can show them I love them." Sure, you can show them you love them. Yet, the best means of showing them you love them is to *tell them you love them,* and then to live behind what you tell them. Some people think, *If I just give them enough . . ."* But you cannot buy or barter love. Love can neither be bought nor sold. Love can only be given. If you truly love your children, take time, make the opportunity, to share that love with them. They deserve a home where there is love.

Think of the pressures and perversions that are forced upon our children today. Through movies, videos, magazines, it seems they all want to push on the public, violence, anger, and sexual perversion. In such a world our homes need to be havens from hate and anger. Love must predominate the home in all that is said, seen, and done. Our kids deserve it!

Our Children Deserve a Home
Where Rules Are Clearly Understood

Lay down the rules and make them clear. So many times we want to be vague in our rules. No organization, government, or ball game—nothing—goes without having rules. Rules must be made plain. They need to be clearly understood.

Here are a couple of rules about making rules. You cannot simply make rules without making rules about rules. (I am sounding redundant on purpose.)

- *When you make rules, make sure they're purposeful rules.*
  Have a purpose behind your rules. Don't just want to show your children who's boss. Be open with them and spell out the purpose for the rules.

• *Rules need to be reasonable.*

The Bible tells us that God expects only that which is *reasonable*. He has never ever been unreasonable. Romans 12:1 stresses that He expects us to obey Him, "which is your reasonable service." Make sure you use a level head when you prescribe rules for your children. Double check to see that the rules are clearly understood. If the kids don't understand the rules for playing the game, they can't be expected to play the game.

Then:

Our Children Deserve a Home Where Discipline Is Given in Love

The Bible presents considerable truth about discipline.

Proverbs 13:24: "He who spares his rod hates his son, But he who loves him disciplines him diligently."

Proverbs 22:15: "Foolishness is bound up in the heart of the child; the rod of discipline will remove it far from him."

Proverbs 23:13-14: "Do not hold back discipline from the child, for if you correct him with the rod, he will not die; although you beat him with the rod, he will not die. You shall beat him with the rod, and deliver his soul from Sheol [hell]" (NASB).

You may ask, "Good grief, Preacher, are you advocating child brutality?" No, that is not what the Word of God teaches, but it does emphasize that you need to give them discipline and direction in love. All of us need discipline, no matter how old or how young. I have actually seen precious little children in the grocery store, tagging along with their mothers, pulling at their dresses or pants legs, virtually begging, "Mama, give me discipline."

Kids often push down the shelves, kick over the cans, do everything their mischievous minds can devise. Do you know what they're doing? They're crying for attention, "Give me the discipline I need." Now, of course, most kids would not agree with this, but I believe it is exactly what they want, and the Bible says that is exactly what they need.

I've heard some parents boast that they would never give physical discipline to their children. Why not? Well, I believe the reason a parent will not discipline his child is because that parent loves himself/herself more than they do the child. What makes a parent fail to discipline his child? It's the fear the child will not love them. When a parent disciplines a child in love and tenderness, they are actually saying, "I care more about your welfare than I do my own. I'm willing to have you criticize me or refuse to love me or have you rebuke me or have you turn your back on me—whatever—just so you might be trained up in the way you should go." Now that is self-sacrificing love!

In 1 Samuel 3 we read the story about how God came to Samuel and spoke with him about a priest named Eli. The biblical record indicates that Eli had reared his own sons, Hophni and Phinehas, in the tabernacle. They were PKs (preacher's kids), but Eli was so busy he failed to discipline them. In 1 Samuel 3:13, God prophesied to Samuel about Eli and his children, "For I have told him that I will judge his house forever; for the iniquity which he knoweth; because his sons made themselves vile, and he restrained them not." Think of it! Eli lost them in the tabernacle of God simply because he failed in their physical and emotional discipline. Rebellion is bound up in the heart of a child, and only the rod of discipline will drive it from him. A child deserves discipline which is given in love.

Children, obey your parents in the Lord: for this is right. Honor thy father and mother; which is the first commandment with promise; That it may be well with thee, and thou mayest live long on the earth. And, ye fathers, provoke not your children to wrath: but bring them up in the nurture and admonition of the Lord. (Eph. 6:1-4).

Fourth:

Our Children Deserve a Home Where Problems and Their Solutions Are Openly Discussed

Do you really communicate with your children? Can you openly talk with them and vice versa? One recent survey stated that out of all the children who run away from home, the major cause is a lack of communication between that child and the parent(s). Often parents don't understand children, and children don't understand parents, and both parties wonder why.

Many times children do not have an open line of communication with their parents because the parents take the small things and make a big deal out of them and take the big things in the child's life that are dear to him, and make a small matter of them. In love we need to understand our children. We must cherish and keep open lines of communication with our children. We must have a wide-open heart and a listening ear. If you lose communication with a child, you have lost the child. It doesn't matter the age of the child. They deserve communication, and you deserve it, too. They must be able to come in and discuss their problems and possible solutions with you.

Also:

Our Children Deserve a Home Where Honesty Is the Best Policy,

where the parents not only teach honesty but practice it themselves. Parents can't teach honesty to their children if they don't set an example. You can't teach that child not to steal from a local store when you cheat on your income tax or in other areas of life.

We must teach our children that honesty really is "the best policy," because they're not going to pick that up from the society in which they live. They're not going to learn that in school, unless it's a Christian school, or by the television or radio. They're surely not going to learn that in rock music. The main way they're going to learn that is because of the life you lead before them. Remember, it's more than likely that your children will never be any closer to God than you are.

I remember a vivid story about a girl who went to a zoo. She and her mother were walking by the wildcat cage. The cat was screaming and growling to the top of its lungs. The child asked, "Mama, what kind of cat is that?"

The mother replied, "Sweetheart, that's a wildcat."

The girl probed deeper, "Why is it a wildcat?"

Mother answered, "It's a wildcat because its father and mother were wildcats."

The reason some of our children are wildcats is because their parents are wildcats! What can the kids expect if their parents constantly bicker, if they talk divorce, if they "run around"—if they live like wildcats? Children deserve a home that teaches them that honesty and civility really are the best policies.

Sixth:

They Deserve a Home Where Each Member
Is Offered Trust and Respect

Do you trust and respect your children? You may comment, "They're not trustworthy. They're not respectable." Listen, I have always noticed that there is an unusual aspect about respect. Respect breeds respect. Trust begets trust. Continue to tell your kids, "You're no good," and they will begin to believe it and live according to your low expectations. You cannot expect your children to respect you until you respect them.

What should we respect about our children?

1. *We need to respect their opinion*. We may be older, but we don't know everything there is to know. Have you realized that yet? Have you recognized that those children may know something you don't know? Maybe that's hard to imagine, but it's nonetheless true.

2. *Respect your children's property.* One's property is an extension of the individual. The clothes you wear, your home, the car you drive, your bedroom, and living room are extensions of your life. When you rob a child of his right to personal property, you're stealing his respectability. Honor their property; reserve their property; respect their property. There are certain possessions that belong to them. When you respect their property, they'll better respect yours.

3. *We need to respect their privacy.* All too often I have heard of mothers sneaking a peek at a daughter's diary. Even if the diary may contain questionable items, mother has invaded her daughter's privacy. Dads have often opened their children's mail. That's not right. Young people need some privacy. Since we expect our teenagers to knock before they come into our bedroom, why don't we knock before we go into theirs? We expect them not to go fumbling through our dresser drawers, why do we fumble through theirs? We expect them not to listen to our phone conversations, why do we listen to theirs? Respect their privacy. They deserve it. No wonder many kids make home sound like a concentration camp.

4. *Respect their individuality.* Let them become what God wants them to become instead of what we might want them to become. A father who is frustrated because he never made the grade in football, pushes his boy to be the very best football player, NFL material. He carries the boy down to an open field and urges, "Come on, Johnny, catch this pass." But Johnny can't catch the ball. Johnny can't kick either. He is a stumble-bum. Dad becomes irate—he's all upset because little Johnny can't catch and can't punt. But dad never did very well. He dropped out of football early. Why should he force football on his little boy who is an individual. He may or may not become a football player, but dad is going about it wrong. God could be making the greatest soul-winner the world has ever known out of that

little boy. Respect your child's individuality. Let him become what God wants him to become.

Seventh:

They Deserve a Home Where the Church of Jesus Christ Fills Its Proper Role

There should be respect for the church of Jesus Christ, for the preachers of God, for the people of God. Don't ever expect your boy or girl to attend Sunday School unless you do. Don't expect your boy or girl to honor the church and pastor and listen to his words unless you do. Are you aware that three out of four American teenagers today receive no religious training?

Three out of five teenagers in the church will drop away when they become adults. Do you know why? It's not because of the gospel. Neither do I think it's because of the church. I think more than all else it's because of certain parents who have not instilled a love for the church into the minds of their children. Parents themselves often have a case against God. They are under conviction. When they come to church and hear the Gospel message preached, they go out grumbling about the church and mumbling about the pastor. The children sit in the backseat of the car and then eat lunch, and hear all this grumbling where the main course is criticism of the preacher, the leaders, and the church in general. The kids don't understand. *Why do Mom and Dad get up and get dressed and go to that awful place every Sunday morning? Why do they make the effort to do it if it is all so bad?* As the years pass by, and the time comes for their own accountability, they make their own decision and say, "I don't want to go to that terrible place Mom and Dad complained about all those years."

Mom and Dad call on the phone and inquire, "Why aren't you at church, at Bible study? Why don't you respect the pastor and the staff?" I'll tell you why. Maybe it's because you didn't. Don't be surprised, if that's been your attitude. Your children deserve a home where the church of Jesus Christ fulfills its proper role, where the church is upheld, where the preacher and leaders are prayed for, where the Gospel is glorified.

Eighth:

They Deserve a Home That Is Committed to Godly Purposes

The purpose of that home is to be a Christian home. What's the purpose of your home? Just to get by? To make another dollar? To have a good time? If that's all, there is not much purpose in that home. Children don't follow God by accident and don't just stumble upon God's will.

By the age of eighteen, it is estimated a teenager has listened to 20,000 hours of radio; he has watched 18,000 hours of television; he has been to school 11,000 hours. That same statistician revealed that a child who is brought up in a church—the average Christian child—has observed only about 1,000 hours of religious education! Then you wonder why we're having problems with teenagers today. It's because parents are not committed to godly purposes in those children's lives.

Do you pray for your children, that God will help you to raise your children in the "nurture and admonition of the Lord"? (Eph. 6:4). Do you pray that God will protect your children when you send them off to school each morning? Do you petition the Lord, "Lord, send your angel to protect them—soul, mind, and body—and watch over them each day"? Do you also pray, "God, raise up godly partners for my children so my heritage may be a blessing to the Lord"? Is that your daily prayer for your children? Or is it, "God, take care of their bodies and just see them home"? Your children deserve more than that. They deserve a life that is fashioned toward a godly purpose.

Ninth and last:

They Deserve a Home That Is
Accustomed to the Things of God

The names of Jesus, the Holy Spirit, and God the Father should be common terminology around the home. We have a family in our church who has a little boy who can barely talk, but I love to be around him. Sometimes in his stammering attempts to talk, he will burst out with, "Praise the Lord!" That family is ingraining in his little heart the custom of being accustomed to the things of God.

What kind of home are you providing for your children? You may feel, "I am afraid I have miserably failed. Is there any hope?" Certainly there is. As long as your dear child is still under your influence, time still remains to train up that child in the way he should go.

8

In the Home—But Lost

Either what woman having ten pieces of silver, if she lose one piece, doth not light a candle, and sweep the house, and seek diligently until she find it? And when she hath found it, she calleth her friends and her neighbors together, saying, Rejoice with me; for I have found the piece which I had lost. Likewise, I say unto you, there is joy in the presence of the angels of God over one sinner that repenteth (Luke 15:8-10).

One of the most interesting parables in the Bible is found in Luke 15. It is about a woman who lost a coin. Not only is it a parable that teaches us about ourselves, and how we should be living, but it also gives us lessons about the loved ones in our family who may be lost without Christ and how we can win them.

There are three obvious parts to this story. *We see a coin,* a precious article, cherished by its owner. That represents a person—a soul. Jesus relates that in verse 10. *We see a woman.* She represents the heart of the home. When we think about a woman, our minds focus on a home, because the mother is the heart of most homes. We think about the family. And then *we*

99

see a house, which is a home. That's where homes naturally exist—in a house.

Jesus employs these short verses to teach us as believers how we are to live among our loved ones who have never met Christ. You may have unsaved loved ones in your home. It may be a son or daughter, a mother or father, a sister or brother. You pray for them, you care about them, and you love them. But somehow, with all your efforts you have not been able to win them to Christ.

Within this parable, Jesus provides for us some dynamic truths that can help us win our unsaved loved ones to Him. Let's think about the woman, the home, and the lost coin.

The first fact is most evident:

The Coin Was Lost

Jesus stated it was lost, but the word He uses there, and in the parable preceding and the parable after, does not mean merely "misplaced." That word in the Greek *apollumi* means it is being destroyed or being wasted. In other words, to be lost spiritually is to have a life that is wasted and is being destroyed by the power of evil. Christ pointed out that the coin was precious. One of the most prized possessions of that day was a silver coin. The souls of our loved ones are also precious. They should be dear and priceless to us. I hardly need to emphasize that.

I would trust that no one likes to think about their sons or daughters being lost and headed for hell. I've never met a brother or sister, a son or daughter, who looked at an unsaved loved one and exclaimed, "I'm glad they're lost." Most don't even want to think about the lostness of their loved ones. They often try to drive the subject from their minds. Yet, the Bible says all people without Christ are lost. It doesn't matter what their relationship to us is, if they're lost, they're lost. They're destined for an eternal hell. That is a horrifying reality.

Many people act as though they think if they live well enough, it will cover the sins of their lost loved ones, but it won't. The

Bible affirms that every man and woman, boy and girl shall give an account of himself unto God. "So every one of us shall give account of himself to God" (Rom. 14:12). You don't and can't give an account for me, and I don't and can't give an account for you. My wife can't even give an account for me. No one can give an account for me, because I will stand alone before God. And so will you, and so will your loved ones.

I realize that sometimes it is difficult to picture our family members as truly lost, unsaved, undone. But they're as lost as the alcoholic down the street, as lost as the prostitute on the street corner. They're totally lost without Christ. But the Bible repeats time and again that even those who are lost have hope, and I intend to share that hope with you.

My mind now moves to the parable which follows this parable. It is the parable of the "prodigal son." Will you imagine with me the father of that prodigal boy? Let's interview him six months before his son rejected him. You ask that father, "Do you know that six months from now your son is going to reject you? Your son is going to reject all the teaching you have poured into him out of love. He is going to turn his back on you, leave, and go off to live in riotous living among the lost."

The father of the prodigal probably would have protested, "You just don't know my boy. You don't know how good he is. I love him and have trained him right. I have taken him and taught him all the rudiments of religion. You say that because you just don't know him."

The problem was: the boy did leave, not because the father hadn't taught him, but the father didn't know the depths of the boy's heart. Salvation is a heart matter. Our relationship to God is a one-to-one heart consideration. You may go to church all you want. You may take your children to church, and I hope you do. You may have all the outward trappings of a life that is pure and holy before God, and that is wonderful, but salvation, our relationship with God, is still a matter of the heart. "For with the heart man believeth unto righteousness; and with the mouth confession is made unto salvation" (Rom. 10:10).

In 1 Samuel 16:7, God speaks of the importance of the heart before Him as He speaks to the prophet Samuel, "Look not on his countenance, or on the height of his stature; because I have refused him: for the Lord seeth not as man seeth; for man looketh on the outward appearance, but the Lord looketh on the heart."

Men judge you by the outward appearance. They comment "She looks saved. He looks saved. He does these certain things; she does this or that." But the Bible says, "God looks upon the heart." Why? Our relationship with God deals primarily with the heart.

I repeat: the coin was lost. As difficult as it is to accept, if we have unsaved loved ones, and if they do not come to Christ, they will spend eternity in hell.

The Coin Was Lost in the Home

It was not lost in a neighbor's house, not lost in the market-place, not lost when a stranger came to visit. It was doubtless during a normal daily activity that the coin was misplaced in the woman's own home. You ask, "How?"

You have seen children who are brought up in certain homes and you have observed, "If there's any way children will ever have a chance of doing right, these kids are going to make it. They have a sweet mother, a loving father, the ideal home." Then when that child grows up, goes in a wayward direction, rejects Christ and home, and winds up in deep trouble, you scratch your head and say, "I can't figure it."

Yet we view another home where a mom and dad are probably not even saved. You look at a child in that home and say, "That kid will never make it. There's no way he'll ever come to know Christ." And then the Holy Spirit works, and that child in the right place and time comes to a saving knowledge of Jesus Christ, and their lives are changed.

You ask, "Why can't we judge homes and children like that?" Because we're dealing with matters of the heart. Certain things happen in homes that are a disadvantage to children to begin with. We recognize it in the life of this lady as she lost her coin. Likewise, you can lose your children. No matter what you do, on your own, you can lose your children unless certain spiritual steps occur.

Here is how you lose them.

First, they can be lost by *neglect*.

You may have the attitude that they're around now and always will be. But that's unrealistic. They will grow up, unless they are severely handicapped. One day he'll be a man, and one day she'll be a full-grown woman. One day you're going to shake your head and say, "I never really thought that would happen." Taking your children for granted can lead to neglecting their development, physically, mentally, and most of all, spiritually.

If you are not caring for your children's spiritual welfare, you are certainly not tending to their needs. We are threefold beings. All of us have a spirit, a mind, and a body. In today's society, all advertisement is beamed toward the two parts that will not matter in the long run—the mind and the body. We feel that if we can nurture their minds, then our children will do right. Wrong. That's not how it works. Yes, we need to cultivate their minds, but that's not the secret. We think if we have indulged them with all kinds of niceties, and if they are strong, stalwart, physical specimens, they'll make it in life. Wrong again.

The real part of a person that matters is his spirit. When you provide for your child's mind and body, and do nothing for his spirit, you are not really caring for the child, because, in essence, the real child is the spiritual nature within him. The child is a spiritual being.

Many people are neglected in that no one seems to care about their souls, their spirit, what's really within them, and that's what counts. In despair David cried, "No man cared for my soul" (Ps. 142:4). And certainly that is the cry of many of our youth today! Not long ago I was having lunch with two men, one of them extremely wealthy. The other was a young businessman. I noticed the young man really liked successful men who were wealthy. The wealthy man had a son who was in prison for the sale of narcotics. As we talked, the young businessman looked at the older tycoon and exulted, "Oh, you're so successful. I would give the world to have the success you have."

Without hesitation the older gentleman replied, "I'd give it all up if my son were right with God. I'd give it all." What had happened? I know that man well. I love him, and he would be the first to confess he gave his son everything he wanted in life. He afforded the son the finest boarding school, clothes, car, and position in life, but he had forgotten to nurture the son's soul. You can lose your loved one by neglect.

Notice also they can be lost *through lack of planning.*

In the business world there is a saying, "If you fail to plan, you plan to fail." How true. What are you planning for your children's lives? Do you plan in your mind's eye how you're going to teach your children about Christ. When each child reaches that certain age, when the Holy Spirit begins to deal with him, will you have planted the seed of the Gospel in the heart of that child so he may readily come to know Jesus?

You see, you must plan for your child's salvation. No, you cannot save them. No, you should not force them to Christ, as it were, but you need to cultivate the Gospel in the heart of that child so he might be saved.

If you neglect that kind of spiritual planning, and simply go along, saying, "Well, I take my child to church every now and then and hope it's going to all work out," I'll guarantee you it more than likely won't work out. You need to plan for the spiritual welfare of your child. You can neglect the child, and you can fail to plan for the child. I quote from Reuben in Genesis 42:22: "Do not sin against the child."

The Coin Was Sought Until It Was Found

Verse 8, "Either what woman having ten pieces of silver, if she lose one piece, doth not light a candle, and sweep the house, and seek diligently till she find it?"

Think with me now. How did the woman find the coin? What did she do to find the coin? Quite frankly, the same thing you should do to win your lost loved ones to Christ. In this one verse Christ gives you all you'll ever need to see that your loved ones come to Jesus. It is a simple plan.

First of all, we see that *she lit a candle.*

The average house in that day was very small and usually had only one window. So it was even dark in the daytime. This lady must have thought to herself, *If I'm going to find the coin I have lost I must have some light.* Who is the Light of the world but Jesus Christ? The Light of Christ needs to be in every home.

You may have witnessed to that loved one again and again. You may have gone through every plan of soul-winning imaginable, but if Jesus doesn't live in a home, if He is not the Light of that home, the family members will never want to know Him. He declared, "And I, if I be lifted up from the earth, will draw all men unto me." He didn't say, "If the church be lifted up," "if religion be lifted up," "if doctrine and dogma be lifted up," although these are good. "If *I* be lifted up . . ." I ask you: Is Jesus in your home? Is His joy resident in your home?

Does your family have a family altar? Have you determined in your home that, even if others in your family don't, you're going to have a time of prayer? Do you pray about the needs of your lost loved ones? The first action the woman took was to light a candle. The first action we must take is to make sure that the Light of Christ is shining brightly in our home.

Second, we note that *she swept her house.* Why is that important? Unless the home was clean and free of clutter, how would she ever find the coin? Here the implication is crystal-clear. It has to do with the cleansing of the heart. How in the world are your loved ones going to desire Christ, if you live like the devil before them—when there is jealousy, anger, frustration, backbiting, and hot tempers in your home? That kind of environment is not conducive to winning family members to Christ.

Perhaps you have an unsaved spouse, and you have been praying for them to be saved. But you may have a bitter grudge against them because of what happened in the past, and you still harbor that grudge deep within. You ask why they will not receive Christ, but the reason could be that grudge, that root of your bitterness standing between them and Christ. How in the world can you expect your loved ones to want to know Christ when Christ doesn't radiate through you?

I cannot expect my loved ones to want Jesus as Savior and Lord unless I sweep up the house. I must keep the house (my heart) clean. Not until I light the candle of Christ in my home, and make sure, through spiritual introspection, that my life is right, will the words I speak ever influence the hearts of those I want to see come to Christ. I must sweep my heart, my life, for only in that can people see there's a difference. "My dad's not the dad he used to be. My mom's not the mom she used to be. My husband or wife is not the person they used to be. They really do care for me, and this business about Christ must be real. Therefore I want to know Him." Those kinds of responses will often emerge if the house is clean.

Third, *she sought the coin until she found it.*

I especially like that. She didn't give up. Did she find it quickly? I don't think so. I think she had to look for it—*diligently.* I can see her down there with the broom as she swept out one little room and then another, carrying the light and going all over the house. She looked until she found it. I think this speaks of importunity in prayer, persistence in prayer, the prayer that goes, "I am not going to give up until that person I love comes to Christ!"

Many of us have had husbands or wives, moms and dads, who prayed for years before their loved one came to Christ. They never stopped. "The effectual, fervent prayer of a righteous man availeth much" (Jas. 5:16b). They kept the candle of Christ lit in the home. They made sure their hearts and lives were clean, and they kept on praying. "Pray without ceasing" (1 Thess. 5:17). That's why Christ taught us, "Ask, and it shall be given you; seek, and ye shall find; knock, and it shall be opened unto you" (Luke 11:9). Those are all progressive verbs. Read correctly, it says, "Ask, and keep on asking; seek and keep on seeking, knock and keep on knocking; and it shall be opened unto you."

Once you grasp the horns on the altar of prayer for that loved one, never, never give up. Mother, never give up. Father, never throw in the towel. Husband or wife, never call it quits. Brother or sister, son or daughter, never lose hope, because if Christ is the Light of your life, and your life is clean before Him, and you pray, you can claim the promise of God that one day your loved one is going to accept Jesus Christ.

What happened? The Bible says she found the coin. Notice last of all:

When the Coin Was Found It Brought Joy

Verse 10, "And when she had found it, she called her friends and neighbors together and said, Rejoice with me for I have found the piece I had lost. Likewise, I say unto you, there is joy in the presence of the angels of God over one sinner that repenteth." I have studied that Scripture many times and have analyzed it, and there's plenty there which is a special blessing to me. There is joy in the presence of the angels. Angels praise and rejoice. They do when a sinner is saved. Does God rejoice? Certainly He does.

Who is in heaven besides God and the angels? Your saved friends and loved ones, all the redeemed of the ages. They're the only others there. Notice that Jesus said, "There is joy in the presence of the angels of God. . . ." Who is there rejoicing when a sinner comes home? God, the angels, and *the redeemed,* including our departed loved ones. Can't you picture in your mind's eye a mother who has prayed for years for her wicked son to be saved, and one day, twenty years after she has gone to heaven, that boy comes to Christ?

Can't you envision a father who has loved his children, and his heart has been broken repeatedly because they have rejected Christ? There in heaven he hears the news that his children have come home. Talking about rejoicing in the presence of the angels! We can imagine the ecstasy of those loved ones.

Years ago I heard about George W. Truett, predecessor to W. A. Criswell as pastor of First Baptist Church of Dallas, Texas. One day he was preaching, and a man came down the aisle, requesting, "Dr. Truett, will you pray with me about my son? He's lost. His mother died many years ago, and I have tried to do my best for my son, but I can't seem to control him. Listen, I love my boy. Pray with me that he will be saved."

Dr. Truett prayed with him. The following day Truett was walking down the street when a young man approached him and reported, "Dr. Truett, I'm the young man whose dad came down the aisle last night and asked you to pray for. I got saved last night, and I met Jesus, and I'm so full of joy."

Truett inquired, "Son, tell me how you came to accept Christ."

"Pastor, last night I came in late, and normally my daddy is at the door to meet me, griping and complaining when I come in late. But last night he wasn't there, and I knew something strange was going on. I went to his bedroom, and I heard him praying, 'God, please save my boy!' Dr. Truett, my dad was crying for me and praying that God would save me. I heard him crying and praying. I went and knelt by my bed and prayed, 'God, I've never asked for anything from You before, but if You're there, and Jesus is real, please save me and let Jesus come into my heart.'"

The boy continued, "Dr. Truett, something happened to me. I went in there, put my arm around my dad, and said, 'Dad, I got saved. I heard you praying, and I got saved.' Oh, Dr. Truett, if only my mother knew I was saved, if only my mother knew."

I somehow believe his mother knew it. There is joy in the presence of the angels when a sinner comes home. This message is twofold; *first of all, to those who have unsaved loved ones, never give up*. Be sure the Light of Jesus Christ is shining in your life. Be sure your heart is clean before Him. If there is sin standing between your witness and the salvation of your loved ones, ask the Holy Spirit to cleanse you before God. Confess it before Him. "If we confess our sins he is faithful and just to forgive us our sins, and to cleanse us from all unrighteousness" (1 John 1:9).

Second, the message is to those who don't know Christ. Someone is praying for you today. Somebody cares and understands. You can reject Christ, neglect Christ, or accept Christ.

Why don't you accept Him today and allow that eternal salvation to enter your heart? Then you won't be lost, like the coin going to waste, but thanks be to God, you'll be found.

Part III

Lord, Send Revival

. . . in Our Churches

9

Lord, Send Revival

If my people, which are called by my name, shall humble themselves, and pray, and seek my face, and turn from their wicked ways, then will I hear from heaven, and will forgive their sin, and will heal their land (2 Chron. 7:14).

My heart has recently been "strangely warmed," to use John Wesley's phrase, by a desire for revival. When I speak of *revival*, I am not referring to having a guest speaker for an evangelistic crusade. Rather, I have in mind God moving among His people as only God can do, God moving "in mysterious ways His wonders to perform."

Promotion or slick publicity cannot bring about real revival. All of our ingenuity cannot create it. I think of the manifestation of God's power among His people that will make us different; that will change us so we will never, in our entire lives, be the same again, once God has moved in our midst.

Have there ever been revivals like that? Indeed there have been. Surely we remember the revival in the Book of Acts, the first revival of the New Testament church. In Acts 2 the Holy Spirit came upon those who were praying in the upper room. As

He descended upon those 120 who were praying. He came like a wind and gave them cloven tongues of fire that sat upon them.

The Bible account records that those followers of the risen Lord fanned out and preached the Gospel with thousands being saved. Those believers changed the face of the world. The Scripture refers to them as world-changers. "These [the Christians] that have turned the world upside down are come hither also" (Acts 17:6). That was the revival in the Book of Acts.

Another remarkable revival called "The Great Awakening" came to America in the 1700s. Out of that revival, nationwide repentance came—John Wesley, George Whitefield, Jonathan Edwards, and other great preachers presented Christ as we need to see Him today.

There was the revival of 1857, an unusual movement that was begun by a layman named Jeremiah Lampere, who began to seek God daily in prayer. On September 23, 1857, Jeremiah went to a prayer room at noon on his lunch hour and began to pray. Twenty minutes later six other men came in and prayed with him.

In one week, twenty men filled the room, and within six months, 10,000 people were coming and praying at noon every day. Revival swept our nation to the extent that from that revival came such preachers as J. Hudson Taylor and D. L. Moody.

Then there was the Welsh Revival, where a young man named Evan Roberts was awakened one night by the Holy Spirit. He lay in his bed and visited with the Holy Spirit in prayer from one o'clock in the morning until four. God set on fire this young man's heart for revival.

He prayed three solid months for revival. He called out, "God, I want 100,000 souls for You from my country of Wales." God, in His omnipotence, moved in that country, and not only were 100,000 saved there, but that revival spread over the face of the earth and hundreds of thousands were saved. It was written that in Wales the judges wore white gloves as a sign there were no criminal cases to try because the criminals had been saved.

There was a mighty revival that came in 1970 at Asbury College in the small town of Wilmore, Kentucky. A group of students gathered together in a chapel service on February 3, 1970. The dean of the college came, looked out at the small group of students gathered there, and suggested, "Instead of preaching to you today, I simply want to have a testimony time."

One after another students and faculty began to testify, and God came to that chapel service. Tears began to flow down their faces as they confessed their sins. They sought repentance, and they experienced joy and peace such as they had never known in their lives. That one chapel service, scheduled to last one hour, lasted continuously for 185 hours around the clock. From all across the land, people drove and flew into that little college to participate in the Asbury revival.

Time and again amazing revivals have occurred throughout history. Do these revivals have anything in common? Indeed they do. As I have studied revivals, I have seen seven major traits that accompany most awakenings. Let me share these with you.

First:

Revival Is Normally Preceded by a Moral and Spiritual Decline in the Churches

Jonathan Edwards said, before The Great Awakening, "I find my church strangely indifferent. I find my church cold." Too many people could testify that about their churches today. When revival comes, it is preceded by a time of deadness in the churches. According to this first trait, we are more than ripe for revival in America today.

Two:

When Revival Comes, God Will Awaken
a Few Individuals to Understand the
Urgent Need for His Moving

Not the mass—but a few. It may be one, two, or a dozen, but God always seems to awaken at least one or two to the urgent necessity for revival. They will give up anything, they will give anything, they will do whatever is called for, for revival to come, because God has laid upon their hearts a divine compunction.

Three:

Although the Spirit of Revival Begins with a Few,
It Grows to Many

You cannot restrict revival to a church, to a town, to a denomination. As God's Spirit begins to move in a revival, revival goes past churches, beyond denominational barriers, and it moves into "the general assembly and firstborn of every believer," the people of God, regardless of denomination (see Heb. 12:23).

Four:

When Revival Comes, God's People Will Enjoy
Long Seasons of Prayer

You don't have to beg them to pray. You don't have to preach about prayer. You don't have to plead with them to come to the altar. In fact, they want to pray, and they will bask in it. It will be an effervescent joy to them. They would rather do that than watch television or dine out—because they are experiencing a privilege far greater than the world could ever afford. The old song goes, "The service of Jesus true pleasure affords, In Him there is joy without an alloy." They are given a peace and joy through repentance and confession of sin, and the power of the Holy Spirit has the joy of the Lord bubbling in their souls. They enjoy long seasons, not only an hour or day—long seasons of prayer.

Fifth:

There Will Be a Renewed Desire for Holy Living

In other words, preachers will preach about sin like they used to in the olden days. They will name specific sins, and receptive people will want to hear about those sins. Why? Because the only means of knowing about sin is to recognize sin. The only way you have of zeroing in on sin, apart from the Holy Spirit, is if that sin is spelled out. As sins are identified, they are then confessed and repented of, and holiness blossoms in people's lives. People will have a hunger for holiness, and sin will be renounced and named, with confession and repentance to follow. That's not popular in today's garden-variety churches where people want a steady diet of new-age positivism.

Sixth:

A Great Harvest of Souls Will Come to Salvation

This will be the result. People won't have to say, "Please come to Jesus." Pastors won't have to beg. They and their staff members won't have to come up with schemes, contests, and bizarre plans to lure people down the aisles. When revival comes, people will yearn to receive the Lord. Great waves of people will be saved.

Seventh:

The True Church of Jesus Christ Will Grow in Numbers

In fact, in the revival of 1857, over a million people joined the churches in America. In Great Britain there were well over a million people who joined their churches during the same time.

We look around us and hope, "Oh God, if we only had revival. Oh, God, will You, can you, do it again?" He can, and He will. Why not believe it? Why not cash in on the promises of God? There's nothing about God that changes. "Jesus Christ the same yesterday, to day, and for ever" (Heb. 13:8). Remember, there's no problem with God. What God was in eternity and before the beginning of time, He still is. What He is today, He has been in the past and will be in the future. What He is in the future, He has been in the past. He is always the same. He asserted, "I am God. I change not."

There never has been nor will there ever be anything wrong with God. The problem is found in you and me. God longs to send revival, but how can we have it? In one of the most powerful Scriptures in all the Bible, God speaks concerning revival: "If my people which are called by my name, shall humble themselves, and pray, and seek my face, and turn from their wicked ways; then will I hear from heaven and will forgive their sin, and will heal their land" (2 Chron. 7:14).

Notice first of all:

God Says He Has a People

Verse 7, "If my people which are called by my name . . ." Who is God talking to about revival? He is certainly not talking to or about unsaved people. Nor does He have in mind promiscuous men or women or the drunkard or the gambler or the robber or the murderer. He calls out to His own people and pointedly challenges them to repentance.

Revival is a mighty movement of God which occurs first among His people, His called-out ones, His bride. In our time, revivals and evangelistic crusades have caused confusion, and that can become deadly. Churches announce they're going to have a revival. They put a sign out front and set up a date. What do most churches have in their minds? Seeing hundreds of people saved in their "revival," but true revival first has to do with God's people. Evangelistic crusades have to do with the unsaved coming to Christ. Let us never confuse the issues, for it can be deadly to our understanding of the necessity for revival.

Yes, if we are blessed enough to have an evangelist come in and have hundreds of people saved, we ought to become excited. We should be. We tell everyone, "We had a great revival." No, you didn't. You had a fantastic soul-winning, evangelistic crusade. You didn't necessarily have a revival.

The only time you will know if revival genuinely comes is when hardened hearts are broken, and people start making up with their brothers and sisters in Christ, begin to apologize and to ask forgiveness—when jealousies, angers, and hatreds begin to be confessed and laid on altars of prayer, and tears begin to flow down faces, not because of the problems the folks are in, but because of the sin that the Holy Spirit has revealed, sin that needs to be purged from their souls. When there is a fresh awareness of the holiness of God, that's what revival is all about, and where does it start? It starts in the house of the Lord, among God's people. He says, "If *my people* which are called by my name." Revival starts with the people of God.

We see also in this Scripture that:

God Hates Human Pride

"Pride goeth before destruction, and a haughty look before a fall" (Prov. 16:18). "If my people shall humble themselves." That's urgently vital. The Bible says God resists the proud but gives grace to the humble. Have you ever wondered why God hates pride so? Because pride is the basis for rebellion, and rebellion is the very essence of sin. Coleridge well expressed it: "And the Devil did grin, for his darling sin / Is pride that apes humility."

In Isaiah 14 we read about Lucifer, Satan, the devil. Lucifer was an angel in heaven. The text describes him as being arrayed with grandiose splendor. There was no angel in heaven above this angel, Lucifer. Lucifer was found to have pride in his heart.

He boasted, "I will exalt my throne; I will be like the most high." God saw his rebellion in heaven and Jesus said, "I saw Satan as lightning fall from heaven." God cast Lucifer out of heaven, and he came to earth.

God had created the Garden of Eden. He had created man and woman, Adam and Eve, to love. He had wonderful communion and love with Adam and Eve. They were his children. But Satan came to the Garden of Eden, and he brought with him pride. He suggested to Eve, "Why don't you partake of the forbidden fruit, for if you do, you will be as God." Pride. *I will not be subject to God's laws and principles,* she must have thought. *If I just partake of that forbidden fruit, I will be a god.* So Adam and Eve sinned against God, and God, in order to restore mankind unto Himself, had to send His only begotten Son, Jesus Christ, to a cross. Christ had to shed His blood upon that cross, and give up his very life's blood.

What cost God's Son His life? Man's pride. No wonder God hates pride. All too often when God looks at his children He sees pride. People too proud to pray, too proud to bend a knee before Him, too proud to give unto God that which belongs to Him. Folks too proud to go to their neighbor whom they have offended and say, "Will you please forgive me?" Too proud to tell their mate, "Honey, I'm sorry, I was wrong." Too proud to say to that husband, "Though I don't agree with everything you agree with, I'm going to be in subjection and love to walk under your leadership as the spiritual leader of our home."

There are thousands of ways pride rears its ugly head. God looks at us and says, "I will not pour out my Holy Spirit when I see pride, for I hate pride." God resists the proud, but He gives grace (unmerited favor) to the humble.

Notice also that:

God Hears Holy Prayer

Verse 7, "If my people which are called by my name shall humble themselves and pray and seek my face and turn from their wicked ways, then will I hear from heaven . . ." When? When two things happen. Number one, not only that we pray, but we seek His face. Notice He says, "Seek His face." I've heard Dr. Adrian Rogers say, "Many of us want to feel the hand of God, but not many of us want to seek the face of God." Why? The hand of God is provision. We hear much preaching today about provision.

But God said if we're going to have revival, we must come seeking His face. What's the difference? When you seek the hand of God, you seek provision, but when you seek the face of God, you seek His holiness. And when you stand in the holiness of God, you see yourself as you really are.

The prophet Isaiah (ch. 6) saw the throne of God, and he confessed, "Woe is me, for I am a man of unclean lips, dwelling in the midst of a people of unclean lips"— because he saw the holiness of God.

Number one, He commanded seek My face, and number two, turn from your wicked ways. What does that mean? Repent of it. Charles G. Finney, the powerful revivalist, preached, "Revival is nothing less than a new beginning of obedience to God." That's good, but I want to add another thought to that. Until you deal with step number one, step number two can never come to be. For revival is not only a new and fresh obedience to God:

Revival Is Always Preceded by Repentance

Revival is when God's children come to repentance and then follow in obedience before Him. Why? Because wickedness can never remain in our hearts if real revival is to come.

We must return to the Scripture, where God teaches us the

right order. Repentance occurs prior to revival's coming. We must not pray, "God, send revival, and then we will repent." That's not how it works. Repentance precedes; repentance comes before revival can ever come to be. Notice the Scripture, "If my people . . . shall pray . . . seek my face . . . turn from their wicked ways . . . then [a simple adverb] will I hear, forgive, and heal their land." "Then" is an exceedingly important adverb because it connotes an event happening before that will cause another event to occur.

We live in a world of cause and effect. All of life is cause and effect. If we're ever going to experience revival, we must understand the cause of revival is repentance among God's people, and the effect of revival will be repentance of the unconverted coming to Christ for salvation.

The question is, "What's the sin in your life?" You might answer, "I don't have any sin." Gipsy Smith once ran into a fellow who claimed he didn't have any sin. Gipsy suggested, "Just get on your knees and guess at a few!" What is the sin in your life? What is the sin in my life that stands between God and revival? The Bible makes it clear that God wants us to have revival. It's His heart's desire. Can we have a life-changing, sweeping revival? Yes, on the basis of Christ's shed blood, we can. What must we do? We must repent and seek His face.

Lastly, notice the Scripture says, "then will I hear from heaven and will forgive their sin and will heal their land." There was His promise:

"Then Will I"

He gave His promise, and God will always keep His promise. What is the hope of America? Revival. What is the hope of the home? Revival. What is the hope of the heart? Revival. How are we going to have it?

I repeat B. B. McKinney: "Lord, send a revival. Lord, send a revival, Lord, send a revival, And let it begin in me."

Do you want revival? Revival will never come until it begins in *you* and *me!*

10

The Old Time Religion

Thus saith the Lord, Stand ye in the ways, and see, and ask for the old paths, where is the good way, and walk therein, and ye shall find rest for your souls. But they said, We will not walk therein (Jer. 6:16).

When I was a boy we used to sing the song, "The Old Time Religion." "Give me that old time religion, it's good enough for me. It was good for our fathers, it was good for our mothers, it was good for everybody, and it's good enough for me."

What did we mean when we used to sing that song? Were we talking about some type of antiquated, out-of-vogue, old-fashioned belief? Were we talking about some outdated religion that happened many years ago, one that is not relevant for the day in which we live? No, not at all. What we were singing about were some basic fundamentals of the Christian faith.

These primary, historic truths of the Christian faith are the only precepts that will transport men and women and boys and girls to heaven. Let us consider these fundamentals. Why do we sing that it was good for our fathers and mothers? Because it was. Why do we say it's good enough for us today? Because it is.

125

I want you to understand why the "Old Time Religion" (I should call it the "All-Time Religion") is good enough to answer any problem, any question, any situation you have in your life.

First, I want you to notice a fact about the old time religion. The old time religion includes a belief in:

A Living, Everlasting God

The old time religion, of course, believed in the existence of God.

You may not realize it, but there was a time in this land when few intelligent people questioned the existence of God. I still believe that's true. I believe a person with half a mind would not question the existence of God. Psalm 14:1 is pointed: "The fool hath said in his heart there is no God." That interests me. "The fool hath said in his heart. . . ." Why would he say it in his heart? Because even a fool wouldn't say it in his head. Even the most foolish person, through reason, would believe in the existence of God.

Creation, the form and design of life, proves there must be a Creator God. When I climb into my automobile, I don't say, "I wonder if this thing was designed by somebody, if there was an engineer for this car, if somebody put this thing together." No, I don't wonder, because I realize that particular automobile has a certain kind of design or form. So design and form mandate there was a designer, a creator.

When I go to the airport and walk into the terminal, and I see the massive buildings and the long concourses, I don't ask, "Do you suppose these things just happened? One day a big bang came to Atlanta, and this airport just came together?" Do I question whether or not an engineer or architect drew the plans for the facility? No? Sheer common sense tells me there were creators for that airport.

When I fly five or six hundred miles an hour across the sky in a plane, I don't say, "I really doubt if one day somebody designed this airplane." No, I know it has a maker.

When I see a bird fly across the sky and I view the clouds above, enjoy the flowers of the field and the mountains and the valleys, the oceans and the plains, the sun and the moon, I don't question whether there was a Creator God, because design mandates there was. Plain common sense about life dictates there is a Creator God.

David must have had this in mind when he gazed up into the sky one night and proclaimed in Psalm 8:3-4, "When I consider thy heavens and the work of thy fingers, the moon and the stars, which thou hast ordained; what is man that thou art mindful of him?" Psalm 19:1, "The heavens declare the glory of God and the firmament sheweth his handiwork."

Educators, philosophers, liberal theologians, and all the rest may try to do away with God. You may enter into their classes and hear them indicate, "There is no God." It doesn't matter what they believe. All that matters is the true existence of God. Educators, philosophers, and astronomers used to believe the world was flat. Galileo and Copernicus disagreed and were persecuted for their stand.

If you had approached certain thinkers in their day and asked, "What is the shape of the earth?" they would have replied, "Everyone knows it is flat." Many of the greatest minds of science and education believed the world was flat, but it was still round. Men can pitifully claim, "There is no God." They're like a dog barking at the moon or a mouse threatening an elephant. There is a God. He said, "I am the I Am. I am Alpha and Omega." His first name in the Bible (Gen. 1:1) was *Elohim,* which means, "I have always been, I am now, and I always will be. I was in the beginning, and I will be throughout the eons of time to come. I am forever and forever." The existence of God poses no question. All that is questioned is your sin and your intelligence if you argue, "There is no God."

The Bible classifies a person who says, "there is no God," in a particular manner. It says, "The fool hath said in his heart there is no God." Give me the old-time religion that believes in the existence of a living God.

The old time religion also includes the belief that:

The Bible Is God's Pure, Holy, Inerrant Word

In 2 Timothy 2:16, we read, "All scripture is given by inspiration of God and is profitable for doctrine, for reproof, for correction, for instruction in righteousness." This does not mean only a certain portion out of the Old Testament and a piece out of the New. It does not include merely that which you think is applicable for today. It doesn't mean a miracle here or a miracle there or that the Book is right here but wrong there. I declare: *all Scripture.*

In certain areas, the old-time religion may not be fashionable today. Those who consider themselves the "intelligentsia" may think the Gospel is passé in the 1990s. But it is neither out of vogue nor foolish nor out of date. If the Gospel is out of date, somebody needs to change his calendar. The Bible is true through and through. It is infallible, and we who know it have an obligation to stand up for that knowledge. The Word of God, though it actually needs no defense, calls for those who know it to be true to stand up and say no.

Why is it so vital that those who believe the Word of God is without error and totally true to stand up and speak for it? We ruminate in our minds, *The Word of God needs no defense. Who am I to defend God's Word?* Yes, the Word of God is all powerful, and able to take care of itself.

But the reason we must stand up for the Bible is that any lie allowed to go unchallenged is one day accepted by many as the absolute truth. This has often happened with evolution.

One time a Christian was ridiculed by her humanist professor. He asked her, "Do you really mean to tell me that you believe the Bible?"

She replied, "I really do."

"If you truly believe that book, and that it's really true, tell me how Jonah went into that fish, stayed three days and nights, and lived again when he came out?"

She came back, "Well sir, I really don't know."

"What? I thought you believed the Bible to be true."

"Yes sir, I do."

"Well, why can't you tell me how Jonah lived after he was in the belly of the fish three days and three nights?"

She said, "Sir, I really don't know, but I'll tell you what I'll do. When we all die, and I get to heaven, I'm going to ask him."

He said, "Well, my lady, what if he's not in heaven when you get there?"

She said, "Then, sir, you can ask him."

The old time religion includes the belief in the Bible as God's Holy Word. Third, the old-time religion includes the fact that:

Man Is a Sinner

Why do we act as we do? Some say, "Well, I am a student of modern psychology and I believe if we act wrongly it is because of the negative influences of our heredity or environment. Certainly I don't believe in this thing called sin." You hear all kinds of ideas.

Some people still believe that all people are inherently good. I wonder, don't they read the newspaper? Don't they watch television? Haven't they heard about Saddam Hussein, Joseph Stalin, Adolph Hitler, or your "run-of-the-mill" serial killer? Where have they been? Do they have their heads buried in the sand? People are not "good." Look at the crimes of our society. Are those the result of basically good people? The Bible covers up nothing. "Wherefore by one man sin entered into the world, and death by sin, so death passed upon all men; that all men have sinned" (Rom. 5:12).

What does that Scripture mean? That without Christ, all

people are in the same sinking boat. You say to me, "Preacher, you don't know who I am." You may say, "I'm rich. I'm a blueblood. I'm well liked. I'm popular. I'm a good man/woman, boy/girl. I'm a religionist. You just don't know who I am."

I may not be aware of your pedigree, but without Christ I know precisely what you are. You're just like everybody else, whether rich or poor, whether highly educated or uneducated—none of those outward signs matter. "Wherefore by one man sin entered into the world, and death by sin . . ." Because of sin, death passed upon all men, because all men have sinned.

It doesn't matter to God where you were born or to whom you were born. It doesn't matter to God whether or not you are an aristocrat or a sharecropper. All that makes the difference to God is whether you've been born again.

In John 3 we read about the rich Pharisee, Nicodemus, who came to see Jesus one night. This influential religious leader confided in Jesus, "Jesus, I'm hoping to learn how to have eternal life. I'm a Pharisee. I've studied all the Scriptures, and I know them quite well. I've studied the prophets and have kept all the Ten Commandments we were given by Father Moses."

Then Jesus commanded him, "Sir, you must be born again." Nicodemus answered, "I don't understand. Can I reenter my mother's womb and be born a second time? That's impossible, Jesus. How can I be born a second time?"

Jesus replied, "That which is born of flesh, is flesh; And that which is born of the Spirit is spirit. Marvel not that I said unto thee, Ye must be born again" (John 3:6-7). Jesus was saying, "I'm not talking about a fleshly birth. That which is born of flesh, is flesh. It would do you no good to be born again physically. But what I am talking about is a spiritual birth of that dead, sinful nature found in the souls of all men, which can be brought to life. Nicodemus, marvel not that I say unto you, You must be born again." Why? Because there is a truth that every person without Christ is a sinner, lost and headed for hell.

Fourth, the old-time religion includes a belief that:

Sin Has Its Consequences

There is indeed, in the words of the late R. G. Lee, a "payday someday"—one day, judgment time; pay time; accountability time for sins unconfessed is coming.

Nations today don't believe that. Even our nation is now receiving some of its rewards for this unbelief. Today we have embraced illicit sexual sins, sometimes called "sexual preference." AIDS is on the rampage. Things that used to be sin, abhorred, and blushed at, are now called "sexual preference." The results? They are evident, and think about the little innocent babies that are being slaughtered by the millions through abortion, seventeen million in the past thirteen years, since the Supreme Court decision. What is it? "The wages of sin." Sin has its consequences.

The Bible speaks at length about liquor and strong drink. Yet, many of the mainline churches think social drinking is OK. The Word of God cries out against alcoholic beverages. Alcoholism in America is running wild. One third of American teenagers admit becoming drunk off alcohol at least once a week. One hundred and fifty thousand people died last year from alcohol-related sickness in America.

You might remark, "Preacher, haven't you awakened to the fact that alcoholism is a disease?" Yes, I have. It's a disease called sin. Someone commented, concerning alcoholism being a disease, "Some say alcoholism is a disease. Right. If alcoholism is a disease, it's the only disease that is bottled and sold. It's the only disease that is self-induced. It's the only disease that requires a store to spread it. It's the only disease that produces revenue for our government. It's the only disease that provokes crime and punishment. It's the only disease that produces battered wives and abused children. It's the only disease spread by the advertisers. It's the only disease that requires a license to spread it. It's the only disease that is spread without germ or virus, and it's the only disease that will bar its patient from heaven."

No, I am not unaware of the chemical dependence one develops for this and any other type of drug abuse, but it all has as its basis—an act of sin. And sin has its consequences, all the time, everytime!

Finally, the old-time religion includes a belief that:

A Person Can Be Eternally Saved
Through the Blood of Jesus Christ

Haven't you wondered what's so great about the blood of Christ? "Without the shedding of blood there is no remission of sin" (Heb. 9:22). The song goes, "What can wash away my sin? Nothing but the blood of Jesus. What can make me whole again? Nothing but the blood of Jesus."

The blood of Jesus Christ that flowed through His veins was the most precious commodity this world has ever known or will ever know. That blood was and is the very life of God's only begotten Son.

Personally, what's the most precious thing in the world to you? Not your car, not your house, not your business, not your cabin on the lake, your golf clubs, or your fancy appliances. What's the most precious thing to you or me? The blood that flows in our veins? Why? Without that blood there is no life. "The life of the flesh is in the blood" (Lev. 17:11).

One day Adam and Eve did the most terrible act that could ever be done. There is nothing more grotesque than sin. They indulged in sin, and on the spectrum of good and evil, on the gamut of right and wrong, mankind stooped to the lowest end of evil and sinned against God. The only way that the balance, called forgiveness, could ensue is that Jesus gave the most precious thing in all the universe. Peter said, "Your salvation was bought not with silver or gold, which is corruptible, but with the precious blood of Jesus Christ" (1 Pet. 1:18-19).

Jesus Christ shed His blood on Calvary that you and I might be saved. Romans 6:23 states: "For the wages of sin is death, but the gift of God is eternal life through Jesus Christ our Lord." Romans 10:9 declares: "That if thou shalt confess with thy mouth the Lord Jesus and shalt believe in thine heart that God hath raised him from the dead, thou shalt be saved." Romans 10:13 says: "For whosoever [means all of us] shall call upon the name of the Lord shall be saved." That is the light, the hope that shines into a darkened world.

I once read a fascinating story of a lighthouse on the eastern shore of New York state. The lighthouse was mammoth, 200 feet high in the air. The powerful beam emanating from the lighthouse was covered with a glass that was over two inches thick.

One morning the people who cared for the lighthouse came down and walked along the ground. There beneath the great structure, they found over a hundred birds of all kinds lying dead on the ground. What had happened was this: the night before, a dense fog had enshrouded the area, and it was so thick that the birds had lost their direction. In panic, they flew toward the light of the lighthouse, and they literally crushed themselves to death, beating against that light.

I think of those who are without Jesus, rejecting Him, beating their souls to death against the glowing light of the Gospel.

If that is the story of your life it doesn't have to be like that. Jesus calls, "Come unto me, all ye that labour and are heavy laden and I will give you rest. Take my yoke upon you, and learn of me; for I am meek and lowly in heart: and ye shall find rest unto your souls. For my yoke is easy, and my burden is light" (Matt. 11:28-30). Why not come to Jesus? Simply come and let Him wash your sins away, giving you abundant life here on earth and eternal life throughout the ages to come. He shed His blood that we might live and have abundant life forever. That's religion at its best—in personal relationship with Jesus Christ as Savior and Lord.

11

What Every Church Should Be Known For

We give thanks to God and the Father of our Lord Jesus Christ, praying always for you, Since we heard of your faith in Christ Jesus, and of the love which ye have to all the saints. For the hope which is laid up for you in heaven, whereof ye heard before in the word of the truth of the gospel; Which is come unto you, as it is in all the world; and bringeth forth fruit, as it doth also in you, since the day ye heard of it, and knew the grace of God in truth (Col. 1:3-6).

As Paul opens the Book of Colossians, he writes to a church he has never attended. "My heart rejoices that I have heard good things about you." Paul had heard of the church's excellent reputation.

Every church should ask itself, "What is our reputation—among other churches and also in the eyes of a lost world?"

You may counter with, "Reputations really don't matter. We don't really care what anybody thinks about us." But you should. Why? Because like the old timers used to remark, "Our reputations precede us." You are, to the person who does not know you, what your reputation is. Your church is, to the person who does not actually know it, what its reputation is.

As Christians, we should walk circumspectly (looking all around) before God and before the world, clean, pure, and with holy lives. Why? That we might have a reputation that honors God.

The Colossian church was most pleasing to the Apostle Paul. It wasn't a church like Corinth where a constant turmoil was going on. Corinth was filled with a party spirit. Some were for Paul, some for Peter (Cephas), some for Apollos, and some claimed to have an exclusive hold onto the Lord Jesus Himself! In the Corinthian church there was controversy over the gifts of the Spirit, and gluttony was even going on at the Lord's Supper. Added to that, one of the leaders in the church was having an incestuous affair with his mother. Talk about being up to their necks in problems! But that was not the case with the church at Colosse. It wasn't a church like several of the others where Paul had to deal with such problems. In fact, he commended the Colossians with, "I have heard nothing but good about you."

Can that be said of your church? Can that be said of its members? Can that be said of you? Hopefully it can. But regardless it can be, and Paul tells us how.

Notice first of all in Colossians 1:3-4, Paul wrote that:

We Should Be a Church Known for Our Faith

Listen to what he says, "We give thanks to God and the Father of our Lord Jesus Christ, praying always for you, Since we heard of your faith in Christ Jesus, and of the love which ye have to all the saints . . ." He is thanking God for their being strong in the faith. Their faith was important because it was placed in Jesus.

Their faith was not centered on programs, personalities, politics, or popularity. The Colossians were firmly rooted in the Lord Jesus. At Caesarea Philippi, Jesus inquired of His disciples, "Whom do men say that I the Son of man am?" Some said,

"You're John the Baptist." Others guessed he was Elijah and still others, Jeremiah.

Jesus pressed the question, "Really, whom do you say I am?"

Peter finally answered. "Thou art the Christ, the Son of the living God!"

Jesus commended Peter, "Blessed art thou, Simon Barjona: for flesh and blood hath not revealed it unto thee, but my Father which is in heaven. And I say also unto thee, That thou art Peter, and upon this rock I will build my church; and the gates of hell shall not prevail against it" (Matt. 16:17-18).

That is invigorating to me. No matter what comes against the church, the very gates of hell cannot prevail (stand against it), since the church is founded upon Jesus Christ. If you build your church on politics, personalities, programs, properties, or percentages, or anything else outside of Jesus Christ, there is no guarantee it will stand.

That kind of church may discover itself deep in trouble. When the difficult, tough times arise, that church may well crumble and fall—but oh, how a church, a family, and an individual's life, once it is founded upon Jesus Christ, has power. It has a firm foundation which all the tempestuous waves and knotty problems of life cannot topple.

> How firm a foundation, ye saints of the Lord,
> Is laid for your faith in His excellent Word!
> What more can He say than to you He hath said,
> To you who for refuge to Jesus have fled?
> . . . .
> "The soul that on Jesus hath leaned for repose
> I will not, I will not desert to his foes;
> That soul, though all hell should endeavor to shake,
> I'll never, no never, no never forsake!"
>
> —John Rippon

God's infallible Word speaks of this solid, sure foundation.

"Other foundation can no man lay than that which is laid, which is Jesus Christ" (1 Cor. 3:11).

He Is the Supreme Foundation

Jesus is our guarantee of success. As believers in Him, we cannot fail. If we follow the principles of the Bible, we will celebrate victory through Christ. As the Lord prepared His disciples before His arrest and crucifixion, He promised:

> These things I have spoken to you, that in Me you may have peace. In the world you have tribulation, but take courage; I have overcome the world (John 16:32, NASB).

We are not only overcomers, but we have already overcome the world, and Jesus has granted that surety. Oh, how I rejoice in that! You and I have already overcome the world. How? Through our all-sufficient Lord and Savior Jesus Christ. He is our Foundation, our Strength, our Guarantee of success.

In the edgy business world, where there is the constant threat of recession or depression, there is no guarantee of success. You could work day and night, follow every business principle there is, and still lose all you have. In fact, you can "bomb" financially in a matter of minutes. But that's not how it is with the Word of God. If you follow its precepts and principles, you are assured success. How? Because God Himself has given us these principles.

He Assures Growth in the Church

How? Through maturity. The church becomes mature when it stays close to Jesus. My grandmother used to counsel, "You are who you run with." She meant you become like the people you hang around. When I was a boy, I had a friend who wasn't the most admirable one a guy could have. This fellow had a bad habit of spitting. He spat constantly and everywhere.

One day I was out in the yard. The spitter had already gone home. Guess what I was doing. Spitting in the yard. I had no idea I was doing it. It had become second nature. My mother looked out and saw me.

She came out, grabbed me by the shoulders, and asked, "Richard, what are you doing?"

"I dunno" was my inane answer.

She chided me, "You're spitting. Ugh, that's terrible. It's ugly, filthy, nasty. You won't be a gentleman if you spit."

Then she summed it up, "I know where you got that habit. You got that from ——— . You're going to have to stop hanging around him!"

I had developed the nasty characteristic of spitting from my buddy. I had, by association, become like him, and that was not good.

Conversely, on the other end of the spectrum, is Jesus. I mean, the closer you associate with Him, the more you become like Him. Then you begin to mature in the faith. How I love the Apostle John's promise, "Beloved, now we are the sons of God, and it doth not yet appear what we shall be, but we know that when we shall see him, we shall be like him, for we shall see him as he is" (1 John 3:2). Isn't that fantastic? We shall be like Him. We will become more and more like Him and assume His characteristics.

When a church remains close to Jesus, that church starts reminding people of Jesus.

That Church Becomes Mature in Faith

The pastor doesn't have to beg, "Look, folks, you ought to tithe. You must give God His tithe, because the church is in need. The world has to hear of Jesus Christ. So please give at least the tithe, and an offering above that." But the mature church, by and large, would be tithing, so that begging wouldn't be essential.

The minister of music won't have to plead for the singers and instrumentalists to fill their places on the Lord's Day. A mark of spiritual maturity is volunteering to serve the Lord without waiting to be begged. What's going to guarantee that sort of maturity? No programs, no personalities. What will do it is that closeness, that spiritual intimacy with Jesus Christ, when a church has built a firm foundation upon Him, unlike any other foundation that can be laid. Closeness to Jesus guarantees growth in maturity.

He Also Guarantees Growth in Stability

What do I imply? The closer you come to Christ, the more you understand the strength of the faith, and the more you understand what Bible doctrines are all about. The Bible states in Ephesians 4:14, "As a result, we are no longer to be children, tossed here and there by waves, and carried about by every wind of doctrine, by the trickery of men, by craftiness in deceitful scheming" (NASB).

One of the problems in the church today, as it was then, is that people are often tossed about with every new teaching that comes along. Always bear this in mind: *the Bible is the complete revelation*. You cannot take from it or add to it (see Rev. 22:18-19). The problem with most of us is we haven't learned to live this revelation.

When you have all the Bible lived in perfection, then you can move onto another revelation. And that will never be! You see, a mature church teaches the Word of God. It teaches its children, its teenagers, its adults, its senior adults the Word of God, that they might mature in the faith, that they might "grow in grace and in the knowledge of our Lord and Saviour Jesus Christ" (1 Pet. 3:18).

When these little children grow up and go off to high school, college, and graduate school, and they are bombarded by some atheistic professor, they won't have time to question their faith and think, *Maybe Mom and Dad weren't right. Maybe my pastor wasn't right.*

The parents won't have to sit at home and worry, *I wonder if Johnny or Susie are going to have trouble with their faith while they're in college or the seminary.* No, because they will have been rooted and grounded in the Word of God. When their faith is challenged in the classroom, they will open the Bible and become a witness to all those hungry souls sitting in that classroom or walking around the campus. How does that happen? It occurs when you love Jesus and are near to His Word.

Jesus guarantees growth in maturity, in spirit, and in stability. But:

He Also Guarantees Growth Numerically

In other words, a church near to Jesus and His heart is going to grow. That church sees people coming down the aisles to be saved; the baptismal waters are stirred; evangelistic activity is always going on. People are continually joining the fellowship. I learned long ago in basic biology that whatever you starve, dies. That which you feed, grows. A church that is growing—alive—must be fed with new converts. People must be born again. Lives must be eternally changed, and that metamorphosis is seen by growth in numbers as people are born into the kingdom of God.

Please understand that numbers represent people, and people are what the church is all about—people being saved, being baptized, being added to the church membership, those people joining Bible study. We count them. Why? Because that helps us understand (it's a thermostat) what's going on in the life of the church.

Some have argued with me, "You're too concerned about numbers." We believers can't be too concerned about numbers. Why? Because numbers in the church represent people, and people are souls for whom Christ died. That's what the mission of the church is all about, isn't it? Precious souls.

I heard of a church in another city that called a new pastor. The church was a great historic church, large in numbers. Six months after the new preacher started in that pastorate, in the pulpit one Sunday morning he announced, "Folks, things around here are not as spiritual as they need to be, so we're going to stop counting people in Sunday School, in the choir, in our worship services, and the like."

What happened was: the church had begun to die under that man's ministry, and he didn't want the people to be aware of it. Today that once-great church is almost dead. It had been a historic church that many wonderful pastors and laity had worked for years and years to grow into a mighty, soul-winning church for God, but they stopped counting numbers.

You might comment, "Dr. Lee, are numbers what it's about so a church might boast and brag on the flesh?" Oh, not at all! But it surely helps you to keep a record of what you're doing or not doing for the kingdom of God.

Paul wrote to the Colossians: "I see you have a faith that is rooted and grounded in Jesus Christ." And that faith produced growth.

Paul also wrote that:

They Were Known for Their Love

Verse 4 goes: ". . . and of the love which ye have for all the saints." *Love*. There have been thousands of songs about love. "What the world needs now is love, sweet love." "Love makes the world go round." "Hip, hip, hooray for love, who was ever too blasé for love?"

But there is no love to compare with the love of Jesus Christ. Paul, empowered by the Holy Spirit, wrote the classic in 1 Corinthians 13: "Though I speak with the tongues of men and of angels and have not charity [love], I am become as sounding brass, or a tinkling cymbal" (1 Cor. 13:1). In other words, without genuine love from Jesus, we are nothing but a discordant noise. All we do must be motivated by Jesus' love. Jesus linked His love with our discipleship. "By this shall all men know that ye are my disciples, if ye have love one for another" (John 13:35).

Why do we as believers do what we do? Why do we meet in a place of worship? Why do we assemble ourselves in the name of Jesus? Ours is a voluntary army. No one can make us come. And I hope the reason you show up is because you love Jesus and you love one another. Every boy and girl, every teenager, every mom and dad, every grandmother and grandfather in the church should know they are loved and cherished.

Several weeks ago I visited a section of our city that many people would not want to enter. I dropped in on a family that had attended our church and shown an interest in joining. When I arrived at their home, it was evident they had not been especially blessed with the material things of life. After being invited in, I pulled up a chair to the table where the people were eating.

As I looked across the table to the little lady of the home, she said, "Pastor Lee, there's one thing I felt about Rehoboth. I felt loved. I have been to many churches, but I've never felt the love I felt there." If she could have written me out a check for $100,000 and handed it to me, it wouldn't have meant as much as those words. Why? Because Jesus didn't teach, "This is the way the world will know you're my disciples—that you preach good sermons, that you sing splendid music, that you erect giant buildings, that you have a huge budget." Instead, Jesus made it crystal clear: "This is the way people will know you're My disciples, because you love one another." Let love, sincere love out of a godly heart, constantly permeate your lives and the ministry of your church fellowship.

Notice another dominant truth. In verse 5:

They Were Known for Their Hope

"For the hope which is laid up in heaven whereof ye heard before in the truth of the gospel." *Hope*. What a word of consolation and encouragement! What does "hope" in the Bible mean? In the Greek, the word is *elpis*. It's not merely a "hope-so" attitude. "Hope" biblically is not just saying, "Oh, I *hope* that comes to pass."

Hope biblically is a confident prior expectation of that which will be ultimately fulfilled. It is fraught with excitement. It's exclaiming, "I know something great is going to happen!" You may not know exactly when, but you know—you have that hope—based upon Jesus Christ in the Word of God that you can expect things to happen.

That should be the main attitude of every worship service and activity of the church. The mind-set of the whole church itself should be a prior expectation that something good is about to happen for the glory of God. When we enter our church buildings, our hope should be that lives are going to be changed at the invitation, that saints are going to be baptized, that the church is going to be added to, and you're going to leave the services, go out, and make a difference in the world day by day. There is the expectation. There is the joyful hope.

That's what the joy of Jesus is all about—knowing we can serve Him and count not only in the church, but in the world, and we can make the world different because of the dynamic of God that rests within us through the power of His Holy Spirit. There is the hope, a positive expectation. It's not an old, negative, draggy face and attitude that moans, "It's so hard serving Jesus. Just pray I'll make it through." If that is your attitude, you don't have the same Jesus the Bible talks about.

Jesus explained, "I am come that they might have life, and that they might have it more abundantly" (John 10:10). That is joy, that is peace, that is contentment, that is challenge, that is hope, that is a positive attitude, not based on some "pop" psychological frenzy, but an expectant, victorious attitude thriving upon the Word of the living God.

I like the story of the little boy who invited his daddy to a soft-ball game. It was the top of the first inning, and the little fellow went into the outfield to play. The opposing team scored five runs, ten runs, fifteen runs, twenty-five runs. Finally, the opposing team made three outs, and the little boy, worn out from chasing the ball all over the outfield, sat down on the bench beside his daddy. He was smiling from ear to ear. Elation was written all over him.

His daddy inquired, "Son, how can you be so excited? How can you possibly smile when you're losing 25 to 0 in the first inning?"

The fellow instantly replied, "Oh, Daddy, I'm smiling because we haven't come to bat yet!" Now there's hope!

That's how it is. Satan, the enemy, the accuser, may try to get you down. He wants to discourage you and try to trample you underfoot. He will do all he can to oppress you, but he doesn't seem to know you haven't gone to bat yet! There is a hope, a steadfast expectation, that God's victory is near in that situation—that God's victory will not only see you through, He'll see you through every single time. Paul uplifted the Colossians with: "I believe in you. I love you. I understand you. My heart goes out to you. I'm excited about you because of your faith, your love, your hope, your expectation."

But notice another facet. He also proclaimed:

They Were Known for Bearing Fruit

Listen to verse 6, "Which has come unto you as it is in all the world, and bringeth forth fruit as it does also in you since the day ye heard of it." What's that? The Gospel. It bears fruit since the day you heard of it. The end result is this: after all the smoke has cleared and all the excuses have played out, the bottom line is how many souls have been won, how many lives have been changed, and how much fruit you are bearing for the kingdom of God.

In Mark 11:12-21 we read of Jesus walking down the road in the vicinity of Bethany. In the distance, "afar off," he spied a beautiful fig tree. He and His disciples were hungry. I can imagine that as Jesus approached the fig tree He began to think to Himself, *Oh, those luscious figs! How good they will taste — how juicy and nourishing.*

But when Christ reached the fig tree, lifted up the lovely leaves, and tried to find the figs, there were none. The leaves were there, green and lush, but there were no figs on the tree!

Christ spoke to the tree, "No man eat the fruit of thee hereafter for ever" (v. 14). They returned the following morning, and "the fig tree dried up from the roots" (v. 20). Why? Not because it wasn't gorgeous, not because it wasn't green, but because it bore no figs. I wonder today, in our churches and personal lives, how we look in balance with the fruit we bear. You see, only by bearing fruit will we ever be able to please Jesus.

I read about General William Booth, founder of the Salvation Army. He was a remarkable man. He was a man's man, and he used to march his Salvation Army band down the streets of London. They would play their brass instruments and beat their bass drums. Crowds would emerge from office buildings, houses, and shops, and follow the procession down the street. When they reached the end of the street, General Booth would stand and preach to the people. The band had gathered them together, and then he could preach to the crowds and see souls won to Christ.

One day the religious hierarchy of the city became upset. The high muckety muck of the religious world thought to themselves, *This is crude. Look at this man preaching on the streets.* So the religious leaders connived together and asked, "Who's going to stop Booth from doing this? He's embarrassing all the religious people of London."

One man volunteered and confronted Booth with: "Mr.

Booth, you are an embarrassment to the preachers of this community. You see, you play those infernal instruments and preach on the street corner to everybody. We want you to stop. After all, when we hear those bass drums pass our churches, all we can hear in our offices; is 'boom, boom, boom, boom.' Mr. Booth, don't you think that's offensive? 'Boom, boom, boom, boom, boom, boom'?"

Booth smiled and replied, "Do you know what, Sir? I don't hear those drums saying, 'Boom, boom, boom, boom.' When those bass drums begin to beat, all I hear are those words, 'Fetch them, fetch them, fetch them, fetch them.'"

I wonder. What is the beat of your heart? Is the beat of your heart, "What's in it for me?" Is the beat of your heart, "What can I gain from Christ?" Or is the beat of your heart, "Fetch them, fetch them, fetch them to a saving knowledge of Jesus"?

A great church is one with a great faith, a great love, a great hope, and a great fruit for the kingdom of God and for the cause of Christ. Is that your church?

12

How to Have a Brand-new Church

Now in the twenty and fourth day of this month the children of Israel were assembled with fasting, and with sackclothes, and earth upon them. And the seed of Israel separated themselves from all strangers, and stood and confessed their sins, and the iniquities of their fathers. And they stood up in their place, and read in the book the law of the Lord their God one fourth part of the day; and another fourth part they confessed, and worshipped the Lord their God. Then stood up upon the stairs of the Levites, Jeshua, and Bani, Kadmiel, Sherebiah, Bunni, Sheribiah, Bani, and Chenani, and cried with a loud voice unto the Lord their God (Neh. 9:1-4).

From the Book of Nehemiah, we are taught how we can have a "brand-new church," even if our particular church has existed *per se* for decades. The historical setting behind the Book of Nehemiah was, of course, Nehemiah's return from Shushan, the capital of the Medo-Persian Empire, to the Holy City of Jerusalem, where he was to engineer the rebuilding of the walls.

As Bible students are aware, the Jews were under the Babylonian Captivity for seventy years, and then God allowed the

Medes and Persians to invade and conquer Babylonia and its capital city, Babylon (see Dan. 5), in approximately 538 B.C.

Nehemiah and a remnant of his fellow Jews returned to Jerusalem. With a brand-new future in front of them, they were excited. God was instituting a brand-new people. The rebuilding of the walls of Jerusalem, the reemphasis on the laws and commandments of God, and the Word of God are all found in the Book of Nehemiah.

It is manifestly clear in Nehemiah that God is showing not only the rebuilding of the walls of the city, not only the reinstitution of His people in their homeland, Jerusalem, but He was also pointing to certain truths we must understand even today.

We desire God to look upon us and to breathe upon us with a new vision because we must have that new vision. The Bible says, "Where there is no vision, the people perish" (Prov. 29:18). What does that mean? That means if a person does not have a vision in his life, he is going to stagnate spiritually and atrophy. That applies to your *personal Christian life*. You must have a vision, a spiritual perspective, in your life for the Lord. It applies to your *family, spiritually*. You must have a vision in your family, or your family will have no sense of God-driven direction.

It also applies to the corporate body of the church. The church must have a vision of the potential for Christ which lies before it. When that vision becomes ingrained in the hearts of God's people, that church is in for a brand-new day.

Here we will look into the Book of Nehemiah and see the plan of God for any church to enter into such a day.

Here God tells them that:

They Must Begin with an Examination
of Their Hearts

In every part of our Christian walk, the very basis of that life is examination. That's why the Bible teaches that we should examine ourselves to be sure we are in the faith.

It's not enough merely to join together in fellowship. It's not enough just to listen attentively to the preacher. It's not enough to become excited when we hear the choir sing. Yes, those worship experiences are wonderful; they are exciting, glad, and joyful times. But the only way we can bring about a change in the Christian life is not by listening to a preacher and shouting "Amen," or listening to the music and applauding. Those manifestations don't bring about a change. The genuine change comes when you begin to examine your life and see how you stack up to Jesus Christ and the Holy Scriptures.

We should thoroughly look at our lives. That's why the Bible urges us to examine ourselves to make sure we are in the faith, that we are depending totally and wholly on the Lord—not our neighbor, not our friend, not our husband or wife. Examine *yourself.* I want to share with you how the Jews examined themselves. Nehemiah 9:1 says:

They Were Assembled with Fasting and Sackclothes, and Earth Was Upon Them

The people of God were clad in sackcloth, fasting before God with the earth upon them. They were humbly laid out before God. They meant business. They were not playing pious, put-on games. They were truly repentant.

Recently I was talking with a fellow minister. He and I spent about forty-five minutes together. We were referring to our prayer lives and were touching on how the people in the Old Testament prayed before God. In most of the great times of repentance, people laid their faces on the ground before God. I mean, they literally laid themselves out before God—faces to the ground, noses and lips in the dust.

There is the picture we view here, the people humbling themselves before God with their faces in the dust before Him. Why would they go to that extreme? They were doing it to confess,

"We realize You are God, and we want to show You as we fast and as we dress ourselves in sackcloth, and as we cover ourselves with dirt, that we are humble before You, Oh God!"

The Bible makes it clear that God was pleased with that—because God's Word states that God loves a broken and contrite heart. "For Thou dost not delight in sacrifice, otherwise I would give it; Thou art not pleased with burnt offering. The sacrifices of God are a broken spirit; A broken and contrite heart, O God, Thou wilt not despise" (Ps. 52:16-17, NASB).

Want to know when revival is going to break out in the church? It's not going to come when you are erecting a new educational building or an impressive auditorium. There are empty, large church auditoriums all across the nation that will proclaim that patent fact today. It's not going to happen when a certain evangelist or preacher steps into the pulpit. Sometimes that has virtually nothing to do with revival. Evangelism? Yes. Revival? No.

Revival comes to a people when they humble themselves before God, when we see men and women at the altars who perhaps have not been there for twenty or thirty years. When a pastor's heart is broken in humility before God Almighty, when the church is filled with people who can no longer stand themselves in pride, for the lack of concern for souls, and not through the coercion of a preacher, but through the power of the Holy Spirit in conviction, when they are sobbing in repentance, and crying for the lost souls of dying men and women, boys and girls—that's what revival is all about!

Oh, that God would give us a heaven-sent revival! Oh, that He would rain revival and let it begin in me. We can have a new church, but the first step is not a new budget, not a new building, not a new attendance in Sunday School, not a new member in worship service, but in seriously humbling ourselves before God.

Notice also in verse 2, that they not only examined themselves and humbled themselves before God, but:

They Separated Themselves Unto God

Verse 2: "And the seed of Israel separated themselves from all strangers." They drew aside to worship. They were dead serious about it. They went alone with God to worship.

That's why we gather; that's why we set ourselves aside on Sunday and other times. Most folks could be many places. My own city, Atlanta, Georgia, is one of the most entertainment-filled sites (and sights) in the world. We have almost every major sport. There's always activity going on. You can eat in an opulent restaurant in this town every single night of your life and never go to the same place twice. That is the character of the city in which we live and minister! In many ways I am blessed to minister in such a metropolis. So when someone comes to our church, Rehoboth, they have done so because they chose to, not because it was the only place in town. I hope they have come for a specific purpose—the purpose of following Jesus and worshiping Him.

So I ask you, "Why don't we do what we came to do?" Why don't we worship like we came for that very reason? You may come back with, "What do you mean, Pastor Lee, worshiping like you came to worship?" I mean by putting aside the world and drawing alone with God.

How many times, as pastors preach, do they look out across the auditorium and see their church members, people who are polite and kind, and even have their eyes open on Sunday night? They may sit there and look at the preacher, attentively watching his every move, but they really are hardly aware he is there. Why? Their minds are somewhere else, maybe a thousand miles away. They are at Grandma's, a friend's home, out joy riding, or at work or school the following day. Young people are taking that final exam in their minds as they hear their pastor preach.

There are so many ploys Satan will concoct to rob us of worship. He will put every kind of errant thought in one's mind he possibly can. He will even have a choir member moving unnecessarily so you will want to focus on them. A person on the pew in front of you will do this or that, and you will feel compelled to watch them. A ten-year-old child will walk across the balcony, and heads will turn to monitor them. What is happening? Satan is trying to distract you from worshiping God.

When we gather together, we are supposed to separate ourselves unto worship. In other words:

We Must Shut Out the World

You need to determine, *I couldn't care less about the payments that need to be made tomorrow. I couldn't care less about work tomorrow. School is not on my mind. I'm not thinking about what I did before worship tonight. I'm not thinking where I'll go after worship tonight. I have come that I might separate myself from all the world, in the very house of God Himself, that I might worship the King of kings and Lord of lords.*

The Bible explains that they separated themselves. We must humble ourselves, shutting out all else. We must fix our minds and hearts upon what God is trying to do to us and for us in the worship service. Separated unto God.

But look at another fact:

They Confessed Their Sins

They confessed their own sins and the iniquities of their fathers (v. 2). When they came down to business, there was a sweeping confession. I do not mean they stood before a microphone and confessed their sins, but they were confessing their sins to God, nonetheless.

You ask, "What kind of sins?" All kinds, I am sure. But perhaps the most severe sin among church members today is they neglect their duty to Christ and His church. Solomon advised,

"Fear God, and keep his commandments: for this is the whole duty of man" (Eccl. 12:13). What is your life all about? It is serving God, obeying God, following God, and keeping His commandments. That's the whole duty of your life. Remember the instructions of Mary to the servants at the wedding feast in Cana of Galilee, "Whatsoever he [Jesus] saith unto you, do it" (John 2:5).

I heard an old-time preacher when I was a little boy. He spoke of the duty that believers have toward God. I still remember his message. First of all, he declared: *They Had a Duty to Attend God's House.* Hebrews 10:25 admonishes, "Forsaking not the assembling of yourselves together . . ." In other words, we have a duty, an obligation, to God's house to come and be together, worshiping together, praying together, serving together, filling the church pews as a personal and public testimony of our love for Christ and His church. Empty pews cry out. They mutely speak to the visitor in a church, "The people of this church are dedicated to God to a degree, but not wholly and totally."

Empty pews give a message to those who view them. People comment, "Well, preacher, we'll be there in spirit." I don't care if you're there in spirit. I want you there *in body.* We sing, "When the roll is called up yonder, I'll be there." That doesn't impress God. Why don't we sing, "When the roll is called in Sunday School next Sunday morning, I'll be there"? Now, that impresses God. I feel you're going to be there if you love Jesus. We have a duty to attend God's house, because it is our spiritual home.

Second, he spoke not only of the duty to attend our church, but: *We Have a Duty to Defend Our Church.* Are you aware that the church in America is standing against an onslaught by the federal government? Do you realize that right now in the halls of Congress there are politicians lobbying day in and day out for the taxation of the church? Sometimes if you go on a visit to Washington, I want you to enter the halls of the Senate and the House of Representatives.

You will see lobbyists, people who are paid to go around and try to induce your senator and/or congressman to vote for a certain issue. They do everything possible, legal and sometimes not so legal, to make your representatives vote in a certain manner. There are powerful gay and lesbian lobbies, a liquor lobby, many anti-church lobbies, including atheists and agnostics who are working to remove all reference to God from our nation—even campaigning against Nativity scenes during Christmas, and working overtime to remove all tax-exempt status from non-profit Christian churches and benevolence organizations. Our forefathers allowed these exemptions, realizing the power to levy taxes on churches and other religious, non-profit organizations is also the power to control, govern, and even destroy.

Perhaps you are sitting at home, eating your evening meal, thinking your senators and congressmen are actually representing the desires of their districts and their states. You feel your interests are their interests, and, in some cases that may well be true, but I challenge you to make a trip to Washington and see what's going on. Your eyes might well be opened. Professionally paid people are lobbying against many of our sacred values to your congressman and your senator at this moment. We have a divine duty to stand and vocally let it be known that no church should ever be subject to control by the government of the United States.

You ask, "Why?" Because this nation was founded for religious liberty, religious freedom to be able to worship as we please. And if we are not vigilant, by the turn of the century we may lose that freedom. It is our duty to defend the church of the Lord Jesus Christ.

Some of you may think, *Surely that's not true. You're exaggerating.* No, I'm not. Many simply have no idea of what is insidiously transpiring all around us in the United States today. Fifteen years ago, or thirty years ago, if I had commented, "One day they will not allow your children to pray in public schools," you would have protested, "Aw, don't tell me that. That's an impossibility in America." But what has happened to us today?

In many school systems it's OK to read dirty books and curse just so long as a kid is not praying or reading God's Book! Isn't that insidious—and ridiculous? In many schools, the Bible, important as it is in the history of the world and of literature, cannot even be referred to as literature. At the same time all kinds of blasphemous, uncouth books are being placed on recommended reading lists. Winston Churchill, considered by *Time* magazine the greatest person of the first half of the twentieth century, emphatically declared, "No person can call himself truly educated without a thoroughgoing knowledge of the Holy Bible."

If twenty-five years ago, I had preached, "One day we're going to have legalized, federally funded abortions of innocent, unborn children," you would have thought I was a radical and you would have paid me no attention. Yet, that is happening today. We had better understand it is our duty to defend what we believe in and to stand for the convictions of Bible-believing, Gospel-preaching churches.

Also: *We Have a Duty to Extend Our Church*. We must grow; we have to grow; we have no choice. Unless the churches of Jesus Christ grow and reach out, Christianity will fade and give in to other isms and religions, and that is happening all around us today. Mohammedan mosques are cropping up all over the nation, along with Hindu and Buddhist temples. Every kind of false cult and religion is spreading like a scourge when we have the glorious Gospel of Jesus Christ and fail to share it. In addition, there are literally hundreds of so-called "Christian" cults flourishing, cults which are usually easy to spot because they water down the fundamentals of the historic Christian faith like the virgin birth of Christ, His Deity, His substitutionary death on the cross, salvation by grace through faith, His burial, His resurrection from the grave, His ascension, His coming again, and other major doctrines which center around Christ's Deity and shed blood.

If a church ever stops growing because of its pastor, it ought to call another pastor. If a church ever ceases to grow because of its staff, it ought to seek another staff. If a church ever ceases to grow because of its deacons, elders, or Sunday School teachers, new deacons, elders, and teachers are called for. The very purpose of the church is to grow, not that they might record on their bulletin a certain number in Sunday School. If that is your feeling, you are wrong—not that they might put a big number on their church letter, or to brag there are so many in their church. The church must grow because growth is an outward, visible indication that souls are being won to Christ. That is why.

Those we see coming for salvation, baptism, and church membership are visible evidences that the church is alive. If they ever stop coming, it means the church is dead. I have been to churches all over this country. I spent years as an evangelist traveling from one church to the other, week after week, night after night. People would remark, "Preacher, we have such a wonderful church, with all these missionary organizations." I would ask, "How many souls have you won?"

They would reply, "Well, we don't do that. We just talk about missions, and let things take care of themselves. We have this wonderful witnessing program we go to twice a year."

Then I ask, "How many did you baptize last year?" They can't even tell you! That's terrible.

We can have all the trappings and look good, but if people are not being put into the water and being baptized, if they're not coming to the altar to rededicate their lives, to be saved, or to come for church membership, your church is flat dead! You cannot allow that to happen because the church doesn't belong to us—it belongs to the Lord Jesus. Jesus forcefully stressed, "Go ye into all the world and preach the gospel to every creature" (Mark 16:15). We must extend the church at all costs.

Last of all: *We Must Commend the Church*. What does that mean? It means to "talk it up." It means to be proud, in the right way, about what God has done for your church. Share the good news. Go to work and brag on Jesus and His church. "You wouldn't believe the music we had at church last Sunday. It was fantastic! And the preaching was terrific too!" Commend the church. If you can't commend your church, maybe the Lord is either leading you to help make it commendable or pointing you toward another church.

Talk up the church. It's *your* church home. Enjoy it. Commend it. That is your duty in Christ. So what did the children of Israel do? They examined themselves.

Second:

They Had a Consideration of Their God

They began to consider the blessings of their God. In Nehemiah 9:5-28, there are four ways they remembered God.

In verses 19-21, *they remembered the provisions of God.*
In verses 22-23, *they remembered the promises of God.*
In verses 24-25, *they remembered the power of God.*
In verses 26-28, *they remembered the patience of God.*

In other words, they set themselves to remembering how good God had been.

They remembered His provisions, His promises, His power, and His patience with them. We must rejoice about how good God has been to us. I have learned in my personal life that the more I thank God, the more He readily gives to me. Thank Him all day and all night. Consider constantly what He has done for us.

Third:

They Determined Their Future

They set in their minds certain things they were going to do for their future. Verse 38, "And because of all this we make a sure covenant, and write it; and our princes, Levites and priests seal unto it." Here is what they did. They determined that they, the people of Israel, were going to do certain things, and they were going to write those things down so God would have a record of them. Now, of course, God knew. He knows everything. Has it ever occurred to you that nothing has ever escaped God? Why? He knows all! Writing the covenant down was more important for the Israelites than it was for God. In the Garden of Eden, God called out, "Adam, where art thou?" You know good and well that the all-seeing, all-knowing God knew where Adam was. The point is that He wanted *Adam* to know where Adam was! And God wanted the people to remember the covenant which was written down and signed by the leaders of the Israelites. They made a covenant with God that they were going to follow certain actions.

Every year in our church we have a budget subscription time. We send out pledge cards. One year I had a person write on his pledge card, "Sorry, I do not believe in pledging." I wonder where they heard that. They may have had a cantankerous daddy who never gave anything, and they thought that since their daddy didn't pledge, they would follow his rebellious lineage and do the same.

It is biblical to pledge in writing, not only verbally, but to pledge unto God. You need to sign a covenant with God. What did the text indicate? They were going to write it down and seal it unto God. There is nothing more apropos in an evangelical church than written, signed commitments, according to the Word of God. Those leaders signed those documents as an unashamed testimony. They were publically and openly dedicating themselves.

What is the gist of a pledge? A written pledge says, "God, I'm not going to be wishy-washy. God, I'm not going to be maybe this or maybe that. God, I want You to know that by faith in You I'm going to do precisely what I write down to do for You." That is a commitment unto God.

Suppose some young man who was about to be married remarked to his fiancee, "We're going to get married, but I don't want to sign any kind of wedding certificate or license. Let's just not have anything written down about it." Of course, millions of couples are "living together" in sin without commitment, and such is an abomination. Do you think your wife would have married you with that kind of commitment? I hope she wouldn't have. Why? Because marriage is a covenant, and God is in the covenant business. If He wrote His Word for us, the least we can do is to make a firm commitment to Him.

They had determined several matters. Number one: *faithfulness*. Note Nehemiah 10:29. They promised to "observe and do all the commandments of God." Not only a few, but *all* the commandments of God. They determined they were going to follow God, regardless, no matter what it cost them. Have you made that determination?

Second, *they made a determination concerning their families*. Look with me at verse 30. Here they promised to do nothing with their families other than to bring glory to God. They pledged, "God, we're going to give You obedience. We're going to obey You, and we're also going to give You our families. We're going to give You our children, our wives, our husbands. We're going to dedicate our entire families to You."

Last, *they made a determination in their finances*. In chapter 10:37, they determined to "bring the firstfruits of our dough and offerings to the chambers of the house of our God, and tithes unto the Levites." They were going to carry tithes into the house of the Lord for use in God's service.

They were saying, "We will write it down that we will bring the firstfruits unto God." And God will move when any church members come to the place that they are willing to humble themselves before God and examine their hearts, plainly and honestly, and pray, "God, if you find pride in our lives, crush it. If you find hardened hearts, plow them up. Do whatever you need to do in and to us to bring us back close to You."

When I was 19 years old I was preaching in Garland, Texas, in a little church that would seat 75 or 80 people. I had recently married Judy, and we drove there for the services. It was summertime, and there was no air-conditioning in the building. But the church had the windows open and the old-fashioned funeral home fans. People were fanning frantically all across the auditorium.

I noticed a Mexican-Indian man who came in and sat down in back. I continued to preach, and as I extended the invitation, he moved to the front and knelt at the altar. All of a sudden, he did something strange—he laid out across the altar. I had no idea what he was doing. I had never seen a soul do that. He had a hobo-type package with him, and he also laid that out beside him. He stretched out full length.

I tried to speak with the man, but he spoke Spanish, and I couldn't talk with him. I asked the pastor, who did speak Spanish, to go down and ask what the man meant. The pastor whispered into the fellow's ear. The man spoke to him, and the preacher came back to the platform and announced, "The man said you told him in your sermon if he wanted to know Jesus to come lay his all on the altar. That's all he has, and he's laying it all on the altar."

Oh, how desperately we need to do that. How we, who have been abundantly blessed, need to bring our houses and our cars, our pocketbooks and our children, our pride and our popularity—all of those—and lay them on the altar before God. Merely lay it out, because Jesus taught that's the only way we can come to Him. We must come and make Him Lord, because if Jesus is not Lord of all, He's not Lord at all! Bring your all to the altar, as a person, as a church, making a firm commitment to personal revival, whatever the cost, and you can expect the power of God upon your life and your "brand-new" church.

Part IV

Lord, Send Revival

. . . in Our Nation

13

What's Happened to America?

And Rehoboam the son of Solomon reigned in Judah. Rehoboam was forty and one years old when he began to reign, and he reigned seventeen years in Jerusalem, the city which the Lord did choose out of all the tribes of Israel, to put his name there. And his mother's name was Naamah an Ammonitess.

And Judah did evil in the sight of the Lord, and they provoked him to jealousy with their sins which they had committed, above all that their fathers had done.

For they also built them high places, and images, and groves, on every high hill, and under every green tree.

And there were also sodomites in the land: and they did according to all the abominations of the nations which the Lord cast out before the children of Israel.

And it came to pass in the fifth year of king Rehoboam, that Shishak king of Egypt came up against Jerusalem:

And he took away the treasures of the house of the Lord, and the treasures of the king's house; he even took away all: and he took away all the shields of gold which Solomon had made.

And king Rehoboam made in their stead brasen shields, and committed them unto the hands of the chief of the guard, which kept the door of the king's house (1 Kings 14:21-27).

Not long ago I sat beside a man on a bench in a major mall. We were watching the people walk by, and I noticed the older gentleman beside me picked up a paper. The headlines recorded where a man had murdered, in cold-blooded style, a young girl, but had been set free because of a technicality in the arrest.

As I looked at his saddened face, I heard him sigh under his breath, "Oh, God, what has happened to America?" I likewise asked myself that same question that day, and I've asked it hundreds of time since. "Oh, God, what has happened to America?" What's wrong with "the land of the free and the home of the brave"? Where is America headed?

What has happened to America when Congress allows a few radical deadbeats to burn her flag? What's wrong with America when an avowed, professing communist, whose friends are Arafat, Castro, and Kadafi, comes to this nation and we welcome him with a ticker-tape parade?

What's wrong with America when we allow unborn, living babies to be murdered in their mother's wombs in this, a land of freedom and democracy? What's wrong with America when we misappropriate taxpayers' money and give those monies to an exhibition of "art" so a degenerate can put together a collection tnof grss blasphemy and pornography financed by Americans?

What's wrong with America when our school boards dictate to our children, "You cannot pray in a school classroom."

Multitudes scoff and ask, "Who is God that we should obey Him?" What is the Judeo-Christian ethic? Our nation was founded on the Bible, yet secular humanists leave it out of our textbooks, and yet in the public schools our children are not being taught the true history of our nation. I ask you, "What is wrong with America?"

In spite of our overwhelming victory in the war against Iraq in the Persian Gulf, and the resurgence of nationalism, and the many references to prayer for our troops, it still seems evident, America is not unlike other nations. Other nations have risen up, as great and powerful as America is today, and those same nations disintegrated quickly. In 1 Kings 14 we read of such a nation, the nation of Judah, the Southern Kingdom of Israel. Judah was an armed, powerful nation, a proud nation of international strength and military might. Their king was Rehoboam. In this chapter we read of this powerful nation's collapse.

King Shishak of Egypt and his pagan armies stormed Jerusalem and pillaged the city, robbing the Temple of God of its treasures, even stealing the shields of gold Solomon had prepared for his royal guard. All the muscle-bound warriors of Judah, along with their sinful king, Rehoboam, actually stood by paralyzed and watched Jerusalem, the city of God, ravaged and laid bare.

Yes, the Bible spells out how Judah fell, but it also teaches how the United States is subject to falling today, how any nation that commits the sins the Bible warns about here will fall.

Notice with me that:

The Nation That Falls Is the Nation That Forgets the Fear of God

Verse 22, "And Judah did evil *in the sight* of the Lord" (author's italics). Judah had an agnostic, atheistic attitude that God didn't exist. The nation was insensitive to the Lord. Judah didn't ever think it would be judged by God. The nation that thinks there is no God and that it will never be judged by God, is one that has forgotten the fear of God.

I like to think about the old days when my dad used to teach me about "God-fearing" men. "You can trust that man, Son, because he's a God-fearing man," Dad would remind me. No longer can we do that, because we have a land that has really forgotten the fear of the Lord. America has bypassed the respect and knowledge of God. As a whole, we are living in infidelity, which either denies the existence of God or ignores Him.

Judah was flaunting its evil in the sight of God, saying, as it were, "We don't care whether or not there is a God, because we won't ever be judged, because after all, God doesn't exist anyway!"

As a young man I read about the German philosopher, Immanuel Kant, who affirmed, "I believe in the existence of God because of the heavens above and the conscience within my heart." Two premises: "I believe in God because of the heavens above." The psalmist sang, "The heavens declare the glory of God, and the firmament sheweth his handiwork." The heavens themselves prove God's existence.

Kant declared, "I just look up into the heavens, and I believe in God." Second, "I look in my heart and because of the conscience there I know God exists." But sin can blind the eyes to the heavens above, and it can numb the heart to the conscience so the eyes cannot *see* the witness of God in creation and the heart cannot *feel* the witness of God.

Only a fool would contend that God does not exist. "The fool hath said in his heart there is no God" (Ps. 14:1). That's why no "educated" person, not one, can possess a true education and not believe in God. Why? Plainly the Bible asserts that those who deny His existence are *fools*. If you gaze at the cosmos, at the solar system, and then look at the stratosphere and the clouds; watch the birds, the trees, the beasts of the field, and the fish of the sea; then study mankind, with our systems that pump and keep us alive, our eliminary, cardiovascular, and respiratory systems running throughout our bodies, and then our minds, and conclude, "Let's be rational, let's be intellectual—all this happened by accident," I'm going to look at you and shake my head at your sheer stupidity. Only an absolute dolt would believe all of this could have happened by accident.

Throughout the centuries the believers have been confronted by scoffers:

> That ye may be mindful of the words which were spoken before by the holy prophets, and of the commandment of the apostles of the Lord and Saviour: Knowing this first,

that there shall come in the last days scoffers walking after
their own lusts (2 Pet. 3:2-3).

I'm reminded of a cynical professor who was farsighted. He
carried his class to the museum, but he forgot his glasses. He was
walking down the hallway of the museum, pointing out the var-
ious portraits, when he came upon one particular piece. He
stood there staring at it. He called the class over and commented, "Look, this is the ugliest, most grotesque picture in all
the museum!"

One of the fellows in the class spoke up and responded with,
"Professor, you'd better be careful because that's a mirror, and
you're looking at yourself!"

When I hear people spout there is no God, when they claim
you can't believe there is a God, and there's no proof, I simply
reply, "I pity you because I know 'the fool hath said in his heart
there is no God,' and the god of this world, Satan, has blinded
the minds of those who believe not."

America will one day stand before God. You ask, "Why is
America not in judgment now?" Quite frankly, because we're living in the day of grace. God has stayed His hand of judgment,
but it will arrive one day. We can recognize it coming step by step
even now. One day judgment will fall; but God has given us the
dispensation of grace in which we are now living. The well-
known black preacher, Frederick G. Sampson, noted, "We're living in the passionate pause that proceeds a pronouncement of
penalty." A nation that falls is a nation that forgets the fear of
God.

In verse 23 we read:

The Nation That Falls Is the Nation That
Forsakes the Worship of God

"For they also built them high places and images and groves
on every high hill and under every green tree." What does he

have in mind? Idol worship. These people had forgotten God, and they had to have a god, so they went out and built images and groves on every high hill.

We live in what we consider an enlightened age. We are an "educated" society, and we consider people who worship stone and wooden images such as the pagans worship, and chide, "That's ridiculous. No one could ever worship a piece of stone or wood." When a man denies *the* God, he tries to find *some* god, because no man can be satisfied without God in his life. So they find some other god. The "New Age" movement, for instance, ultimately teaches that God is none other than man!

We're really not so enlightened, because we have our own gods, our own idols, today. You ask, "What do you mean, 'If I don't have the true and living God, I have some other god'?" Yes, you certainly do. What, or who, is your god? is the question. It may be the god of sports or music. It may be the god of the physical physique. You worship the body in which your spirit dwells. You may ask how to find the god you are worshiping. This is easily done. Where do you spend your time? What is the most important factor in your life? Is the most important thing in your life worshiping the true God?

When it comes time to attend God's house to worship, do you let anything in the world keep you from worshiping Him? Is that the highlight of your week? Do you look forward to the time you can arise in the morning and say, "This is the day which the Lord has made; Let us rejoice and be glad in it"? (Ps. 118:24, NASB) Do you come to Bible study and the worship service, and does your heart overflow?

Or, do you live for the ball game—the sport? Do you live for the social club to which you belong? Do you live for that job and ignore family and Christ for it? Your god is whatever you put before the true and living God.

These people had made a severe mistake. Our nation is making that dread mistake today, because we put everything the mind can comprehend before our God, and He is no longer the God of the hearts and minds of most Americans.

Also:

The Nation That Falls Is the Nation That Embraces the Abomination of Immorality

Verse 24: "And there were also Sodomites [homosexuals] in the land, and they did according to all the abominations of the nation which the Lord cast out before the children of Israel."

Now it requires little imagination today to understand the abomination God is talking about. If you don't understand the perverted sexual society we're living in, you don't understand where America is living today. Merely look at the ads and billboards. Glance at the magazines and newspapers and be repulsed by the filth in them. Turn on the television and look closely at what America is all about today. Notice the twisted sexual sin of this nation.

Many people today, even in the church, have become so accustomed to sexual perversion that they almost think it's normal. Dr. James Dobson observes, "Sometimes I think we're so blind to evil that we wouldn't recognize immorality if it were an elephant coming through the church door. Somebody in the church would say, 'Why, that's just a mouse with a gland problem,' and everybody would believe!"

People refer to it as "sexual preference." They call it "the new morality." But call it what you will, it is still *sin*, and we must look at what God judges. The Bible underscores that God judges sexual perversion. Why did He destroy Sodom and Gomorrah? Because He found homosexuality and lesbianism, and He destroyed those cities. I have heard that if God doesn't destroy America for its sexual sins, He will have to write a letter of apology to Sodom and Gomorrah.

What has our perversion cost America? We now have five sexual diseases for which there is no cure. They are the direct result of sexual promiscuity and perversion. And many of the churches are not speaking against it. Listen to the Scripture, "And there were also sodomites in the land who did according to all the abominations of the nations which the Lord cast out before them." That means such filth was in front of the children of Israel. The people of Judah knew better, but they were not standing against it. This sexual perversion was no doubt practiced by a small group, but God brought judgment upon the entire nation because of the sin of a few.

The sin was not simply the sin of the few, because those who did not speak against it also aligned with sin by their guilty silence. When we allow a few to ruin our nation with sexual perversion, and to contaminate our blood systems, hospitals, and society, and we sit within the four walls of the church, thinking all is well with America, that's not how it is. We are guilty, if we don't from the highways, the street corners, and the pulpits speak the truth of God to this nation.

Fourth:

The Nation That Falls Is the Nation That Stands Idle at the Loss of Her Values

Verses 25-26,

> And it came to pass in the fifth year of King Rehoboam that Shishak, king of Egypt, came up against Jerusalem, and he took away the treasures of the house of the Lord, and the treasures of the king's house. He even took away all the shields of gold which Solomon had made.

What happened? Shishak gloated as he saw a once-great nation now a pitiful nation. He sneered, "Men, let's go over and take it for ourselves." Shishak led his soldiers into Jerusalem, into the very temple of God, stripped it of all the sanctified objects Solomon had placed there to give honor and homage to God.

No doubt the Egyptians razed the land, robbing and pillaging whatever they desired.

One would think King Rehoboam would have been there with his sword, defending his nation. Where was he? No one could locate him. Where were the mighty men, the soldiers trained to defend the land? They were nowhere around. Where were the religious people? Where was the remnant which remained? You would think someone would have challenged, "Let's go to war and defend our nation. Let's stand against Shishak." But there were none. When Hitler's storm troopers marched into Paris in 1939, it was estimated that thousands of French soldiers were in bistros and bordellos.

Why was Judah defenseless? Because the nation had not only forgotten God, they had turned cowardly in the face of opposition. We live in a land founded on the Judeo-Christian ethic. No matter how humanists try to expunge truth from the history books, such is true. Anyone with one eye and "half sense" (like Granddaddy used to put it), with any knowledge whatsoever of true American history, realizes this nation was founded on a Judeo-Christian foundation. America is "one nation under God."

But let me ask you, where are the gallant men and women of God today? Where are the Christian soldiers? We used to sing the song,

> Onward Christian soldiers,
> Marching as to war.
> With the cross of Jesus
> Going on before.

Where are the gallant, believing soldiers who will cry out, "Enough. This shall not go on. We will not permit it at the voting booth and at the picket line. It shall not go on?" These outspoken Christians are few and far between.

What has happened? Many have traded in their armor. As Vance Havner expressed it, "They have traded in their helmets for a night cap." They have traded in their breastplates for a clerical collar. They have traded in their swords for a crutch. That is the situation in America today. But let us awaken and acknowledge what God has entrusted into our hand. I, for one, don't want to go through the experience of the righteous judgment of God Himself.

Last of all, notice:

The Nation That Falls Is the Nation That Ignores the Opportunity for Repentance and Forgiveness

The Jews simply were not interested in repentance, and they totally ignored God's forgiveness. You ask, "Is there hope for America?" Yes, there is. Where is there hope for America? Throughout the Word of God. You cannot talk about the hope for America unless you turn in your Bibles or in your memory to 2 Chronicles 7:14. That must be the most appropriate Scripture in the entire Bible for America today. It's the promise of God. Who is the promise to? His children. It's not to the lost man, the harlot or the drunkard, the robber or embezzler. God loves them, and I'm thankful He does. God cares about them, and I'm grateful He does. There's hope of forgiveness for them.

But God is speaking to His people in 2 Chronicles 7:14. He promises, "If my people [that's us] which are called by my name, shall humble themselves, and pray, and seek my face, and turn from their wicked ways; then will I hear from heaven, and will forgive their sin, and will heal their land." We live in a land that is in dire need of healing, and it can still be healed, thank God. Not only will God forgive our land, He will *forget* our sins.

Why? Because that's what He's made of. No matter who you are or what your situation is, God not only wants to heal and forgive you, He wants to forget your sin. It used to boggle my mind to think about the fact that God could not only forgive but also *forget* my sins. "As far as the east is from the west, so far has He removed our transgressions from us" (Ps. 103:12-13). Then one day I heard a pastor tell about a mother who had an unruly boy who had grown up in the church. He was in trouble all the time.

When the boy grew up, he was the worst teenager in the youth group. Then in early manhood, he was wicked and spent several years in prison. Later, when he left prison, he gave his life to Christ and became a deacon in his church. One day the pastor visited the boy's mother, and he asked, "Mrs. Smith, do you remember when Billy was such a bad boy? Do you remember all the trouble he gave us?"

As the pastor was talking to the mother about all the sins Billy had committed, she looked at him with sincere eyes and said, "Preacher, you're not talking about my boy, because Billy has always been a good boy." How did that mother forget the boy's past? A mother's love—the only way. She had forgotten all the trouble the boy had, because of a mother's love.

A far greater love is available today: the love of Jesus Christ. Jesus assures us, "I'll take every mistake, every time you've 'blown it,' and wash it in the sea of my forgetfulness, never to be heard from again."

God loves America, and America still has a chance if she will come back to God. On our coinage we stamp, "E pluribus unum" (from many, one). America is not merely a land of masses. America is a land of one and one and one, each person individually. As much as God loves America—and God can bring America to repentance, and God can help America: the heart and desire of God is to draw you unto Himself.

14

God Bless America

Blessed is the nation whose God is the Lord; and the people whom he hath chosen for his own inheritance (Ps. 32:12).

"God bless America!" Surely that is the prayer of all our hearts. If I were able to speak for all of my readers, I believe we all love America, our nation, our land.

America is a homeland given to us by God and continues only by the grace and mercy of Almighty God Himself. Sometimes we Americans don't really realize our Christian heritage. We do not recognize the nation God has given us and the faith of many that has kept our nation great.

I love what Francis Scott Key penned in the second verse of "The Star Spangled Banner." We seldom hear this verse.

> Oh thus be it ever
> when free men shall stand
> Between their loved homes,
> the war's desolation;
> Blest with vict'ry and peace,
> may the heav'n-rescued land
> Praise the pow'r that hath made

179

and preserved us a nation!
Then conquer we must,
When our cause it is just,
And this be our motto,
"In God is our trust!"
And the Star Spangled banner
in triumph shall wave
O'er the land of the free,
And the home of the brave.

Key was right when he wrote we should praise the power that has made us and preserved us a nation. But I ask you, "Is America praising the power that preserved us and made us a nation?" Are we Americans today in a position that God can bless us? Are we what we ought to be even after our leadership in the Persian Gulf War? Have we now become puffed up because of our high-tech military success? Have we given God the glory? In spite of a resurgent nationalism, is our nation closer to God?

I want to answer that by a simple understanding of America— where she began, where she is now, and where she can be in the future.

Think with me a moment about the history of America. Where did we come from? How did we begin?

Most of us who study history know that on August 3, 1492, Christopher Columbus knelt to take holy communion, then boarded his ship, and set out to sea in search of this new land. Later Columbus was to write in his personal diary the reason he went. It wasn't for economic gain. Why did he set forth to discover a new world? He penned in his diary, "I set forth. I was led of the Holy Spirit to carry the message of the Gospel to undiscovered lands."

The Puritans, when they arrived in America, were tired of the repression of the Church of England, and they realized the official church had backslidden from God. They fled to America, hoping to build one nation under God, that all the nations of the world would understand what would happen to a people under God and blessed by God.

We have read the charters. We also have seen the compacts of the early Americans, the Plymouth Charter, the Delaware Charter, the Maryland Charter, the Virginia Charter, and the Rhode Island Compact. Why and how were all these monumental agreements and statements of faith reached? All of them emphasized they were given to propogate the Gospel of Jesus Christ, to spread the Christian Gospel!

In 1776 the Continental Congress met, and it discussed the nation's freedom, signing the Declaration of Independence. The representative from Pennsylvania stood and protested, "I'm against any declaration of independence." But John Adams rebutted, "I must make a speech. I must have my say in this matter. Before God I believe this hour has come. I am for this declaration. It is my living sentiment, and by the blessing of God, it shall be my dying sentiment—independence now, and independence forever!"

The Declaration of Independence, the Revolution, the Constitution. And our vast land grew and grows today. But for a long time the tapestry of the United States has frayed. Somewhere in our history America has not become the nation our forefathers envisioned it to be.

America, once known as the most moral nation in the world, is now infamous for its immorality. In spite of our seeming benevolence, we are often hated and despised around the world. We are often called "The ugly Americans!" America, the nation once known to have the most stable economy, is now a debtor nation to the tune of almost four trillion dollars. A nation once known as "one nation under God," is now a nation which has not only turned its back on God, but often disavows the very existence of God Himself.

Still, God has blessed America. There has never been a nation in the history of the world blessed as we have been. Not one!

The blessings we are enjoying today could have come from no other hand than that of a sovereign, Almighty God.

Why has God blessed America? There are several reasons, I believe. First of all, I believe God has blessed America because:

America Was Founded Upon Christian Principles

Do you understand that? The atheists didn't found America. Neither did agnostics found America. Christians founded this nation upon the bedrock of God's Word. This nation was born upon God and upon Christian principles, by Christian people.

The late and great theologian-philosopher, Dr. Francis Schaeffer, noted, "If you study the Constitution and the Declaration of Independence (and all of us should study them) you'll see America was founded by people with 'a definite Christian consciousness.'" In other words, a Christian mind. As we see, throughout these charters we have already mentioned, there's not one charter that does not somehow refer to Jesus Christ and the propagation of the Gospel of Christ. Notice our coinage, our bills. What is written? Our national motto: "In God We Trust."

Dr. Schaeffer was right: we are a nation founded by people of Christian consciousness, a consciousness given to our forefathers and set forth in the Judeo-Christian ethic. I want to share these seven principles used historically to forge our Christian nation.

The seven principles of the Judeo-Christian ethic are:

Principle One:
The Principle of the Dignity of Human Life

That principle forthrightly states that you have a right to live. That principle teaches that your life has some inherent worth. You may inquire, "Have Americans turned their backs on the principles of the dignity of human life?" Have they? Four thousand little babies are destroyed every single day in America. Did you hear me? Four thousand murders take place every single day in America by abortion. We remember Hitler's regime, the SS and the prisoner of war camps, and moan, "What a shame! How could anybody on the face of God's earth ever commit genocide, the Holocaust?" Our nation is doing that today. Not only have we forgotten the principle of the dignity of human life, we have absolutely turned our backs on it in the American mentality today. Abortion is practically smiled on in many areas.

Principle Two:
The Principle of the Traditional,
Monogamous Family

There is to be one man and one woman who come together under God in marriage, a holy institution. Out of that marriage, if God blesses it especially, comes children. Those children have a right to a mother and daddy in a Godly Christian home. What is that? The principle of the traditional family. Yet, this is less and less the case in America.

Principle Three:
The Principle of the Work Ethic

That merely means that if you're going to eat, you ought to work, unless you are aged or severely handicapped. The Scripture says in 2 Thessalonians 3:10, "That if any would not work, neither should he eat." We're talking about the fact that every able-bodied individual ought to work. What have we done? We have blasted the Word of God in our welfare system today. If a man should eat, that man ought to work, and there should be a reemphasis of the work ethic in America.

Principle Four:
The Principle of a God-Centered Education

This means that little boys and girls have the right to understand that the creation in which they live came from a Creator God. No one can begin to comprehend the creation until they are acquainted with the Creator. To claim we have a creation from a "big bang" or a form of evolution is ludicrous. To argue we have a creation without a Creator strikes death to every kind of rationale and intellect God has given the common sense of common man. Every boy and girl deserves a God-centered education.

You ask, "Preacher, don't you believe in the separation of church and state? When you talk about education don't you think there should be a secular education and Godly education?" Yes, I do believe in the separation of church and state, but whoever taught the education of our children should belong to the state?

Principle Five:
The Principle of the Abrahamic Covenant

What does that mean? It implies if a nation honors God, God is going to bless that nation. God made a covenant with Abraham. He promised him, "Abraham, if you will raise your children to honor me, I will bless you above all the nations on the face of the earth." Psalms 33:12 tells us, "Blessed is the nation whose God is the Lord." Our founding fathers realized that a nation would be blessed if God was their Lord. They believed in the principle of the Abrahamic Covenant.

Principle Six:
Common Decency

This is the principle that Americans are going to do the decent thing, the right thing, not only in our nation, but around the world. Americans will do that which is decent and right. The

French historian Alexis de Tocqueville wrote: "America is great because she is good. When and if she ceases to be good, she will cease to be great."

Principle Seven:
Our Accountability to God

One day every one of us will give an account of himself to Almighty God, the great and small, the big and little. America has basically turned its back on its Judeo-Christian heritage, and because of that we are virtually empty of moral character today.

Daniel Webster, the powerful Christian statesman, was once addressing a class one day, and the students wanted to ask him several questions. One young man lifted his hand, stood up, and asked, "Mr. Webster, we know of your intellect. We know of your statesmanship. I want to ask you one simple question. Can you possibly tell us the greatest thought that has ever passed through your mind?"

Without hesitation Webster replied, "Young men, young ladies, the greatest thought that has ever crossed my mind is my personal accountability to God."

Why has God blessed America? First, *because this nation was founded by Godly, Christian people.*

Second, I believe God has blessed America *because God sees that America has blessed Israel.* When God made a covenant with Abraham in Genesis, we read in chapter 12 that God meant what He said and said what He meant. Genesis 12:2-3: "And I will make of thee a great nation, and I will bless thee, and make thy name great; and thou shalt be a blessing: And I will bless them that bless thee, and curse them that curse thee: and in thee shall all families of the earth be blessed."

When God made that covenant with Abraham, He meant it. "Abraham, I'm going to make your people like the sands of the sea. I'm going to give you a nation, a country, that you might sojourn in and live. It's going to be your homeland. And listen,

Abraham, if a nation in the world blesses your nation, and honors my people, I'm going to bless them. But if they curse you, I will curse them."

America has stood as a monumental blessing to Israel. We all know that. It is almost superfluous to make that statement. We do not agree with all Israel does, but America has understood the importance of Israel, not only prophetically, but because of its relationship to America. Sometimes Americans complain, "Why should we bother with Israel? Why do we give them all that foreign aid. Why do we put up with them? Why do we help them?"

In our foolish piousness, sometimes we think we can make it without Israel, but can we? Do you realize Israel is the third most powerful nuclear nation in the world? Do you realize, when we have confronted Russia the main reason they do not challenge us more is because America and Israel are together?

The Bible predicts that God is not only to bless those who bless Israel, He is going to place them under His hand of protection. We certainly have seen God's protection upon our land in recent days! America's standing in the world behind Israel has been our national policy for years. In addition think of this: there are more Jews living in the United States than in Israel.

Third, I believe God has blessed America *because the majority of our citizens still claim to be Christians*. A recent Gallup Poll estimated that 95 percent of Americans believe in a God. Eighty-seven percent of Americans believe in heaven, and 67 percent believe in hell. That same Gallup Poll indicated that more than 100 million Americans claim they have some exercise in Bible study and prayer every week.

Fourth, God has blessed America *because America is a key in the prophetic future*. You must understand that is what keeps Russia's or Iraq's or Iran's aggression from taking over the Middle East. If Russia ever controlled the Middle East, it would hold the major oil reserves, the riches of the earth in its hand, and it would have dominance and power over the world. What's keeping such aggression from overtaking the world? America is keeping them from it. All we have to do is consider America's role in the recent Persian Gulf War.

God has blessed America because of these reasons and many more. It's not by accident that we've received these blessings of God. But then we ask, "What is America's future?" What *is* our future? The answer is not found in our welfare systems. The answer isn't found in balancing our budget or having great military technology, even though these are pivotal. Yes, we need to balance our budget, and that seems unlikely. We need enough military force; we must be able to stand against the wiles and tricks of nations like Iraq, Russia, and Iran, and the rest of the communistic, socialistic world.

What is the hope of America? The hope of America is found in the book of 1 Peter 4:17. The Apostle Peter presented this as the hope of America. "For the time is come that judgment must begin at the house of God: And if it first begin at us, what shall the end be of them that obey not the gospel of God?" What is God speaking to us today? He is saying it is time that we believers in America started walking, talking, acting, thinking, and being what Christians are all about.

Do you remember Israel? Throughout the Old Testament, Israel was constantly wandering from God. Time and time again the nation rebelled against God. But again and again God repeated, "I will save Israel." Why? *For the remnant,* that group of Godly ones who served Him and lived in righteousness. God said, "I will save Israel for the remnant."

In Genesis 18 there is the account of Abraham going to God. He was beseeching God to spare Sodom, a hideously wicked city that God looked down upon and beheld involved in perverse activities that were sickening to Him. So God warned He would rain down fire and brimstone from heaven and destroy Sodom and its sister city of the plain, Gomorrah.

Abraham fell down before God. He had a nephew, Lot, who lived in Sodom. Abraham pled to God, "Oh God, would you spare Sodom if you could find just fifty righteous people?"

God answered, "I will, for fifty righteous."

Abraham bargained, "But, God, would you spare Sodom for forty or thirty or twenty righteous people?"

The merciful God said, "I will."

Finally, Abraham begged, "Oh God, Oh God, will you spare the city of Sodom even for ten righteous people?"

God replied, "I will."

God looked to and fro across Sodom and couldn't even locate ten righteous people. So a righteous God rained down fire and brimstone from heaven and destroyed that city. What was God looking for? He was looking for a little righteous remnant, a handful of believers, that He might spare that city.

What is the hope of America? It is found in the righteous remnant. It is found in *you and me!*

In Acts 17, as Luke recorded, it points out that believers looked at the New Testament Christians and exclaimed of them, "They're those people who are turning the world upside down." Do you hear that? Most of secular society today feels the church should maintain itself within its four walls, but within the four walls of any building is not the church—the church is in the hearts of the believers! If the believers are in society, the church is in society, and if the church is in society, it will make a difference in that society.

We should be active and aggressive for the King of kings and Lord of lords. We should beseech the Lord, "God, what can I do as a believer to help change the nation in which I live?" I remember reading about the Italian philosopher and poet, Dante, of the thirteenth and fourteenth centuries. His writings made an indelible impression upon my heart as a young man, "The hottest places in hell are reserved for those who maintain their neutrality in a day of moral crisis," he penned. Dante was challenging us to stand up for what is right. We Christian Americans *can make a difference*. I want to share with you how.

We must pray. God instructs us in His Word that we are to pray. We are to pray for our presidents, our senators, our congressmen, and our local politicians. We are to pray about those individuals. How are we to pray? May I suggest that you pray, "God, thank You for this individual. I lift this individual up to You, and I pray that You will prosper them and maintain them as Christians in public office"?

What about if they are anti-God? What if they vote against that which is moral and against the principles that are right? Then I pray, "God, remove them from office, and put in their place someone who stands for You." You see, we must understand that we have power with God. Surely we have power in society, but more than that, we have power with a sovereign God who does as He wants, not only in heaven, but on earth as well!

Daniel 2:21 says, "God removes kings and sets them up." When we face a situation whereby we see an injustice in the American system, the first step is: we should pray.

We must participate. This simply means we must vote and become active in the political process. If you don't vote, you don't have a right to speak a word. As Christians we should find out what our politicians believe, how they have voted in the past, and we should vote our conviction. I don't believe a pastor should tell you how to vote. (Although if you do not know, he ought to be well informed enough to share the names of those politicians and information on the issues as they relate to Christian standards.) I don't believe a church should be a political organization to instruct you how to vote, but I believe the Holy Spirit is willing to direct your voting every time.

We must persist. That means we must keep it up. If there is wrong in our society we need to vote and continue to vote and speak out until that wrong is made right. I want you to know the Scriptures teach us that righteousness will ultimately prevail.

George Washington, the first President of our nation, was a general at one time. General Washington fought nine battles with his troops, and he lost six out of that nine, but you see, he kept on, and he won the war! It's not how many times you lose, it's how many times you hang in there until you ultimately win.

We are to pray, we are to participate, we are to persist, and lastly, *we are to proclaim the truth of the glorious Gospel of Jesus Christ.*

The only way a nation can be changed is if the people are changed. All that will effect a permanent change in the people of America is the Gospel of Jesus Christ. If the people of America hear the Gospel, and come to repentance, God promises today, "I'm going to hear from heaven. I'm going to forgive their sin and heal their land." When an Almighty Creator God, who gave us this nation and has watched over it, sees us returning to those principles of righteousness upon which our land was founded, then He is going to be able to bless America.

May God bless America!